The Long War

The Long War

CENTCOM, GRAND STRATEGY,
AND GLOBAL SECURITY

JOHN MORRISSEY

THE UNIVERSITY OF GEORGIA PRESS
Athens

This publication was grant-aided by the Publications Fund of National University of Ireland, Galway, and by a Publication Prize awarded by the Senate Publications Committee of the National University of Ireland.

Most University of Georgia Press titles are
available from popular e-book vendors.

Printed digitally

Library of Congress Control Number: 2017936845
ISBN: 9780820351049 (hardcover: alk. paper)
ISBN: 9780820351056 (paperback: alk. paper)
ISBN: 9780820351032 (ebook)

For Darragh and Adrian

CONTENTS

ILLUSTRATIONS

Figures

Tables

ACKNOWLEDGMENTS

This book began in the autumn of 2007 in a small apartment in the East Village in New York City. I was about to spend a year as a fellow at CUNY Graduate Center in the Center for Place, Culture, and Politics. I had a wonderful year at CUNY, reading, thinking, and writing with brilliant, multidisciplinary colleagues. Their thoughts and probing questions mark this book in numerous ways. A heartfelt thanks go to the following: Padmini Biswas, Bruce Braun, Jeff Bussolini, Patricia Clough, Greg Donovan, Zeynep Gambetti, Chris Gunderson, Tina Harris, Peter Hitchcock, Elizabeth Johnson, Cindi Katz, Ervin Kosta, Ros Petchesky, and Charlotte Recoquillon. I must single out the late Neil Smith for special thanks. I was very close to Neil at CUNY, struggling like others to help him as the seriousness of his illness became clearer. I look back now with a deep sense of loss on our many conversations around geopolitics, imperialism, and the essential insecurities of our time. I remember Neil mostly though with fondness: fondness for a lion-hearted man who somehow managed to combine incisive, defiant critique with hope and romanticism, fondness for a man who sought his whole life to shake up the world with ideas and deeds, and fondness for a friend I miss.

On my return to NUI Galway, I reconnected with fantastic colleagues and students, to whom I am variously indebted for the support they offered as the book came to fruition. Thanks especially to the following: Dan Carey, Pat Collins, Ursula Connolly, Nessa Cronin, Shane Darcy, T. J. Hughes, Phil Lawton, Sharon Leahy, Valerie Ledwith, Marie Mahon, Killian McCormack, Niall Ó Dochartaigh, Kevin O'Sullivan, Kathy Reilly, Anna Stanley, and Ulf Strohmayer. I have long received great support from the broader academy too. I am grateful particularly to John Agnew, David Beckingham, Mark Boyle, Kate Brace, Joe Campbell, Padraig Carmody, Dan Clayton, Mat Coleman, David Dawson, Erin Delaney Joyce, Klaus Dodds, Mona Domosh, Lorraine Dowler, Paddy Duffy, Jim and Nancy Duncan, Jamey Essex, Matt Farish, Colin Flint, Amanda Frie, Emily Gilbert, Fergal Guilfoyle, Tom Harrington, Jennifer Hyndman, Nuala Johnston, Rob Kitchin, Steve Legg, Mike Leyshon, Denis Linehan, Francesca Moore, Alison Mountz, Cian

O'Callaghan, Simon Reid-Henry, David Ryan, Matt Sparke, David Storey, Mary Thomas, Karen Till, Gerard Toal, and Katie Willis. I want to give a special thanks to Deb Cowen, Simon Dalby, David Harvey, and Marilyn Young: thank you for your belief in me and in the critique at the heart of this book.

I wrote much of this book during fellowship stays at Fitzwilliam College and Emmanuel College, Cambridge, in 2013/2014. My time at Cambridge was a joyous one, and that owed much to the fellows I shared conversations with every day over coffee, lunch, and dinner. At Fitzwilliam, my thanks to Kasia Boddy, Dominic Keown, John Leigh, and Nicola Padfield. At Emmanuel, my thanks to Ivano Cardinale, Bérénice Guyot-Réchard, Lawrence Klein, David Livesey, and especially Phil Howell and Alex Jeffrey. While at Cambridge, I presented many of the arguments in the book in Emmanuel College, Sidney Sussex College, and the Geography Department; I am grateful for the excellent questions and ideas offered. I also presented the book's findings at various international conferences over the years, including a number of annual conferences of the American Association of Geographers, Geographical Society of Ireland, and Royal Geographical Society—Institute of British Geographers. My thanks to the audiences at these events and also to those who attended research seminars I gave in recent years at Maynooth University, Royal Holloway, University College Cork, University College Dublin, University of Exeter, and Virginia Tech.

My final thanks to individuals in the academy are for Derek Gregory, Craig Jones, Gerry Kearns, and David Nally. Derek has been an inspiration since I was an undergraduate studying geography, and this book is all the richer from his support of my research over the last ten years. Thank you, Derek. Craig Jones has become a dear friend in recent years. His reading of the book at a late stage pushed me to extend discussion in a manner that I did not expect to enjoy as the end line neared; that I did wholly reflects the remarkable thoughtfulness of Craig's own work. Thanks, Craig. For the longest time, my two closest colleagues have been Gerry Kearns and David Nally. Thanks to you both for your inspiring empathy as human geographers, your boundless sense of intellectual commitment, your conversational joy, and your wonderful sense of fun.

I am especially proud to have this book published in one of the most important collections in critical human geography, the Geographies of Justice and Social Transformation series. My thanks to Nik Heynen, Deb Cowen, and Melissa Wright for believing in the book from the very beginning. At UGA Press, I am also indebted to a number of individuals who have made writing the book an ease. Thanks to Mick Gusinde-Duffy for his steadfast encouragement from the start, to Christina Cotter and Beth Snead for all their assistance, and to Jennifer Comeau and Jon Davies for their careful reading and advice on the text. It was a pleasure to work with you all. My thanks too to Bobbie O'Brien, Paul Courtnage, and the *Tampa Bay Times* for the credited usage of various images, and to John Wiley and Sons, Routledge, Sage, and Taylor and Francis for permission to draw on previously published empirical material in *Antipode*, *EPD: Society and Space*, *Geopolitics*, the *Geographical Journal*, and the book *America and Iraq*, edited by David Ryan and Patrick Kiely. Thanks also to my former colleague at CUNY, Jochen Albrecht, for drawing the book's maps, and, finally, I wish to gratefully acknowledge the grant aid received from two publication awards for the book from the National University of Ireland and NUI Galway.

To finish, I want to thank my family and friends for their ongoing support of my work, which I have always appreciated. In recent years, I have begun my own family with Olive, and my thanks to her for being on that journey with me. Her heart and empathy are a joy to be around. We have two little boys now, Darragh and Adrian—I dedicate this book to them and to the dream of a better future for children everywhere, one in which knowledge still counts, even in a post-truth political world.

JM
Galway
September 2016

ABBREVIATIONS

AFB	Air Force Base
AOR	Area of Responsibility
CDHQ	CENTCOM Deployable Headquarters
CENTCOM	United States Central Command
CINC	Commander in Chief
DoD	Department of Defense
GCC	Gulf Cooperation Council
ISIS	Islamic State of Iraq and Syria
JAG	Judge Advocate General
RDF	Rapid Deployment Force
RDJTF	Rapid Deployment Joint Task Force
SOFA	Status of Forces Agreement
USAID	United States Agency for International Development

The Long War

CHAPTER ONE

"Shaping the Central Region for the 21st Century"

CENTCOM's Long War

Of all the enemies to public liberty war is, perhaps, the most to be dreaded [. . .]
No nation could preserve its freedom in the midst of continual warfare.

James Madison, "Political Observations," 1795

The initiation of United States Central Command (CENTCOM) in January 1983
was a watershed moment for contemporary U.S. geopolitics. It signaled a new
era of U.S. global ambition in the aftermath of military failure in Vietnam, solidified a refocused U.S. foreign policy on the most energy-rich region on earth,
and set in motion a security mission whose legacies and ongoing wars we are
still witnessing today. In no other region has the U.S. military established more
bases, lost more troops, or spent more money in the last thirty years than the
Middle East and Central Asia. From its inception, CENTCOM was tasked with its
military-economic securitization, the safeguarding of commercial opportunities
therein, and ultimately the policing of a pivotal yet precarious space in the broader
global economy. CENTCOM calls this its 'Long War', a war underpinned by a range
of entangled geopolitical and geoeconomic visions and involving the use of the
most devastating Western interventionary violence of our time. This book tells
the story of that long war.

In any ways the story of CENTCOM began with President Jimmy Carter's State
of the Union Address in January 1980, when he declared that an attempt by "any
outside force to gain control of the Persian Gulf region will be regarded as an
assault on the vital interests of the United States of America, and such an assault will be repelled by any means necessary, including military force" (J. Carter
1980). Two months later, the initiation of the Rapid Deployment Joint Task Force
(RDJTF) was the first formal commitment of U.S. forces to protect the region, and
with CENTCOM's succession in 1983 the U.S. government had fully committed to
the Carter Doctrine. CENTCOM would become the most active command in U.S.
military history. Its critique is vital to understanding the recent global ambition of
the United States and its ongoing grand strategy to shape global security.

For the past thirty years, CENTCOM has been the foremost appendage of the U.S. national security state in implementing U.S. foreign policy in one of the most important spaces of global security, the Middle East. Yet there has been remarkably little critical examination of CENTCOM's security mission, nor has there been any sustained interrogation of its discursive production of inherent Middle Eastern volatility and threat—the reductive, strategic geographical knowledges that have been instrumental in unleashing interventionary violence in the region. There have been a small number of insider books on the command's ongoing wars in recent years, describing issues such as command structures, the use and extent of intelligence, and interpersonal rivalries.[1] Such accounts, however, have not considered CENTCOM's leading role in shaping and actioning U.S. foreign policy, nor have they located its story within existing scholarly debates on neoliberalism, imperialism, and geopolitics or addressed key questions of territory, the law, and what counts as war in our contemporary moment.[2]

Operating since 1983 from MacDill Air Force Base (AFB) in Tampa, Florida (figure 1.1), CENTCOM has played a pivotal role in international affairs over the last thirty years. In the book, I position the command centrally in the story of U.S. global ambition over this formative period by documenting its efforts to spearhead a global security grand strategy defined in military-economic terms and enabled via specific legal-territorial arrangements. In intersecting CENTCOM's evolving grand strategy with a range of recent debates in the broader academy addressing questions of ongoing Western interventionism, the book offers a focused

FIGURE 1.1. MacDill Air Force Base, Tampa, Florida. Photo by the author.

critique of the interventionary logics and modalities of a crucial instrument of U.S. national security on the global stage. Through the course of the book, I draw on extensive archival sources, including CENTCOM's declassified strategy papers, posture statements, mission reports, command histories, and press briefings, together with key Department of Defense (DoD) publications, namely *National Security Strategy* and *National Defense Strategy* documents, Unified Command Plans, Overseas Basing Commission reports, and relevant Congressional Research Service reports to the U.S. Congress. I also draw on a valuable interview conducted with the serving CENTCOM command historian, David Dawson, at CENTCOM Headquarters at MacDill AFB.[3]

In employing a wide range of materials,[4] my aim is to deconstruct the core formulations of current U.S. grand strategy on the Middle East and Central Asia and to illustrate the focal import of CENTCOM's securitization discourse, representationally and performatively, in prominent forums of geopolitical knowledge production in the United States. CENTCOM occupies a pivotal position in the U.S. national security state, enveloping both foreign policy making and foreign policy practice; its annual posture statements, for instance, are important speech acts at the very nexus of the military-political establishment in Washington. Although policy making and policy enactment become muddied in all sorts of ways, what becomes clear when reflecting upon the connections between 'text' and 'practice' in CENTCOM's securitization discourse is how consistent it has been in its focus on military-economic security, deterrence, and policing—and moreover how that interventionary discourse has been operationally put into action repeatedly and largely successfully over the course of thirty years. CENTCOM's interventionary rationale serves to underpin an enduring discursive mechanism of Western imperialism: the identification of threat and instability coupled with the scripting of necessary correction and security measures. Its mission brief appears not only necessary but indeed therapeutic to the liberal urge to improve. Documenting the liberal imperial hallmarks of contemporary Western geopolitical imaginaries is an essential part of a still necessary postcolonial critique, directed ultimately toward the "transformation of epistemologies" and the "establishment of new forms of discursive and political power" (Young 2001, 428). Part of that critique in geography is to counter abstracted geostrategic knowledges, such as those permeating CENTCOM's securitization discourse, and to this end, denaturalizing the 'essence' of the region's insecurity and insisting upon the region's human geographies is vital.

'Guardians of the Gulf'

CENTCOM's 'Area of Responsibility' (commonly abbreviated to AOR) is seen in figure 1.2. It is one of six regional commands in the U.S. military's Unified Command Plan in which the world is divided up into "Areas of Responsibility" with

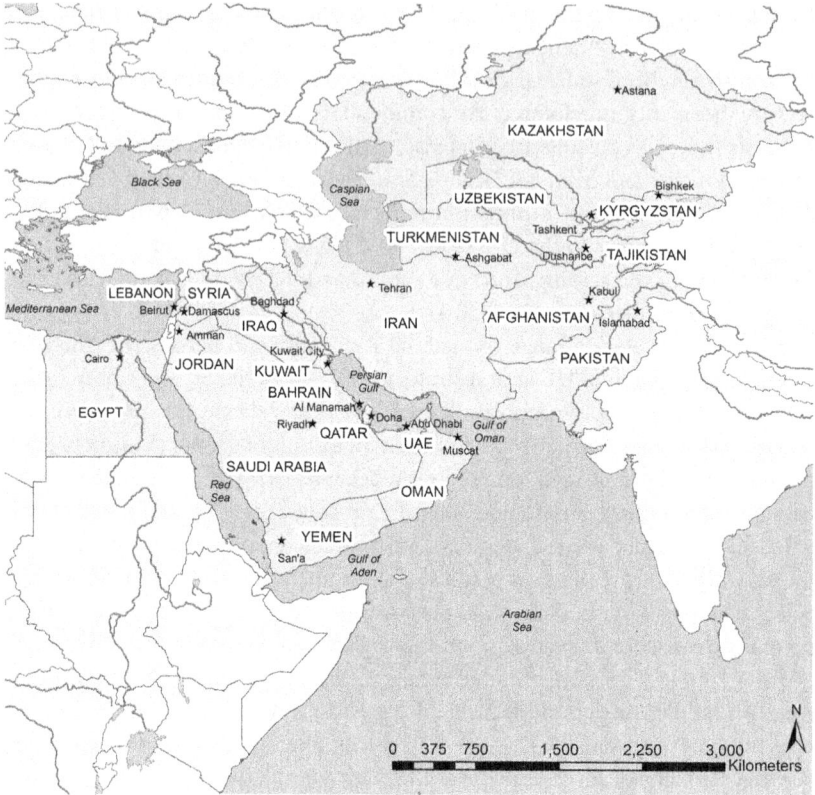

FIGURE 1.2. CENTCOM 'Area of Responsibility', 2016.

specifically assigned "missions and geographic responsibilities" (U.S. Department of Defense 2016a; see figure 3.3).[5] Producing a map titled "The World with Commanders' Areas of Responsibility" mirrors a deeply assumptive imperialism, of course, that naturalizes both the essence of regions (however arbitrarily constructed) and the assigning to the U.S. military of global responsibility to secure them. The bounded regions within the map are framed and known through a security lens, and such knowledge is reinforced in a wider discourse of securitization that includes Country Books, for instance, where the heads of commands such as CENTCOM are regularly furnished with "a single-source document" of "data on countries" (U.S. Central Command 1985, 143–144). Such abstracted mappings encapsulate the most dangerous geographical formulations of area studies (Gibson-Graham 2004; Szanton 2004); and it is this reductionism, present elsewhere in the U.S. global imaginary too, that is the prerequisite to drawing the world into 'Areas of Responsibility'. Reprising the colonial tactic of renaming, CENTCOM calls the vast Area of Responsibility under its military watch the

'Central Region'.[6] It is 'central' for CENTCOM primarily in three ways, central to the global economy; central to global energy assets; and ultimately central to global security. In tracing the geopolitical and geoeconomic arc through which the region has been discursively produced in recent years, CENTCOM's narrative and performative role at the nexus of military and political circles between the DoD and the U.S. Capitol stands out. In their annual posture statements to the U.S. Congress, CENTCOM commanders have perennially presented their armed forces as "Guardians of the Gulf," authorized with the role of safeguarding the free-market global economy (Palmer 1992; Morrissey 2009). The command's mission statements and strategy papers have been equally consistent in communicating a 'neoliberal policing' responsibility (U.S. Central Command 1985; U.S. Central Command 1999a). A 1992 CENTCOM-commissioned strategy report, for example, noted how the end of the Cold War and "the loss of the Soviet Union as a foe of the United States" had "not diminished" the remit of the command as "the guardian of the Persian Gulf"—it would continue its "main mission" of "guarding Gulf oil" (Pelletiere and Johnson 1992, v). 'Guarding Gulf oil' is undoubtedly a central element of the story of CENTCOM, but its interventions across the Middle East and Central Asia have not just been concerned with securing the regional spigots of energy assets (Harvey 2003; Vitalis 2006; Mitchell 2011; Bacevich 2016); rather, they form part of a wider U.S. regional grand strategy to facilitate a 'controlled' neoliberal global economy, which I draw out and explore through the course of the book. As the report above makes clear, the "name of the game" for CENTCOM is "control": "we are trying to control what goes on in the Gulf in order to maintain the status quo" (Pelletiere and Johnson 1992, 17).

CENTCOM has long exhibited a particular consciousness of the need to communicate to the American people its vital, mandated security brief (Reveron and Gavin 2004; Wrage 2004).[7] A core command concern outlined in its chief strategy document from 1999, *Shaping the Central Region for the 21st Century*, for instance, was to "[e]ducate key leaders and the American public on the mission of CENTCOM and the importance of the Central Region" (U.S. Central Command 1999a, 8). The command's principal mission objective was also set out plainly:

> Protect, promote and preserve U.S. interests in the Central Region to include the free flow of energy resources, access to regional states, freedom of navigation, and maintenance of regional stability. (U.S. Central Command 1999a, 7)

Ten years later, its 2009 mission statement laid out a more universalist agenda, presenting the notion of U.S.-led international "cooperation" and "development" and erasing explicit references to U.S. national interests:

> U.S. Central Command, working with national and international partners, promotes development and cooperation among nations, responds to crises, and deters

or defeats state and transnational aggression in order to establish regional security and stability. (U.S. Central Command 2009a)

The discursive shift here mirrors what Mark Duffield and others have shown as the blurring of war and development in our contemporary moment via a broadened vernacular of security, peacekeeping, and market creation (Duffield 2001; Essex 2013). It reflects too an effort to garner renewed international support for the ongoing U.S.-led war on terror under the auspices of the Obama administration in early 2009. It also masks U.S. national ambition in declarations of a universalist 'special mission' (N. Smith 2003a, 2005), and it reveals once more a familiar contradiction in both historical and contemporary scriptings of U.S. interventionism, what Mona Domosh calls the "borderless world of commercial mobility vs. the territorial prerogatives of national interests" (Domosh 2013, 963). Yet in all of this CENTCOM's Long War rationale remains constant, and it necessitates long-term posturing of military force.

Military posturing for a long war requires an identified threat, and the Middle East has, of course, been habitually represented in the West as a space of insecurity afflicted with a 'barbarism' that requires a 'civilized' Western response (Said 1978, 1993; Gregory 2004). The Middle East's barbarism today is personified by ISIS (Islamic State of Iraq and Syria) fighters. Shocking descriptions of their abhorrent disregard for human life echo familiar accounts of the violent cruelty of their predecessors, al-Qaeda and the Taliban. As CENTCOM's interventionary violence has become more and more 'unseen' as a result of careful military media management, we have increasingly 'seen' the violence of ISIS as the representation of radical Islam (Gregory 2005, 2011).[8] This discursive differentiation of violence reinforces a dominant geopolitical rationale for an enduring U.S. presence in the Middle East, spearheaded by CENTCOM. In addition to a geopolitical interventionary imperative, a distinct geoeconomic interventionary imperative has featured even more prominently in U.S. regional grand strategy since the initiation of CENTCOM. Over the last thirty years, both at CENTCOM and in wider defense circles in Washington, strategizing for intervention in the region has identified the prime ambition of neoliberal securitization for 'the good of the global economy'. The late Jack Kemp, a former Republican congressman, captured this ambition well:

> My friends tell me I sound like a broken record pleading for a 21st-century Marshall Plan for Arab and Muslim countries in the Middle East and Central Asia. That's because I am passionate about doing everything we can to bring the Muslim nations of the regions into the 21st-century global economy. Not only does the health and welfare of the Muslim people depend on it, the security of the free world depends on it. (Kemp 2004)

Kemp's vision mirrors a now prevailing U.S. national security discourse on the Middle East and Central Asia, a discourse that conflates U.S. military and economic interests in a region with wider global security implications. For CENTCOM, military-economic securitization has always been the mission and successive commanders have repeatedly convinced the U.S. Congress of the necessity of 'forward presence' in the name of U.S.-global economic security.

The Long War to Shape the Middle East

In January 2006, President George W. Bush used the phrase 'long war' for the first time in his State of the Union Address. "Our own generation is in a long war against a determined enemy," Bush declared, "a war that will be fought by presidents of both parties who will need steady bipartisan support from the Congress" (Bush 2006). The phrase had been used before, of course; in the early seventeenth century, it was the name given to the Ottoman Empire's fifteen-year campaign to extend its territorial sovereignty in the Balkans. A few days after President Bush's address in the Capitol, the *Washington Post* reported that his administration had formally embraced the phrase and in so doing "turned a simple descriptive phrase into an official name for the war on terrorism, and possibly catapulted it into the ranks of such other names as 'Cold War' and 'World War'" (Graham and White 2006). The phrase 'Long War' had already been adopted by CENTCOM as a descriptor for its mission several years earlier. After taking over at CENTCOM in July 2003, its new commander, General John Abizaid, quickly departed from the operational focus of his predecessor, General Tommy Franks, on specific military interventions in largely disconnected conflicts. Abizaid was convinced that CENTCOM "did not face a series of local conflicts" across its AOR but rather faced a regional "pan-insurgency," which could be defeated only by "strategic thinking" and a "sustained, integrated effort" (Dawson 2010, 21). Marking a new direction in policy, Abizaid set up a Commander's Advisory Group at CENTCOM Headquarters (figure 1.3), charged with formulating a long-haul strategy to counter this regional insurgency. The group's meetings became known as the 'Long War Briefs'. CENTCOM command historian David Dawson was a member of Abizaid's advisory team, and he recounts that the group primarily addressed how not enough "strategic thinking" had been invested in Operation Enduring Freedom and Operation Iraqi Freedom (Dawson 2014).[9] In formulating a new strategic-level approach, the advisory group came up with a mission plan with the working title 'The Long War', and although the group "disliked" the phrase because it "implied long-term major combat" and "reinforced the idea that the United States was at war with Islam," it was nevertheless adopted as they were "unable to come up with a better short term" (Dawson 2010, 33). The reluctance of Abizaid's advisory team to adopt the phrase mirrors no doubt the pressure on successive U.S. governments to be seen to end specific military operations, despite their seemingly always imminent reignition across the Middle East and Central Asia (as recent

FIGURE 1.3. CENTCOM Headquarters, MacDill Air Force Base. Source: Bobbie O'Brien, WUSF Public Media.

years have shown). CENTCOM's embracing of a 'long war' grand strategy reflects, however, the extent to which the 'new wars' thesis of unending nonconventional war has been understood in recent years (Kaldor 1999)—new wars for conflated military, developmental, and humanitarian security (Duffield 2001). Signaling temporal concerns is important here too: a long war to secure a future of uncertainty and volatility possesses a compelling interventionary rationale.

In all of this, language is crucial. As Terry Jones (2001) quickly observed soon after the 'war on terrorism' was declared, "how do you wage war on an abstract noun?"—and, of course, how can there ever be an endgame (Chomsky 2003)? It is a war that is, in fact, unwinnable and thus a "forever war" (Filkins 2009; cf. Bacevich 2007). In this sense, CENTCOM's embracing of the phrase 'The Long War' is at least linguistically a more appropriate descriptor. Since 2004, the phrase has been increasingly used to signify both the long-term temporality of CENTCOM's project in the Middle East and Central Asia and its wider strategic approach—comprising also "political and economic measures," as emphasized by General Richard Myers in his last press conference as chairman of the Joint Chiefs of Staff in September 2005 (Graham and White 2006). The designation has also been popularly embraced by a range of strategic studies experts; Bill Roggio at the defense think tank Foundation for the Defense of Democracies even set up *The Long War* journal in September 2007 (Roggio 2014; The Long War Journal 2014; see also Carafano 2003). The larger point on nomenclature, however, is that CENTCOM's

Long War began much earlier than its formal adoption of the phrase in 2004. As Dawson notes, the command has been on a "continuous war footing" since the Gulf War (Dawson 2014). From 1992 until the invasion of Iraq in 2003, it implemented Operation Southern Watch, the regulation of the Iraqi no-fly zone south of the Thirty-Second Parallel. Ground deterrence was a constant feature of operations, with military maneuvers such as Operation Vigilant Warrior, Operation Desert Spring, and Internal Look entailing regular mobilizations of CENTCOM's forward-deployed ground troops and military arsenal. And since CENTCOM's first major intervention in the Persian Gulf during the Tanker War in the mid-1980s, it has maintained a continuous forward naval presence in the region.

In April 2007, Brigadier General Al Riggle from the U.S. National Counter-terrorism Center gave a presentation at a leading defense industry association conference in Miami, Florida. In an instructive address titled "The Global War on Terrorism: The Long War," Riggle outlined how the United States had been "a nation at war" in the Middle East and Central Asia since the late 1970s (Riggle 2007). Among key identified events in a protracted timeline, Riggle listed the Iranian hostage crisis of 1979 as the first instance of the Long War, which ever since has comprised various attacks on U.S. embassies, facilities, troops, and citizens in the region. He cited Lebanon in 1983, 1984, and 1988, Saudi Arabia in 1995 and 1996, Palestine in 1995, 1996, and 1997, Yemen in 2000, and the 9/11 attacks in the United States in 2001 as part of an ongoing conflict against "a transnational movement of extremist organizations, networks, and individuals—and their state and non-state sponsors—which have in common that they exploit Islam and use terrorism for ideological ends" (Riggle 2007). It may be persuasive of Riggle and others to foreground terrorist threat and geopolitical instability in summations of U.S. commitment to a long-haul strategy in the Middle East and Central Asia, but what is absent in this reasoning is acknowledgment of what has in fact been the most dominant discourse of intervention since CENTCOM's inception: 'geoeconomic securitization'. Through the course of this book, I show geoeconomic securitization to be both an active interventionary discourse and an apt descriptor of the security operations of CENTCOM in practice. In interrogating the command's geoeconomic rationale in 'shaping' the Middle East and Central Asia, I focus in particular on the tactic of deterrence. My aim is to tease out the dimensions of geoeconomic shaping being anticipated, the kind of capitalism envisaged, and if this altered over a period marked by the advent of globalization and a less-bounded global economic system.

Geoeconomic Securitization

CENTCOM's geoeconomic interventionary logic has always been especially neb-ulous, perhaps not by accident. The absence of precisely formulated contours has in fact further enabled an anticipative message of interventionary intent being successfully declared. The command's discourse of 'necessary' intervention for the 'global common good' possesses the attributes of universalist rhetoric that render its message both promissory and persuasive. In deconstructing the 'kind of capitalism' the U.S. military seeks to practically facilitate and safeguard, I am disinclined to theorize it as one of 'neo-mercantilism', akin to imperial Britain's efforts to facilitate capitalist enterprise (cf. Sassen 2010; McMichael 2013). Like others, I am also reluctant to ascribe it as *simply* 'neoliberalism', largely because I think this term and its associated economic determinisms need to be broken down more frequently to explicate the intricate workings of late modern capitalism (Peck 2013). What I present as CENTCOM's geoeconomic grand strategy is more ambitious in terms of global economic shaping than localized forms of mercantilism, but the endgame is ultimately loosely formulated around concepts such as 'free trade' and 'freedom of movement'. It is a strategy in which a neoliberal universalist rhetoric is deployed, yet the outcome is always one of 'messy capitalism' (Morrissey 2017). I explore this concept in an effort to think through the relationship between military force and late modern capitalism, or more specifically the import of military force in the contemporary global economy's spaces of insecurity.

CENTCOM has consistently articulated universalist economic objectives for its military ground presence across the Middle East and Central Asia. David Dawson, for instance, is keen to recount its efforts to foster regional economic growth and cites the Northern Distribution Network and New Silk Road initiatives in Central Asia in recent years as substantial developments toward that end:

> CENTCOM supports anything that strengthens regional economies, and believes that free trade strengthens economies and fosters economic growth. Since about 2004 CENTCOM has been all about regional partnerships. We see regional cooperation as one of the best ways to foster stability. (Dawson 2014)

The grand narrative here is one loosely reflecting a belief in free trade, infrastructure, and economic stimulus to initiate development and "foster stability." When asked about the specific challenges of uneven economic development, the extractive nature of transnational capitalism, and common absence of local leadership and participation, Dawson responded thus: "very few [military officers] have well developed theories of economics; I think most military officers maintain a contradictory view of economics—they combine a general belief in free markets with a healthy skepticism of the profit motive" (Dawson 2014). Dawson's reply mirrors CENTCOM's long-standing if nebulous accounting of its military-economic remit. There is undoubtedly a 'general belief in free markets' at CENTCOM—this belief comes through annually in commanders' posture statements to the U.S. Congress—and what becomes clear when reading the command's conception of its mission is that it sees its primary assigned responsibility as militarily securing

the vital nodes of a globally pivotal regional economy, to enable economic liber
alization and incorporation for all.

In considering CENTCOM's envisioning of its mission responsibility, I orient a
particular critique of the geoeconomic contours of its interventionary logic and
grand strategy. Such a focus on geoeconomic discourse owes much to 'critical
geopolitics', whose emergence marked a significant moment in political geography
in the early 1990s, not only in countering classical geopolitics but also in opening
up a wide range of accounts of geopolitical statecraft and the role of geographical
knowledges therein (Dalby 1991; Ó Tuathail 1996; Kearns 2009).[10] Earlier work in
political geography, influenced by Immanuel Wallerstein's world-systems theory
and Antonio Gramsci's writings on hegemony, is an important forebear too (Agnew and Corbridge 1995; Flint and Taylor 2011).[11] Much work in geoeconomics
attends to questioning the forms of imperialism and spatial organization we are
witnessing today in a globalized economy dominated by transnational capitalist accumulation (Cowen and Smith 2009; Sparke 2013). Among other things,
this has served to illuminate the impact of both geopolitical *and* geoeconomic
calculation in the ongoing shaping of uneven development, and the perpetu-
ation of international conflict (cf. Dalby 2007; N. Smith 2008). In CENTCOM's
interventionary rationale, both geopolitical and geoeconomic registers have
been interchangeably deployed as "geostrategic discourses" (Sparke 2007, 345)—
they have coalesced seamlessly in the successful articulation of the command's
mission.

In interrogating CENTCOM's security mission, I am drawing on the security
studies conception of the term 'securitization'—employed particularly by the
constructivist Copenhagen School of International Relations—in which potential security risks become discursively mobilized to legitimize actions to counter
national security threats (Buzan, Wæver, and de Wilde 1997; Buzan and Wæver
2003; Williams 2007). I am also drawing on broader work on risk, preemption,
and governmentality that has variously critiqued the interventionary discourses
and strategies that increasingly seek to manage danger and insecurity in our contemporary world (Beck 1992; Dean 1999; O'Malley 2004; Mythen and Walklate
2006). As I show later, CENTCOM commanders have consistently relied on a
risk-flagged securitization discourse to argue for, and legitimize, their interventionary mission of managing threat and insecurity. The meaning of securitization in actuarial science also resonates with my use of the term, particularly how
risk-laden financial interests become bundled into securities in the market that
can be insured against (Bougen 2003; Lin and Cox 2008). In a similar fashion,
CENTCOM's grand strategy posits the assets and liabilities of the political economy of the Gulf region as "insurable risks," and moreover deserving of "continued future insurance-risk securitization activity" (Cox, Fairchild, and Pedersen 2000, 157). Its security project intricately conflates political and economic
interests. As Randy Martin (2007, 17) notes, pressing on the "political meaning of

security" always "brings its economic double to the surface." I am mindful too of other overlapping regulatory and disciplinary logics underpinning visions of security at CENTCOM, particularly in the realm of biopolitics, which I explore by focusing on the use of the law to enable the biopolitical capacities of the command's armed forces in its various 'fields of intervention' (Foucault 2007; cf. De Larringa and Doucet 2008; Mason and Zeitoun 2013).

Ultimately, I hope to expound how CENTCOM's mission in the Middle East and Central Asia is predicated on a global security vision in which the region is seen as pivotal for a functioning global economy yet unpredictable as a geopolitical dynamic, and therefore necessitating a regulatory military presence. I detail how CENTCOM's grand strategy has been discursively underpinned by a geoeconomic imagination replete with universalist claims about guarding the free-market global economy. But I want to highlight too how CENTCOM's project of security seeks to facilitate geoeconomics in practice on the ground in the form of commercial markets. Here, I emphasize the command's territorial tactics and, in particular, the legal armatures that enable the critical operational mechanism of deterrence.

Territory and Access

In his oft-cited 1990 commentary in *The National Interest*, Edward Luttwak anticipated the emergence of a style of international relations in the post–Cold War era in which geopolitical and military statecraft would be replaced by a form of geoeconomic statecraft wherein "competitively, or cooperatively, the actions on all sides would always unfold without regards to frontiers" (Luttwak 1990, 17). Deb Cowen and Neil Smith (2009) lay bare the essentialism of Luttwak's argument, underlining instead the dialectics and contradictions wrought by contemporary capitalism's uneven development. On the question of territory and security, Cowen and Smith see "territorial borders" as historically representing "a solution to security projects" whereas today posing "a key problem" for them (2009, 30). I wonder, however, if this is overstating the historical dichotomy somewhat. Lauren Benton, in her analysis of early modern European empires, is particularly instructive on this point:

> Territorial control was, in many places, an incidental aim of imperial expansion. While an iconic association with empire is the pink shading of British imperial possessions in nineteenth- and early twentieth-century maps, that image, and others like it, obscures the many variations of imperial territories [. . .] Even in the most paradigmatic cases, an empire's spaces were politically fragmented; legally differentiated; and encased in irregular, porous, and sometimes undefined borders. (Benton 2010, 2)

Borders, in other words, have always posed security problems and were perhaps historically more permeable and perpetually problematic than our imaginary of the colonial worlds of the past allows (no doubt static cartographic representations have much to do with this, as Benton suggests).[12]

The other important question here is whether the "control of territory" is just a "tactical option" rather than a "strategic necessity" for contemporary Western interventionism, as Cowen and Smith (2009, 42) contend. They draw a key distinction between 'geopolitics and territory' and 'geoeconomics and territory':

> Where geopolitics can be understood as a means of acquiring territory towards a goal of accumulating wealth, geoeconomics reverses the procedure, aiming directly at the accumulation of wealth through market control. The acquisition or control of territory is not at all irrelevant but is a tactical option rather than a strategic necessity. (Cowen and Smith 2009, 42)

As I argue through the course of this book, CENTCOM's operations in the Middle East and Central Asia have consistently required what the U.S. military calls 'forward presence'—to secure 'land nodes' and 'choke points'. Territory for CENTCOM is not about acquisition or administrative control in terms of traditional understandings of historical colonialism; rather, it is about 'strategic control'. Its primary operational mechanism of deterrence is dependent on territorial access, and this access is sanctioned and facilitated via specific legal-territorial constellations confirming access rights, operational limits, and rules of engagement. CENTCOM's strategy to territorially 'open up' markets, resources, and commercial and transportation networks via deterrence comprises on the one hand a promissory neoliberal vision about 'free markets' yet on the other a military mechanism that seeks to 'control' and 'regulate'. Neoliberal capitalism has never equated to *laissez-faire* economics; rather, it has always involved intervening to "further the game of enterprise" (Gordon 1991, 42). As David Harvey reasoned some thirty years ago, the corollary of Marx's observation that capitalism requires spatial expansion is that it must also require spatial production, comprising "spatial organisation" and "regulatory institutions" (Harvey 1985, 145). Capitalist production entails inherent contradictions, of course, entwining conflicting territorial logics and occurring at multiple scales (Hardt and Negri 2000; Harvey 2005; Donzelot 2008). As Jamey Essex (2013, 5) usefully puts it, "a deterritorializing logic of economic connection exists alongside and, at turns, intertwines with and contradicts a territorializing logic of political control and closure." My hope is that addressing the question of territory will aid in further documenting the modalities of imperial interventionism we are witnessing in late modern capitalism. One of the ways in which to do that, I think, is to pay greater attention to the law and the legal specificities enabling territorial access. In highlighting CENTCOM's grand strategy of deterrence, my aim is to attend not only to the binding of military and economic logics in practices of intervention but also to their crucial governing legal requirements.

War, Law, and Geography

CENTCOM's Long War involves an intricate deployment of the law. As Walter Benjamin (1978, 283) observed nearly a century ago, there is a "lawmaking character" at the heart of war—in its battlespaces, in its territorial, naval, and aerial occupations, in its extraterritoriality, and in its adapted usage of a multitude of legal armatures (Morrissey 2015). For the U.S. military today, its JAGs (Judge Advocate General's Corps military lawyers) play a central role in the juridification of its military operations, from legally conditioning the battlefield to regulating the circulation of troops, optimizing their operational capacities, and sanctioning the privilege to kill (and to kill with impunity, of course—war being the ultimate 'state of exception'; Agamben 2005). They also play a vital, often overlooked communicative role, and this role is important in considering how the law is used *strategically*—in other words, how it is selectively used in "identifying openings that can be made to seem persuasive," as legal scholar David Kennedy (2006, 121) explains. The law's power to persuade is precisely why harnessing it and defining it is key to communicating 'legitimacy'. As outlined on the first page of the U.S. military's *Operational Law Handbook*, the law's function in communicating missions and structuring "public statements" is made crystal clear for military lawyers:

> the success of any military mission abroad will likely depend upon the degree of domestic support demonstrated during the initial deployment and sustained operation of U.S. forces. A clear, well-conceived, effective, and timely articulation of the legal basis for a particular mission is essential to sustaining support at home and gaining acceptance abroad. (U.S. Army Judge Advocate General's Legal Center 2016, 1)

Craig Jones (2016, 221) notes that "processes of juridification are a defining feature of late modern war," yet geographic accounts of war have "generally not considered the role that law plays in its conduct." Addressing this shortfall of critical engagements with "the weaponisation of law," Jones shows how the recently coined concept of 'lawfare' "provides geography with a series of entry points" into urgent debates surrounding "the legal geographies of war" (C. Jones 2016, 223; cf. Kennedy 2006; Weizman 2009; Gregory 2010; Braverman et al. 2014). In my account of CENTCOM's framing and mobilization of the law, I reverse the conservative definition of lawfare, in which it is understood to mean "the use of law as a weapon of war" by 'illegitimate terrorists' or an 'occupied population' attempting to impose "reputational costs on the belligerent" by "alleging violations" (Dill 2014). On the contrary, I am concerned with 'state lawfare', in which the law is selectively adapted and employed in a wide range of military operations and occupations by the 'state belligerent'. Lawfare in this sense, as Janina Dill remarks, is partially the use of law to "circumvent legal obligations in order to be able to continue to claim compliance" (Dill 2014; cf. Halper 2014). It is a tactic too of legally protecting forward-deployed troops, or "offensive lawfare," as I have outlined elsewhere (Morrissey 2011b, 280).

My concern for the legal geographies of CENTCOM's interventions and operations centers on teasing out the entanglements of what, following Blomley (1989) and Jones and Smith (2015), can be usefully described as the 'war-law-space nexus' of late modern war.[13] I want to divulge why the law and its specificities matter for CENTCOM, particularly respecting territorial access, occupation, and the regulation of military conduct. I wish to signal too how the law is indispensable to the recent broadening of what counts as 'war' (Kennedy 2006; Gregory 2011; Taw 2012). My engagement draws especially on Michel Foucault's lectures on security, territory, and biopolitics at the Collège de France in the late 1970s (Foucault 2007, 2008). It also draws on a range of critical work on colonial governmentality and the historical legal conditioning of political, social, and cultural relations (Scott 1995; Kalpagam 2000; Duncan, 2007; Legg 2007; Howell 2009; Nally 2011; Morrissey 2012; Wickramasinghe 2015). From at least the early modern period, as Lauren Benton (2010, 3) has documented, imperial administration has depended on "the exercise of delegated legal authority" in which "a fluid legal politics" produced multiple "territorial variations." Today as much as ever, as Jamey Essex (2013, 6) argues, there is an "incompleteness and contingency" to forms of "territorial control," and this perhaps prompts the kinds of legal-territorial ambiguities we are witnessing in the biopolitical management practices of our contemporary moment (Mountz 2011, 2012). Territory, as Stuart Elden (2013, 10) reasons, is ultimately a mode of "spatial organization" that is "dependent on a number of techniques and on the law," which are "historically and geographically specific." In the case of CENTCOM, its extensive military presence in the Middle East and Central Asia is dependent on an amalgam of specific bilateral legal agreements with nation-states across its Area of Responsibility. They are crucial in enabling CENTCOM's Long War for regional and global security.

Interrogating CENTCOM's Long War

Over the next five chapters, I interrogate key elements of CENTCOM's Long War. Chapter 2 explores CENTCOM's origins and focuses on the discursive production of both 'military' and 'economic' security logics at the heart of U.S. foreign policy toward the Middle East and Central Asia from the late 1970s. I outline the Cold War anxieties and imperial rivalry with the Soviet Union, along with the various regional geopolitical and geoeconomic crises, that formed the backdrop for envisioning a need for U.S. interventionary force. I pay particular attention to the concept of 'rapid deployability', a concept that has become strategized anew in recent years as a core tactic of U.S. global military posturing.

Chapter 3 deconstructs CENTCOM's discursive representation of the Middle

East and Central Asia. The chapter considers the command's reductive scripting of its Area of Responsibility as essentially a space of insecurity requiring continual intervention. In seeking to denaturalize CENTCOM's abstracted formulations of security and insecurity, I reflect upon a still-functioning Orientalist discourse of Middle Eastern volatility that is ahistorical in denying the effects of prior U.S. interventionary violence yet profoundly powerful in advancing the notion of a corrective U.S. special mission. The chapter also charts the broader U.S. geopolitical envisioning of the Middle East from the early 1980s, and the concomitant burgeoning of strategic studies institutes that have persistently championed U.S. military interventionism.

Chapter 4 examines the legal-territorial dimensions of CENTCOM's security project by detailing the legal and biopolitical modalities of power that facilitate the command's posturing across its Area of Responsibility. My aim is to illuminate what Foucault calls the 'mechanisms of security', including Status of Forces Agreements, the now standard form of asymmetric bilateral security agreements of CENTCOM, which enable the command's interventions and battlespaces. I outline the operation of what I call 'full spectrum law' and dissect the practices of lawfare that legally condition and protect CENTCOM personnel in forward-deployed areas.

From the first deployment of CENTCOM forces in the Persian Gulf in 1987, the command has convincingly fashioned itself in its annual posture statements as the 'Guardian of the Gulf', tasked with militarily patrolling, policing, and protecting a region that is pivotal for the global economy. Chapter 5 interrogates CENTCOM's deployment of this universalist register of neoliberalism at the heart of its military-economic securitization discourse, a discourse that has consistently acquired U.S. congressional support. I focus especially on the strategizing of deterrence, which the DoD appositely describes as "shaping activities" (U.S. Department of Defense 2001a, 32).

CENTCOM's key grand strategy document in the late 1990s, *Shaping the Central Region for the 21st Century*, sets out the command's long-term mission in the Middle East and Central Asia of safeguarding against future military threat and shaping the global economy. In spearheading the U.S. military's war on terror, the command continued its discursive practice of binding senses of future uncertainty to necessary practices of securitization in the present. The concluding chapter focuses on this interventionary rationale of 'future insecurity', increasingly oriented by CENTCOM and the wider U.S. military in recent years—a rationale that enables the securitization of the most broadly understood 'instability' and sanctions the ongoing use of forward-deployed forces in an era of persistent conflict. The barbarism that ISIS now represents forms part of a longer Orientalist narrative of Middle Eastern volatility and threat that Edward Said chronicled a generation ago (Said 1978).[14] That narrative continues to be drawn upon geopolitically, morally, and otherwise in new strategies of violent interventionism today—however expedient, historically forgetful, or counterproductive they may be (Cockburn 2014).[15] Such grand strategizing habitually works to occlude history and geography and to conceal context. By critically deconstructing the imperial gaze and grand strategy of CENTCOM, the spearhead of U.S. interventions in the Middle East and Central Asia for the last thirty years, my hope is to provide a different narrative that insists on history and geography—their contexts and ongoing consequences.

CHAPTER TWO

CENTCOM Activates

Cold War Geopolitics and Global Ambition

> Let our position be absolutely clear: an attempt by any outside force to gain control of the Persian Gulf region will be regarded as an assault on the vital interests of the United States of America, and such an assault will be repelled by any means necessary, including military force.
>
> **U.S. president Jimmy Carter, State of the Union Address, 1980**

In his State of the Union Address in January 1980, U.S. president Jimmy Carter first enunciated what became known as the Carter Doctrine. It signaled his administration's firm commitment to militarily securing the Persian Gulf, a region his national security advisor, Zbigniew Brzezinski, had earlier termed an 'arc of crisis' (J. Carter 1980). With the launch of the war on terror some twenty-one years later, the 'arc of crisis' became part of an 'axis of evil', yet its geoeconomic importance remained the same. In 1980, what was at stake, according to then defense secretary Harold Brown, was "the economic and political well-being of the United States and its allies," and if they were "deprived of access to the energy resources of the Gulf," the result would be "collapse of our allies and the world economy" (Brown 1980). With the war on terror in full swing, the bipartisan Council on Foreign Relations declared that "the United States alone has the capacity to protect the global oil trade against the threat of violent obstruction" and that there was an enduring need for "a strong U.S. military presence in key producing areas and in the sea lanes that carry foreign oil to American shores" (Klare 2007). This chapter offers a critical reading of the emergent geostrategic discourse of U.S. intervention in the Persian Gulf from the late 1970s and early 1980s. It explores the geopolitical and geoeconomic registers of insecurity, threat, and U.S. special mission that framed the formation of U.S. Central Command and examines the broader discursive production of military and economic security logics at the heart of a refocused U.S. grand strategy. It considers too the backdrop of the region's various contemporary political and economic crises, which, together with U.S. Cold

War anxieties vis-à-vis the USSR, coalesced in the envisioning of necessary rapid deployment of U.S. military force—CENTCOM's activation.

Interventionary Ambition

CENTCOM's extensive network of bases, access sites, and pre-positioning locations in the Middle East and Central Asia today are critical to the successful projection of U.S. foreign policy. The current extent of CENTCOM's forward presence, however, represents a high point of U.S. interventionary ambition and capacity in the region, and one that in the early years of the command's formation could only have been dreamed of by strategists in Washington. In the early 1980s, in the vast region extending eastward from Turkey to Southeast Asia, the United States held no military bases. As then undersecretary of defense Robert Komer lamented, countries across the Middle East and Central Asia at this juncture "emphatically" refused any formal basing arrangements with the United States (U.S. Department of Defense 1980, 484).[1] This geopolitical backdrop prompted the DoD to pursue four alternative objectives to secure regional strategic reach: the extension of facilities on the Indian Ocean island of Diego Garcia (purchased from Mauritius by the United Kingdom in 1965—see Vine 2009); the diplomatic procuring of contingent access sites across the region; the development of enhanced sea- and air-lift capabilities for rapid troop and equipment transport; and the creation and maintenance of Maritime Prepositioning Ships in the Indian Ocean (U.S. Department of Defense 1980, 318).

The latter policy of pre-positioning had become popular with the DoD from the early years of the Kennedy administration, when the U.S. Army began directing the pre-positioning of vehicles and other military hardware for two divisions stationed in West Germany. In 1964, the Combat Equipment Group—Europe was established and began its Prepositioning of Material Configured in Unit Sets (POMCUS) program to prepare for any potential Soviet attack.[2] Since the 1960s, pre-positioned equipment on ships as well as on land had been considered a vital strategic asset for the U.S. military's global expeditionary posture, particularly in regions where the United States did not have an abundance of friendly host governments to rely on. By the time CENTCOM came into being in 1983, pre-positioning ships in the Indian Ocean had become crucial to regional "strategic mobility"—providing "a stockpile of combat and support equipment for immediate use by arriving forces" (U.S. Congressional Budget Office 1983, 38).[3]

A common concern of contemporary military planners in Washington, however, was that pre-positioning was a limited interventionary tool in the long run, especially in terms of the emerging DoD deterrence strategy against the Soviet Union in the Middle East. Jeffrey Record at the Institute for Foreign Policy Analysis, for example, repeatedly argued that "military access ashore in the Persian Gulf" was the key to effecting U.S. foreign policy in the region (Record 1981a, 109). For Record, land access was imperative: "To get ashore, intervention forces must have access to ports, airfields, and other reception facilities[, and to] stay ashore, they require continued access to proximate logistical support bases" (1981a, 112). His strategic studies colleagues were similarly anxious to underline the challenge of "developing a deterrent strategy" and applying it "in areas of political instability and, if necessary, without the cooperation of local states" (Waltz 1981, 69; cf. Brzezinski 1983; McNaugher 1985; J. M. Epstein 1987). Such anxieties reflected a "frighteningly pessimistic" assessment of contemporary U.S. deterrent capabilities in the Middle East, at a point when the Soviets had twenty-four infantry divisions stationed just north of Iran, while the Americans had far fewer divisions based thousands of miles away in the United States (J. M. Epstein 1981, 127).

With this backdrop, the new Carter Doctrine prompted an active DoD strategy to incrementally forge more direct military links in the region, with efforts initially focused on inaugurating joint military training exercises with partner countries. Egypt quickly emerged as an important ally—the Carter administration heralding the military exercise Bright Star, initiated in 1980, as the first step in establishing a regional foothold for the U.S. military. Exercise Bright Star took place again in 1981, 1983, 1985, and 1987 and saw up to ten thousand U.S. troops at a time training with troops from Egypt, Jordan, Oman, and elsewhere (U.S. Central Command 1985; U.S. Central Command 1987). With the enunciation of the Carter Doctrine, the DoD concurrently pursued a policy of securing military access rights with several countries across the Arabian Peninsula and Horn of Africa (Rapid Deployment Joint Task Force 1981). Agreements were reached with Oman, Somalia, and Kenya, for instance, to include "standard access and status of forces arrangements" (Record 1981b, 58). By the mid-1980s, the U.S. Air Force had attained facilities use and logistics capacity at the Egyptian air bases of Qena and Cairo West, and a significant U.S. military presence had also been set up in Saudi Arabia through support for Saudi airbase modernization programs as well as through the loaning of Airborne Warning and Control System aircraft (Gold 1988).

The Rapid Deployment Force Concept

All of the DoD's initial efforts to enact the Carter Doctrine's call to secure the Persian Gulf revolved around one core idea: the 'Rapid Deployment Force' concept. Although the Persian Gulf had been on the radar of U.S. foreign policy since the end of World War II (and indeed earlier), the crisis-dominated 1970s of oil embargoes, revolution, and Soviet global ambition hastened the designation of the region as an area of U.S. 'vital interest' and accelerated plans for rapid response capabilities in the U.S. military. Ideas of rapid response have had a particular currency since the launch of the war on terror, not just in military circles but more broadly in the prevailing governmentalities of Western life.[4] In considering the interventionary governing protocols of contemporary liberal democracy, historicizing the military origins of rapid response is important. For the U.S. military, the idea of rapid response, in the form of a force that could be efficiently dispatched to a crisis region, is far from new and has long included the discursive mobilization of affective senses of risk, insecurity, and emergency—securitization registers that we see prominently functioning today (Buzan, Wæver, and de Wilde 1997; O'Malley 2004). Historically, the U.S. Marine Corps performed the role of rapid response and indeed was deployed in the Middle East in precisely this manner in the post–World War II period—in Lebanon, for example, in 1958. In 1961, the first attempt at a unified command Rapid Deployment Force (RDF) occurred, when U.S. Strike Command was set up at MacDill AFB in Tampa, Florida. The declared objective was to "provide an integrated, mobile, highly combat-ready force" for military deployment in critical "remote areas" (U.S. House of Representatives 1963, 3296). This ambition was technologically supported by the development of a new strategic transport aircraft, the C-5A, and a new sealift vessel, the Fast Deployment Logistics ship—both, in theory, facilitating the deployment of such a force directly from MacDill AFB. Strike Command failed, however, largely due to the noninvolvement of the Marine Corps and Navy and the wider context of the U.S. military being overextended elsewhere in Southeast Asia during the Vietnam War (Morrissey 2009). It was replaced in 1971 by U.S. Readiness Command, but this initiative too met with failure due to a series of bureaucratic impediments that rendered it effectively a noncombatant command, occupied primarily with planning and training (Gamlen 1993).

The U.S. military's failings in the early 1970s to cohere a unified command with responsibility for rapid deployment to crisis regions was brought into sharp relief by the emergence at the same time of what has become the quintessential 'crisis region': the Middle East. The oil crises of 1973 and 1974 firstly illuminated the region's key geoeconomic import, and they quickly prompted calls for U.S. military intervention to take an active role in the management of such crises (J. M. Epstein 1981). As the new Democratic administration of Jimmy Carter took shape in 1977, U.S. commitment to militarily securing access to the region became official policy. In mid-1977, an influential National Security Council review identified the Persian Gulf region as the 'new frontier' in Cold War relations (Record 1981b). The review was conducted with an eye on the aim of nuclear strategic equivalence with the USSR and highlighted countering Soviet threat in the Persian Gulf as imperative to the successful projection of U.S. geopolitics globally. One of the review's architects, national security advisor Zbigniew Brzezinski, was intent on strategizing anew for 'global forward presence', which would enable the U.S. military to reassert pride in the aftermath of failure in the Vietnam War (Brzezinski 1983). The new focus of U.S. global forward presence—safeguarding access to energy assets in the Persian Gulf—was subsequently underscored in Presidential Review Memorandum 10 from the Office of the Secretary of Defense. Several consequent National Security Council decisions then culminated in Presidential Decision 18 (PD-18) in August 1977, which recommended the establishment of a "quick-reaction" force composed of mobile light infantry and backed by strategic air- and sea-lift capabilities (U.S. Joint Chiefs of Staff 1982).

In March 1978, President Carter announced the imminent initiation of a new RDF to "defend our interests throughout the world" (Gamlen 1993, 218). Leaked press reports of PD-18 confirmed that 'world' as specifically the Persian Gulf region, and for its defense the United States was committing one hundred thousand troops, four aircraft carriers, and three air force wings totaling two hundred planes (Acharya 1986). The new force was designed especially for "strategic mobility independent of overseas bases and logistical support" (Gold 1988, 55). However, no budgetary support for PD-18 came until early 1980, in the aftermath of President Carter's signal State of the Union Address and in the fallout of a turbulent 1979 that had raised the RDF concept to the status of urgent.[5] On March 1, 1980, the Rapid Deployment Joint Task Force (RDJTF) was officially activated, with its headquarters set up at MacDill AFB and the following mission declared: "to plan, jointly train, exercise, and be prepared to deploy and employ designated forces in response to contingencies threatening U.S. vital interests" (Rapid Deployment Joint Task Force 1981, III-1).[6] Heralded as the key instrument to implement the Carter Doctrine, it was given the 'geographic responsibility' of "Southwest Asia," a region spanning from the Horn of Africa across the Red Sea, Arabian Peninsula, and Persian Gulf to Iran and Afghanistan.[7] The 'area of concern' (figure 2.1) mirrored the various crises that had developed across the Middle East and Horn of Africa in the late 1970s—the geographical focus, however, being very much on the Persian Gulf from the outset.[8]

From its inception, a conflated U.S.-global economic imaginary predominated in how the RDJTF was strategically envisioned. Here is RDJTF commander Lieutenant General Paul Kelley outlining the overlapping "Free World" economic stakes to the U.S. Senate Armed Services Committee's Subcommittee on Seapower and Force Projection in the command's first posture statement in March 1981:

> Since the United States imports roughly 13% of its oil requirements from the Persian Gulf, there is little doubt that if forced to do so we could find alternatives. It is highly unlikely, however, that Germany, which imports 45% of its oil requirements from the gulf, or Japan and France, who import approximately 75% of theirs, could find reasonable alternatives should this source be denied. [W]ithout Persian Gulf oil, Western Europe and Japan could be in economic chaos in a matter of months. I need not remind you of the potential consequences to the United States and the rest of the Free World. (Rapid Deployment Joint Task Force 1981, v)

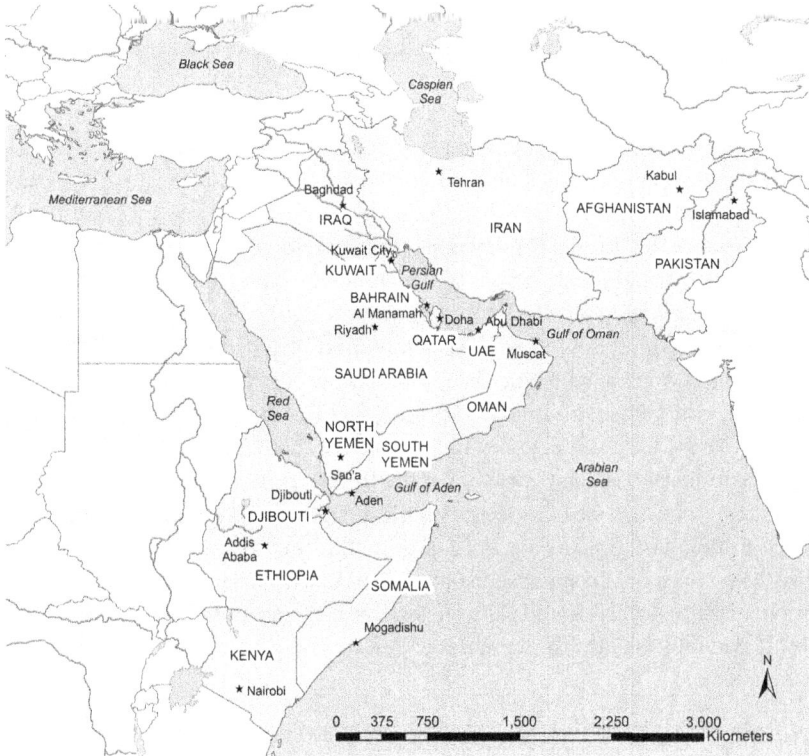

FIGURE 2.1. Rapid Deployment Joint Task Force 'Area of Concern', 1980.

The universalist interventionary remit of 'global economic security' would become a key discourse of military-economic risk management for both the RDJTF and later CENTCOM. As Lieutenant General Kelley remarked in August 1980 to the National Security Commission of the American Legion, "our security is tied directly and irrevocably to that of our allies and friends; as long as they are dependent, so are we" (Rapid Deployment Joint Task Force 1981, E3). This interventionary logic was inflected too by contemporary Cold War anxieties to deter and match Soviet global ambition. For Kelley, the "military power of the Soviet Union and the will the Soviets have shown to use it" was the "most serious" threat to the United States and its Western allies on an increasingly global geopolitical stage: "during the last decade and a half, we have seen the Russians developing a more global perspective to their military capabilities, especially in Africa and Southwest Asia" (Rapid Deployment Joint Task Force 1981, vi). Kelley variously expressed a concern that the United States should not be seen as a "Paper Tiger" on the global stage, which seems oddly overstated given the U.S. military's global interventionary capabilities today (Rapid Deployment Joint Task

Force 1981, iv–ix, E1–E7). The concern, however, highlights part of the Cold War apprehensions driving the emergence of the RDJTF. Military inferiority complexes were present both inside and outside the U.S. military in the aftermath of the Vietnam War. Kelley, for instance, felt compelled to dispel what he perceived as a widely circulated myth that painted a potential combat scenario of the "U.S. serviceman sitting at the edge of his foxhole, smoking marijuana or eating Big Macs or doing something like that, while the Soviet is leaning forward in his and he's ready to go to war" (Rapid Deployment Joint Task Force 1981, D5).

In his command's first posture statement, Lieutenant General Kelley underlined two words that were "basic" to the RDJTF's ability to oversee a credible deterrence program in Southwest Asia: "rapid" and "deployment" (Rapid Deployment Joint Task Force 1981, vii). The idea of a deterrence force, primed in forward positions, war-gamed, and ready for rapid deployment equates, of course, to a preemptive military strategy, and this was seen as something altogether new to the U.S. military. At a news briefing at the Pentagon in June 1980, Kelley could not "remember anytime in modern American history where the Americans have taken ground forces into a potential area of conflict first" (Rapid Deployment Joint Task Force 1981, D7). In any case, a new cycle of U.S. military interventionism had begun, and the RDJTF would be a preemptive presence in the Persian Gulf that would geopolitically transmit a series of "strong and powerful" signals, as Kelley expounds:

> To the Soviets it says that we will not tolerate military adventurism. Such threats to our friends and allies may constitute an assault on the vital interests of the United States, and when they do, we have a military capability to respond. To our friends and allies, it says we are indeed a nation to be reckoned with. (Rapid Deployment Joint Task Force 1981, E2)

The RDJTF, furthermore, would be compelled to initiate "sustained combat operations" if U.S. interests were threatened in the "Middle East/Persian Gulf region," as the command's first official history outlines:

> The Rapid Deployment Joint Task Force was not developed as an invasion force. Rather, it was structured chiefly as a force to deter aggression from outside the Persian Gulf region and to assist nations in the region in resisting aggression from outside the region [. . .] The presence of such a force would be intended as a signal to potential adversaries that movement of their armed forces into the area could result in direct confrontation with the United States. If deterrence failed, the Rapid Deployment Joint Task Force would be prepared to conduct sustained combat operations in the region. (Rapid Deployment Joint Task Force 1981, II-1)

Such a scripting of reluctant yet determined resolve to commit military force to safeguard U.S. and global security interests resonates with ideas of global policing and conjoined military-economic interventionism, themes I explore in detail for CENTCOM in chapter 5. However, it was CENTCOM's predecessor, the RDJTF, that first established the contours of a preemptive grand strategy of military policing and deterrence in the Middle East and Central Asia.

As with its forerunners, Strike Command and Readiness Command, the RDJTF was burdened by bureaucratic and organizational issues from the beginning, particularly given that its assigned forces (from all four armed services, in the RDJTF's case) would have to come from other commands worldwide. It did accomplish a number of important military objectives over its three years of existence, however, before it was superseded by CENTCOM: it built up important military connections, especially in Egypt, Bahrain, and Oman, via official command visits; it initiated a territorial presence in the region via joint training exercises; and it developed U.S. regional deterrence capabilities via an accelerated pre-positioning program. All these steps coalesced a policy of "operations with no forces stationed" that nonetheless demonstrated "American resolve and commitment to the region" (Rapid Deployment Joint Task Force 1984, 79, 102).[9] For many analysts, however, this level of commitment was not enough. The chief specialist on the Middle East at the Institute for Foreign Policy Analysis in Washington, Jeffrey Record, considered the RDJTF a "fatally flawed military instrument for the preservation of uninterrupted U.S. access to vital Persian Gulf oil—the principal rationale underlying the force" and believed that unless the task force was urgently reformed, "the uninterrupted flow of oil from the Persian Gulf" would remain a "threatened and inadequately defended vital U.S. interest in the region" (Record 1981b, vii, 1). Record's concerns were quickly addressed by the new Republican administration of Ronald Reagan, which committed a budget increase for the RDJTF of 85 percent for the fiscal year 1982 and proposed spending an additional $17.5 billion on its reform over the next five years (Gamlen 1993). In April 1981, Reagan's new secretary of defense, Caspar Weinberger, announced that the RDJTF would be upgraded to a regional geographic command, with full responsibility concentrated on the Middle East and Southwest Asia (U.S. Congressional Budget Office 1983, 4). Later that year, he confirmed a clear shift in U.S. national security discourse, arguing before the House Committee on the Budget that the United States faced a greater military threat in the Middle East than in NATO Europe and Northeast Asia combined (U.S. House Committee on the Budget 1981, 9). Against the backdrop of this new security focus for the U.S. military's global operations, the RDJTF was officially replaced on January 1, 1983, by United States Central Command, CENTCOM[10]—the first new unified command with specific geographic responsibilities in thirty-five years. The U.S. military's Unified Command Plan, the expression of its global ambition of 'full spectrum dominance', was changed accordingly, with nineteen countries being incorporated into the new command's Area of Responsibility (AOR), seen in figure 2.2.[11]

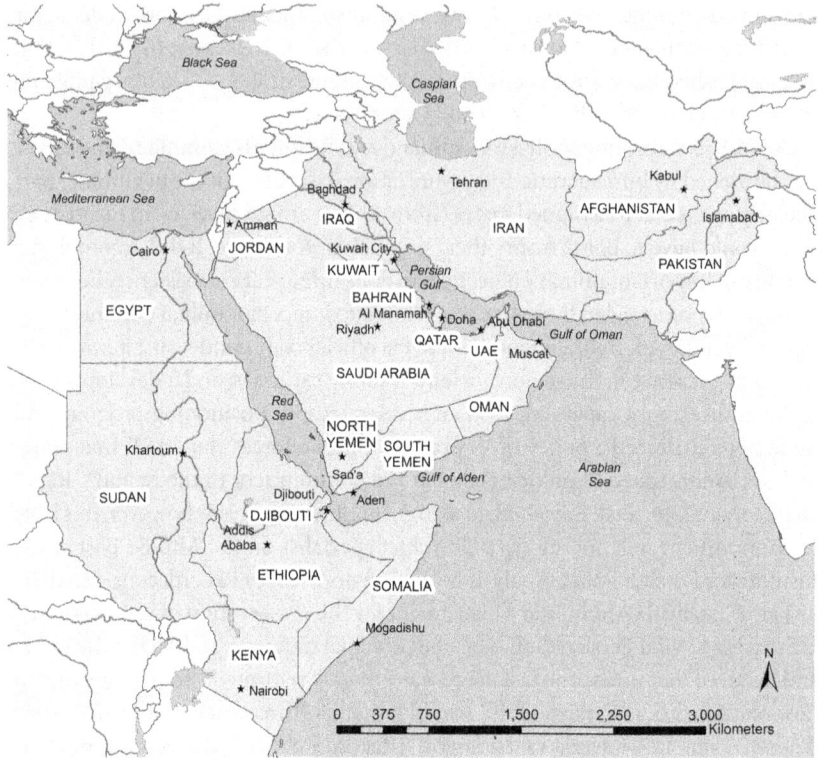

FIGURE 2.2. CENTCOM 'Area of Responsibility', 1983.

CENTCOM Emerges

CENTCOM immediately assumed the role of militarily spearheading the new geographical security focus of U.S. foreign policy on the Middle East. Its original mission was declared thus:

> The mission of the United States Central Command is to achieve U.S. policy objectives in its area of responsibility. These national policy objectives include the following basic goals: assuring Western access to adequate supplies of oil, deterring Soviet aggression, preserving regional stability, and halting the spread of Soviet influence, reversing it wherever possible. (U.S. Central Command 1985, 10)

As its first official command history made clear, there were "two primary threats to the key resources located in USCENTCOM's area of responsibility and to the sea lines of communication needed for U.S. forces to get there: local instability and the Soviet Union" (U.S. Central Command 1985, 11).[12] In its own words, CENTCOM's initiation "indicated a more active U.S. policy toward the Middle East," it "emphasized the importance of this area to American interests," and it "underscored the fact that the United States was ready to take military action to defend those interests" (U.S. Central Command 1985, 9–10). In essence, the command had "evolved as a practical solution to the problem of projecting U.S. military power to the Gulf region from halfway around the world" (U.S. Central Command 2007a). Imperial assumptions about "the problem of projecting U.S. military power" are writ large in such declarations (a theme central to chapter 3), but interestingly CENTCOM commanders and strategists seemed aware of the potentially negative reactions to such assertions at the outset of the command. When General George Crist assumed leadership as commander in chief (CINC) in November 1985, for example, he noted that CENTCOM was regarded by many nations in the region as "little more than a major intervention force designed to operate solely for U.S. purposes without their consultation or participation" (Hines 2000, 44; cf. Telhami 2002). At this point, CENTCOM's Public Affairs Department had set out specific "public affairs themes" for the command, with a view to maintaining a "low profile with the media" and minimizing the reporting of military actions that "would generate media interest" because doing so would "help defuse host nation sensitivities" regarding their involvement with the U.S. military (U.S. Central Command 1985, 194–195). In addition, CENTCOM mission declarations were increasingly framed to reflect universalist motivations and inflected by efforts to be culturally sensitive. In late 1983, for example, the United States Information Agency (USIA) produced a twenty-minute video featuring CENTCOM's first CINC, Lieutenant General Robert Kingston, and U.S. secretary of defense Caspar Weinberger, among others, explaining CENTCOM's "broad military and diplomatic role in its area of responsibility"; the video was brought "to the field," shown to "country teams" at various U.S. embassies, and used to prompt ambassadors to instruct their staff to get on message when communicating the interventionary good of CENTCOM's security mission (USIA later produced voice-over copies in Arabic and several other regional languages to "permit wide use throughout the AOR") (U.S. Central Command 1985, 247–248; see also U.S. Central Command 1987, 180–182).

In its early years, CENTCOM's focus was on building up military interventionary capabilities in its Area of Responsibility. Doing so required developing a range of technical, logistical, and legal mechanisms and systems oriented to enable rapid intervention, and these were honed, revised, and refined via joint training exercises, such as the aforementioned Bright Star (U.S. Central Command 1985, 1987).[13] Enabling CENTCOM's interventionary capacity on the ground involved a wide spectrum of initiatives, including multiple engineering and construction projects;[14] the development of potable water and well drilling facilities; fuels depot management in forward-operating locations; cargo, naval, and aircraft mobility enhancement programs; telephone and communication systems streamlining; planning for electronic warfare activities; diplomatic agreements for facilities access, pre-positioning programs, and naval fleet support; and the ne-gotiation of legal Memorandums of Understanding for supplies and services for forward-operating ground forces.[15] All these initiatives were part of a carefully di-rected military strategy whose objective was to "cement relationships" with coun-tries across the command's Area of Responsibility by technically and legally fa-cilitating "joint coordination and planning for future operations"—which would, it was hoped, demonstrate "American commitment to the region's security" and promote "acceptance of U.S. military presence" (U.S. Central Command 1985, 98).

In 1987, U.S. president Ronald Reagan issued CENTCOM its first major oper-ational assignment. It was a specific geoeconomic mission for 'the good of the global economy': to ensure the continuous flow of oil through the Persian Gulf at the height of the Iran-Iraq War. In conjunction with the newly formed U.S. Special Operations Command (also headquartered at MacDill AFB since 1987), battleship battle groups, carrier battle groups, and surface action groups from the Navy's Third, Sixth, and Seventh Fleets patrolled and regulated the flow of naval traffic through the Persian Gulf from July 1987 to September 1988 in an operation code-named Earnest Will. It was the biggest U.S. naval operation since World War II. By reflagging Kuwaiti tankers with American ensigns during the so-called Tanker War between Iran and Iraq, the operation demonstrated what Reagan called U.S. commitment to "the free flow of oil" (cited in Palmer 1992, 122). As the CENTCOM Office of History later recounted, "Washington sought to ensure safe passage" for "merchant shipping," leading to "the command's first combat operations" (U.S. Central Command 2007a).

A commitment to safeguarding energy assets and the free flow of commerce in the Persian Gulf region has been a core element of CENTCOM's mission since its first interventionary operation in 1987. From this point forward, the United States effectively assumed the role of military-economic 'Guardians of the Gulf' (Palmer 1992). After the Iraqi invasion of Kuwait in August 1990, the command quickly amassed a five-hundred-thousand-strong defensive force to form a 'Des-ert Shield' against the possible invasion of its vital oil-exporting ally in the region, Saudi Arabia.[16] Its devastatingly successful Operation Desert Storm subsequently left the U.S. military with a dominant regional posture—its hegemonic strate-gic reach coinciding with the breakup of the Soviet Union. Paul Wolfowitz, then chair in national security strategy at the National War College of the National Defense University in Washington, observed that the Gulf War "transformed the security structure of the Persian Gulf—a region that will remain the principal source of energy needs well into the next century" (Wolfowitz 1994, 123). Ten years later, Wolfowitz would be a key architect of the Bush administration's extension of CENTCOM's energy security mission in the Middle East and Central Asia into the new century. Wolfowitz considered the Gulf War a universalist intervention to prevent "something truly terrible": a "nuclear war by a tyrant in control of most of the energy supplies that are the lifeblood of the industrialized democracies of the world" (Wolfowitz 1994, 124). He was echoing the same kind of U.S.-led universalism espoused by President Reagan in the 1980s in scripting CENTCOM's first major security mission in intervening, the Tanker War: "The Persian Gulf will remain open to navigation by the nations of the world" (cited in Palmer 1992, 124).

The success of the rhetoric of a (U.S.-led) universalist 'special mission' was a central factor in the swift and unprecedented passing of twelve UN Security Council resolutions against Iraq prior to the CENTCOM-led allied attack in 1991. Six months before Saddam Hussein's invasion of Kuwait in 1990, CENTCOM CINC General Norman Schwarzkopf declared to the Senate Armed Services Committee that "the greatest threat to U.S. interests in the area is the spillover of regional conflict which could endanger American lives, threaten U.S. interests in the area or interrupt the flow of oil, thereby requiring the commitment of U.S. combat forces" (U.S. Central Command 1990). Schwarzkopf was, in effect, announcing the necessity of another major CENTCOM intervention in the Middle East. It would later become known as the Gulf War. CENTCOM's geoeconomic mission to protect U.S. vital interests in the Gulf compelled it to intervene in early 1991. Its success in intervening confirmed its role as 'Guardian of the Gulf', and in the war's aftermath a series of CENTCOM-sponsored studies recommended a focused mission for the command thereafter, revolving around two core concepts: 'critical economic interests' and 'forward deterrence'.[17] The 1992 study *Oil and the New World System: CENTCOM Rethinks Its Mission*, for example, set out an active deterrent strategy for the command in defense of vital U.S. economic interests. The strategy vision identified a military-economic 'policing' function for CENTCOM and flagged at length the global economic stakes:

> The new international system that has replaced bipolarity cannot survive without oil from Saudi Arabia. The industrialized West not only must be assured of dependable supplies but the price also must be acceptable. (Pelletiere and Johnson 1992, v; cf. T. C. Jones 2010)

Calling for a geographical concentration of CENTCOM resources and operations in the most pivotal nodes of energy assets, the authors advised the command to "narrow its focus" to what they termed an "Area of Concentration" centered on the Persian Gulf because, put plainly, the command's "only useful indeed vital mission" was "to keep oil moving from the Gulf to the West" (Pelletiere and Johnson 1992, 13–15).[18] In order to do so, the command would have to "cooperate with various civilian agencies (of the United Nations, the World Bank, and the U.S. Government)" in coercing states such as Iraq and Iran "into preserving the stability of the Gulf," but its "specific role" would be "to take over the coercion process whenever a crisis arises" (Pelletiere and Johnson 1992, 17). CENTCOM fully embraced this role in the aftermath of the Gulf War in establishing an extensive regional deterrence strategy in the name of energy security and, more broadly, global economic stability.

Reprising Imperial Interventionism

The new Democratic administration of Bill Clinton in 1993 continued political support for CENTCOM's now firmly fused military-economic security mission. President Clinton's chief security document for the Gulf region, *United States Security Strategy for the Middle East*, outlined "America's enduring interest in the security of the Middle East" as centrally revolving around "assured access to Gulf oil" (U.S. Department of Defense 1995a, 6). Then U.S. secretary of defense William Perry introduced the document thus:

> One of the most controversial questions the United States faces in the aftermath of the Cold War is when to use military force in this complex world. But there is little dispute that we must be prepared to use force to defend our vital interests: when the survival of the United States or its key allies is in danger, when our critical economic interests are threatened, or when dealing with the emergence of a future nuclear threat. Nowhere are these criteria met more clearly than in the Middle East. (U.S. Department of Defense 1995a, ii)

In this statement Perry rehearses a well-versed geographical representation of the Middle East as inherently unstable and threatening to global security (largely in economic terms). He also advocates a necessary U.S.-led response based on a persuasive risk-securitization binary that reprises older imperial logics of liberal interventionism and remaps them onto contemporary security needs for the global good. Such imperial continuities were already evident in CENTCOM's grand strategizing at this point:

> For years the Gulf was a British sphere of interest. When they left, they handed the job of protection over to the Shah. Now, the United States is doing the job. (Pelletiere and Johnson 1992, 18)[19]

By the mid-1990s, CENTCOM was well positioned geographically and militarily to 'do the job' of imperial intervention—its deterrence operations at key nodes across the Middle East were confidently executing U.S. foreign policy. In 1995, for instance, CENTCOM CINC General James Peay outlined his command's operational successes to *Joint Force Quarterly* by citing the rapid deployment of CENTCOM troops during Operation Vigilant Warrior a year earlier:

> On October 6, 1994, reports poured into the command center that two Iraqi Republican Guard divisions were moving by both rail and heavy equipment transporters southward from their garrisons near Baghdad to assembly areas south of the Euphrates [. . .] CENTCOM at once modified on-the-shelf operational plans and orchestrated the deployment of units from all services in what became known as Operation Vigilant Warrior. Postured to prevent Iraqi aggression against Kuwait and Saudi Arabia, the command built both on the combat power of U.S. forward

deployed and coalition forces and on American prepositioned equipment ashore and afloat to emplace a defensive force. On October 10, as the first U.S.-based aircraft began landing at airfields in the Persian Gulf and lead companies of the 24th Infantry Division began moving to tactical assembly areas, Iraq announced the withdrawal of reinforcing Republican Guard divisions thus defusing the situation. (Peay 1995b, 32)

For Peay (1995b, 32), CENTCOM's mission was ultimately vital for one key reason: maintaining "regional stability and security in the Persian Gulf," which was "integral to the political and economic wellbeing of the international community."

The Clinton administration sought to advance a global national security posture in tandem with a dominant global economic posture as the twenty-first century approached (Institute for National Security Studies 1999; cf. Morrissey 2009). Militarily, these conjoined ambitions centered on extending a forward deterrence strategy of safeguarding 'critical economic interests'. By the turn of the new century, CENTCOM had proven itself in successfully executing deterrence operations in the Persian Gulf, especially in the aftermath of the Gulf War; Operation Desert Spring, for example, comprised frequent training exercises that effectively resulted in a "continuous presence" in the region to "deter conflict, promote stability, and facilitate a seamless transition to war, if required" (U.S. Central Command 1997a, 5). Throughout the 1990s, CENTCOM's security objective, espoused in its annual posture statements, had affirmed an unproblematic vision of using force "to protect the United States' vital interest in the region—uninterrupted, secure U.S./Allied access to Gulf oil" (U.S. Central Command 1995, 1; cf. 8–9). Such envisionings were replete with universalist claims of 'special mission'. General Peay, for instance, told the House Appropriations Committee's Subcommittee on National Security in 1997 that any disruption in the flow of petroleum from the Persian Gulf would "precipitate economic calamity" (U.S. Central Command 1997b). His successor as CENTCOM CINC, General Anthony Zinni, echoed these sentiments and located CENTCOM's geoeconomic mission precisely in his 1998 report to the Senate Armed Services Committee:

> America's interests in [the Central Region] reflect our beliefs in access to free markets [and] regional energy resources [. . .] The vast quantities of oil, gas, and other resources present in the Gulf region, which includes 69 percent of the world's known oil reserves plus significant natural gas fields, are essential to today's global economies. Much of the oil exported from the Arabian Gulf countries passes through at least one of three important maritime choke points: the Strait of Hormuz, the Suez Canal, or the Bab el Mandeb between Yemen and Eritrea. When the Central Asian States are added to CENTCOM's AOR in 1999, the addition of their energy resources, currently estimated at 15–25 billion dollars of oil, will only increase the importance of the region to economies worldwide. (U.S. Central Command 1998)

The succeeding Republican administration of President George W. Bush did not alter CENTCOM's core operational mission: forward deterrence in defense of energy assets. As U.S. secretary of energy Spencer Graham declared to the House International Relations Committee in 2002, "energy security" was, after all, "national security" (U.S. House International Relations Committee 2002). It is worthwhile to remember too that coinciding with the Bush administration's aggressive military interventionism in CENTCOM's Area of Responsibility in the wake of September 11, 2001, was an ongoing and simultaneous security strategy of economic interventionism targeting "economic liberalization and integration" (Katzman 2006, 26–29; cf. Dalby 2007; N. Klein 2007; Martin 2007). Herein lies a clear bipartisan continuum of U.S. foreign policy. Similar to the 1990s in the wake of the Gulf War, negotiated free trade agreements with various Gulf Cooperation Council (GCC) states in the aftermath of the launch of the Iraq War opened up markets for a range of multinational oil and gas companies, including, for example, Exxon Mobil, Royal Dutch Shell, and Totalfina Elf. The Bush administration's *National Defense Strategy* from 2005 further illustrated its dual strategy for military "strategic access" and economic "global freedom of action," oriented toward four conjoined military and economic concerns: safeguarding "the security of the United States"; ensuring "freedom of action"; helping "secure our partners"; and protecting "the integrity of the international economic system" (U.S. Department of Defense 2005a, 6).

CENTCOM's securitization rationale has always been inflected too with more overtly political and cultural concerns of 'bringing freedom and democracy' in the face of 'cultural barbarity and political repression'—thus reprising a long history of colonial discourse denigrating whole nations and monopolizing the moral compass for their political, social, and economic correction (Gregory 2004). I take up the story of this instrumental interventionary discourse in chapter 3. In any discussion of military-economic securitization, it is important to recognize the attendant cultural logics that representationally and performatively underpin and support it. We sometimes fail to fully acknowledge that capitalism itself is an inherently cultural as well as political and economic system. CENTCOM's capitalist security project has long conflated political, economic, and cultural visions of liberal interventionism. In 2003, bringing Iraq back into an 'open', 'free-market', and 'progressive' global political economy was the dominant discursive register of U.S. occupation. Consider, for example, the first news briefing on reconstructing and stabilizing Iraq given by Paul Bremer as head of the Coalition Provisional Authority (CPA):

> Now that [our] sanctions have been lifted, it's important for Iraq to reenter the world economy. The most obvious example of that is the sale of Iraqi oil, the first sale of Iraqi oil directly into the world market by the Iraqis [. . .] And that is good news; it means Iraq will have reentered the world petroleum market. (U.S. Department of Defense 2003a)

For Bremer, the "main emphasis" was "restoring economic activity," because doing so would have the effect of not only enhancing global economic health but simultaneously showing the Iraqis that they were now better off (U.S. Department of Defense 2003a).[20] Such an abstracted vision negates the flagrant oscillations of the U.S. foreign policy toward Iraq since the early 1990s: military destruction, followed by over a decade of crippling, punitive economic sanctions, followed by renewed military destruction and invasion, before an invitation to "reenter the world economy." In all of this, we see the deeply contradictory logics of U.S. military-economic grand strategy and the occlusion of its profound human geographical consequences, whether through repeated interventionary violence or so-called nonviolent sanctions.

Conclusion

With the backdrop of the Cold War, President Jimmy Carter's State of the Union Address in 1980 solidified the United States' renewed commitment to the security of the most energy-rich region on earth. The speech's identification of the geostrategic import of the Middle East and Central Asia could not be clearer:

> The region which is now threatened by Soviet troops in Afghanistan is of great strategic importance: it contains more than two-thirds of the world's exportable oil. The Soviet effort to dominate Afghanistan has brought Soviet military forces to within 300 miles of the Indian Ocean and close to the Straits of Hormuz, a waterway through which most of the world's oil must flow. The Soviet Union is now attempting to consolidate a strategic position, therefore, that poses a grave threat to the free movement of Middle East oil. (J. Carter 1980)

For Carter, the region's escalating geopolitical volatility demanded "resolute action, not only for this year but for many years to come" (J. Carter 1980). In many ways, this moment marked the beginning of the scripting of the 'Long War' and the idea of 'rapid response', for which the RDJTF and soon thereafter CENTCOM assumed the spearhead. As the key appendage in enacting a refocused U.S. foreign policy in the Middle East and Central Asia, CENTCOM quickly adopted an interventionary discourse that championed a military-economic security strategy for the good of a neoliberal global economy. It is a securitization discourse built on long-established registers of liberal imperialism, and one that has remained remarkably consistent for over thirty years at CENTCOM. In the following chapter, I examine how CENTCOM's mission reprises older imperial logics of interventionism and remaps them onto contemporary Western security needs and, more specifically, U.S. global ambition.

CHAPTER THREE

Envisioning the Middle East

New Imperial Regimes of Truth

> No history is mute. No matter how much they burn it, break it, and lie about it, human history refuses to shut its mouth. Despite deafness and ignorance, the time that was continues to tick inside the time that is.
>
> **Eduardo Galleano, *Upside Down: A Primer for the Looking-Glass World***

In any critique of imperial geography, past or present, lies the danger of reifying the regimes of truth of the metropole. A rarely identified contemporary metropole is MacDill Air Force Base in Tampa, Florida. It was an unlikely candidate for ever becoming one when it was slated for closure in the early 1960s, prior to the Cuban Missile Crisis. Yet today U.S. interventionary power in the most cited strategically vital region on earth is directed from within its confines at CENTCOM Headquarters (figure 3.1). In the story of CENTCOM's abstracted discursive production of the Middle East and Central Asia, the human geographies of its Area of Responsibility 'on the ground' frequently become hidden. Insisting upon the latter, linking the two, and avoiding a command institutional history in which the focus is on those who produce the discourses rather than those who are subject to them is admittedly difficult. This chapter considers CENTCOM's reductive representation of its Area of Responsibility as essentially a space of insecurity requiring continual intervention. In seeking to denaturalize the command's abstracted formulations, the chapter reflects on a still deeply registered Orientalist discourse of Middle Eastern volatility, framed repeatedly in the context of its corollary: corrective U.S. special mission. The chapter also explores the wider U.S. national security vision of the Middle East from the early 1980s and the role played by a burgeoning assemblage of defense policy institutes and strategic studies centers in reinforcing a powerful geographical imaginary of Middle Eastern instability that serves to deny the effects of prior U.S. interventionism yet champion the need for ongoing U.S. security missions.

FIGURE 3.1. Seal of United States Central Command, CENTCOM Headquarters. Source: Bobbie O'Brien, WUSF Public Media.

Populating the Landscapes of War

When the U.S.-led war on terror was extended to the attack on Iraq in 2003, in the face of the biggest global protest in the history of the world, there was a palpable sense of being overwhelmed by military-political monopolizations of words and interventionary rationales, if not, of course, by bombs. Documenting and insisting on the populated landscapes of the West's late modern wars has been vitally important in academic discursive and political efforts to challenge essentialist formulations of interventionary violence. Geographers have been especially keen to highlight the use of strategic understandings of space and security to sanction the use of U.S. military force (Dalby 2007; Gregory and Pred 2007; Hyndman 2007; Amoore 2009), while there have been valuable contributions from history, political science, and elsewhere in examining the imperial and colonial past's echoes in contemporary U.S. interventions (Little 2002; Dodge 2003; Gardner and Young 2007; Ryan and Kiely 2009; Bacevich 2016). The colonial legacies reverberating through the present have been addressed by geographers too—Derek Gregory (2004, 16) showing how the war on terror reified colonialism's deeply registered cultural tropes "that mark other people as irredeemably 'Other' and that license the unleashing of exemplary violence against them." The intimate connections between the violence of war and geographical knowledge can be traced back to the emergence of geography as a discipline at the zenith of European colonialism in the nineteenth century (Heffernan 1996; Woodward 2005). Surveying and cartography, in particular, facilitated what Edward Said (1993, 271) called "acts of geographical violence," in which spaces were "explored, charted, and finally brought under control." The twentieth century's two world wars saw the discipline of geography play an even more significant role in both the practices of war and the codification and legitimation of its interventionary violence, while the advent of satellite-enabled remote sensing, global positioning systems, and geographic information systems during the Cold War and beyond saw geography further expand its military utility (Farish 2006; Barnes 2008).

Cartography's key role in late modern war continues, owing much to its enduring capacity for abstraction and distancing, as Trevor Paglen (2008) notes:

> The "God's eye" view implicit in much cartography is usually not helpful in terms of describing everyday life, nor in describing the qualities of the relationships that cartography depicts. Because of what cartography cannot represent [. . .] it becomes pretty clear why it, and the forms of power that the cartographic viewpoint suggests, have traditionally been such powerful instruments of both colonialism and the contemporary geopolitical ordering of the world.

The rise of extraterritorial violence via drone warfare by the U.S. military in recent years relies on particular forms of prestrike cartographic surveillance and poststrike cartographic explanation. Sifting out the disconnected geographical knowledges from surveillance to strike poses a considerable challenge. As Derek Gregory (2014) remarks, "thinking about the multiple 'situations' folded into a single air strike orchestrated by a drone" prompts us to consider "their lack of connectedness," the "dispersed, uneven and labile formation of what Foucault called a dispositive." Gregory continues:

> Thinking explicitly about how to stage all this [the multiple situations that inflect any given incident] is a way not only of presenting research differently but of conducting research differently. Because once you start to think in these terms, you begin to see things that were otherwise at best at the very edges of your field of view.

Gregory's interest in the specificities of the 'situational' not only attends to the levels of disconnection in the construction and circulation of dominant forms of instrumental geographical knowledge, it intimates too a core postcolonial concern for insisting on those marginalized 'out of view'.

Circulating prioritized, instrumental geographical knowledge is something CENTCOM and the wider U.S. military does very well. The repeated designation and casting out of 'enemy combatants' in the war on terror as 'the worst of the worst' or 'less than human' forms much of the discursive terrain from which the ideological justification for interventionary U.S. violence emerges. This legitimates the U.S. military not only in offensive mode but also in defensive mode, as exemplified by the legal armatures that were instigated post 9/11 to facilitate 'enhanced interrogation techniques' or torture (Savage 2015). In the spaces of extraordinary rendition and torture throughout the world, the 'Other' is not only reduced to bare life but largely erased from view. Even in the recent exposure by the U.S. Senate Select Committee on Intelligence of the extent of torture performed by U.S. intelligence personnel, much of the subsequent debate was dominated by questions of intelligence effectiveness (or not) rather than on the plight of those tortured or on the vital questions of law, human rights, and accountability (Guardian Editorial 2014; Timm 2014).

The hegemonic Western response to the *Charlie Hebdo* shootings and coordinated November attacks in Paris that bookended a terrible 2015 for the French capital also divulges a selective imperial regime of truth about violence, empathy, and outrage. Markha Valenta's commentary in the wake of the first attack captured this selectivity:

> everything that might be said about revolutionary Islamist movements—when it comes to global violence—could be said about global Americanism and U.S. foreign policy. It has been ruthless, cruel, illiberal, anti-democratic. It has wreaked havoc, killed innocents [. . .] It does so in our name. In the name of democracy. And those who expose this, as did Chelsea Manning, are shut up ruthlessly, cruelly and in ways designed to degrade. (Yet we did not march then). (Valenta 2015)

Valenta's insistence on context echoes Derek Gregory's thoughtful and carefully reasoned reminder of why the "ghosts of a colonial past continue to haunt the colonial present" in contemporary France (Gregory 2015b). Imperialism's structural violence and the regimes of truth that commonly erase it from view warrant our critical attention as much now as ever. Today, locating and defining difference remains integral to perpetuating new regimes of truth about imperial violence. In violence's differentiation, we are presented with a separation and erasure of place and culture, and we are witness to an effacement of the pain of 'Others' (Gopal 2014). The imperial story is yet again codified into truth hegemonically, and its deconstruction demands particular attention to the formative grids of power-knowledge. For CENTCOM, it demands an unmaking of the worlds of its intervention.

Scripting CENTCOM's World

CENTCOM Headquarters in South Tampa is separated from the worlds of its interventionary forces by thousands of miles. As the command explains, its headquarters is "not located in its theater of operations because of sensitivities in some of the region's nations" (U.S. Central Command 2007b; cf. Prados 2001). Those sensitivities have not prevented CENTCOM from developing an extensive basing structure in its 'theater of operations,' however: in the early twenty-first century, the command supported 128 operating bases across its Area of Responsibility, by which time it had also developed a mobile deployable headquarters, CENTCOM Deployable Headquarters (CDHQ), in Camp As Sayliyah outside Doha in Qatar (Raytheon 2003; U.S. Central Command 2006b). CENTCOM has been keen to intersect its forward-deployed troops with the militaries of its various host countries (via joint training exercises, in particular), but the primary goal is always strategic: to maximize interventionary capabilities.[1] Furthermore, across its Area of Responsibility, its troops are based in isolated compounds for security reasons, far removed from any opportunity of local encounter, as Mark Gillem (2007) has documented. Even in the 'field of intervention' at CDHQ in Qatar, where field commanders ostensibly "maintain seamless connectivity" with "command staff at their main headquarters at MacDill Air Force Base" (Raytheon 2003), the predominant gaze is backward to the metropole, just as throughout colonial history. And when CENTCOM's gaze *is* directed toward its Area of Responsibility, it is underpinned by a liberal 'world policeman' sensibility. Command historian David Dawson, for example, commented thus on "the main obstacles to regional cooperation" and why the U.S. presence is imperative:

> They are often more willing to work bilaterally with the United States than with each other. But a series of bilateral relationships with the United States enables CENTCOM to act as a de facto link between the countries. In the past few years we have seen a significant increase in willingness to participate in multi-lateral exercises. (Dawson 2014)[2]

From its inception, CENTCOM has confidently asserted its assigned role in a U.S. global security mission in which unified commands have "divided up the world" (U.S. Central Command 1986a, 5). The cartographic representation of this division, titled "The World with Commanders' Areas of Responsibility" (figure 3.3), features CENTCOM's AOR at the center of the map. It is a profoundly imperial mapping, reifying a global securitization discourse in which the world is divided up into regions and the U.S. military is assigned "geographic responsibilities" to patrol, police, and intervene therein (U.S. Department of Defense 2016a). With its establishment, CENTCOM assumed 'responsibility' for "a specific portion of the earth's surface," and its representation of that portion of the earth has been instrumental in the 'making' of the region as intrinsically a space of insecurity requiring intervention, regulation, and ultimately saving from itself (U.S. Central Command 1986a, 4). The command's focal discursive tactic is familiar to any reader of colonial history: the identification of threat, disorder, and volatility, with the simultaneous signaling of liberal correction and universalist special mission. In its 1999 strategy document, *Shaping the Central Region for the 21st Century*, such a special mission is outlined plainly:

Our friends in the region have and continue to support our presence in the region. Their contributions to our engagement in the region have included access to bases and ports, logistical and equipment support, infrastructure improvements and cost sharing of ongoing operations. Since 1990, we have made great progress in our ability to deter and, if needed, respond rapidly to aggression through improvements in our prepositioning programs, infrastructure improvements and force projection capabilities. (U.S. Central Command 1999a, 10)

There are several rhetorical and imperial claims here, but two are foremost: the first is the patriarchal identification of "friends" who "continue to support" the U.S. presence in CENTCOM's Area of Responsibility (this also involves a profound silencing of any resistance); the second is the dichotomous positing of 'good' and 'bad' forms of interventionary violence, one that is implicitly necessary and as-signed a regulatory function, and another that equates to "aggression" and is cast as illegitimate (Sidaway 1998; Coleman 2003; S. Graham 2005).

Shaping the Central Region for the 21st Century sets out an imperial vision for the Middle East and Central Asia that tasks CENTCOM with securing the unstable future of a pivotal regional geography for the global economy. Three core elements of CENTCOM's imperial mission are evident even in the title. First, the word 'shap-ing' reflects the urges of liberal empire in advancing global geoeconomic ambition. Since 1983, CENTCOM's shaping has been undertaken from the confines of a U.S. Air Force base in Tampa, Florida, yet such a level of abstraction has not prevented its framing of its Area of Responsibility as vital to the shaping of the global econ-omy. Second, the title reprises the colonial tactic of renaming vast regions, reduc-ing a multiplicity of peoples and places from an all-seeing Cartesian and Western perspective. The 'Central Region' is central in terms of what the U.S. military calls 'full spectrum dominance'—dominance of global U.S. interests, ongoing military threats, and emergent geoeconomic challenges. And third, the temporal signaling of CENTCOM's mission is to secure the future: 'for the 21st Century'. Well before the war on terror began, CENTCOM was openly planning for the securitization of the future of the Middle East and Central Asia and the perennial requirement of intervention and deterrence. Even when specific operations such as Operation Enduring Freedom are officially declared over (as President Obama announced on December 28, 2014, to end the 'longest war in U.S. history'), the Long War goes on. U.S. troops remain and Afghanistan continues to be considered an 'area of active hostilities' (Gregory 2015a).

In CENTCOM's long-haul mission, its initial focus on securing and safeguarding energy assets and transportation networks partly explains why its Area of Respon-sibility did not include Israel and the Occupied Territories (Gold 1988).[3] Apart from illustrating the emphasis of U.S. national security interests in the region, the policy of separating Persian Gulf issues from Palestinian ones also mirrors the imbalance between the diplomacy of the U.S. State Department and the military strategy of the DoD. For the fiscal year (FY) 2015, the base budget for the DoD was $495.6 billion, while the FY 2015 base budget for the State Department and the U.S. Agency for International Development (USAID) was $40.3 billion—a ratio of more than 12–1 (U.S. Department of Defense 2014, 1-1; U.S. Department of State 2014, 1). The emphasis on military force rather than diplomacy was present from the onset of the Rapid Deployment Force concept in the early 1980s. As then prominent national security expert Jeffrey Record opined: "[i]t should go without saying that military reputation, or the ability to use force successfully in defense of declared national interests, is desirable in a world where force remains the final arbiter of international disputes" (Record 1981b, 39). The Goldwater-Nichols Defense Reform Act of 1986 seemed to reinforce this understanding about the primacy of military force in international relations: in an important policy shift for CENTCOM CINCS, thereafter they "had a unique chain of command arrangement, reporting directly to the Secretary of Defense rather than through the Joint Chiefs of Staff" (Wrage 2004, 186). Ever since, CENTCOM CINCS have played a much more active, rather than attendant, role in enacting U.S. foreign policy in the Middle East, especially compared with their diplomatic counterparts in the State Department. Former CENTCOM CINC general Norman Schwarzkopf, for example, recalled in his memoirs how he reveled in a role akin to "a kind of military ombudsman," "overseeing advisors' work" and "solidifying relations with rulers and generals" (Schwarzkopf 1992, 271).[4]

Other than financial resources and greater governmental access, CENTCOM CINCS have always had one additional advantage over their State Department colleagues in effecting U.S. national security policy overseas: their military brief does not compel them to "implicitly or explicitly pass judgment on the internal politics or regimes with which they do business" (Robbins 2004, 172). As James Robbins (2004, 172) puts it, the "promotion of human rights or political change" is not the "primary province of the combatant commander." CENTCOM's pragmatic alliances with various repressive regimes in its Area of Responsibility since 1983, from Saddam Hussein in Iraq in the 1980s to the Northern Alliance in Afghanistan in the early years of the new millennium, demonstrate this plainly. Where do human rights lie on CENTCOM's list of interventionary priorities? And has the recently heightened military consciousness of international law, in what Eyal Weizman terms 'the humanitarian present', significantly featured in CENTCOM's operations (Weizman 2011; cf. Douzinas 2007)? I take up these questions centrally in later chapters in considering CENTCOM's legal grand strategy and the extent to which, rhetorically at least, the command has embraced the language of humanitarianism in orienting its 'stability operations' over the last ten years. It is clear that in the early 1990s, however, humanitarian definitions of 'stability' did not substantially inflect CENTCOM's mission. The previously cited CENTCOM-sponsored study, *Oil and the New World System: CENTCOM Rethinks Its Mission*, is particularly revealing of the kind of interventionary practices the command should pursue, and those it should not. The report came out a year before the CENTCOM mission in Somalia failed, with a loss of eighteen Army Rangers. Yet even before this incident, the authors warned of such operations taking CENTCOM's focus away from its long-term military-economic mission: "Somalia type operations should be approached with extreme caution, and under no circumstances should they be allowed to escalate because they have the potential to wreck the system" (Pelletiere and Johnson 1992, v).

In CENTCOM's wide range of discursive productions of its Area of Responsibility, from posture statements and grand strategy reports to mission declarations and 'Country Books',[5] whole nations like Somalia are geographically reduced and represented via Orientalist discourse. In such representations, there is never an acknowledgment of the effects of prior U.S. and Western interventions in the production of the region's terror and volatility. The CENTCOM-commissioned strategy study above repeatedly references a decontextualized, intrinsic Middle Eastern volatility. "In the Gulf one does not have to go looking for trouble," it declares; the area is "volatile as it is" (Pelletiere and Johnson 1992, 26).[6] CENTCOM, furthermore, has "no brief to involve itself in hole-in-the-corner disputes" because "neither the United States, nor any other major state, is vitally interested—or even strategically anymore—in countries like Somalia" (Pelletiere and Johnson 1992, 12–13). Apart from a hierarchical scripting of strategic value, what also becomes clear when reading such discourses is how political and cultural denigrations are linked to a consequent security imperative that is logically required. Consider how Qatar, Bahrain, and the United Arab Emirates are referred to in the report above: "[t]hese countries are little more than collections of tribes; they are true Potemkin villages." The Orientalist script then serves to set up the security declaration that follows: "we do not think that making them the 'shield of the Gulf' is a good idea" (Pelletiere and Johnson 1992, 12).

Strategic Studies in DoD Service

The interventionary rationales of CENTCOM and the wider U.S. military have for many years been championed by the discipline of strategic studies and its array of defense and security experts. These experts have played a prominent part in the rise in recent decades of a distinct militarism in the United States, whose pervasiveness and seductiveness Andrew Bacevich (2005) has detailed so well. As I have explored elsewhere, since the late 1970s, strategic studies has increasingly called for CENTCOM's securitization of the Persian Gulf region, in particular (Morrissey 2011a). Such pleas have echoed broader calls for a renewal of U.S. global ambition (N. Smith 2003b)—for instance, the memoirs of President Jimmy Carter's national security advisor, Zbigniew Brzezinski, divulge the contemporary

Cold War anxieties of Washington strategists and their desires to reestablish 'global forward presence' in the aftermath of various U.S. military failures in the 1970s (Brzezinski 1983). In 1979, defending the energy-rich Middle East from potential Soviet attack became a U.S. strategic priority in the wake of the fall of the Shah in Iran and the Soviet invasion of Afghanistan (J. M. Epstein 1981; Waltz 1981). As the DoD began planning for the securitization of the Middle East, Washington's strategic studies policy institutes played a key supporting role (see, for example, Record 1981a; cf. B. S. Klein 1994). In the early 1980s, a number of such institutes, focusing particularly on U.S. national security concerns in the Middle East, emerged in Washington, including the Defense Budget Project (1983), the Institute for National Strategic Studies (1984), and the Washington Institute for Near East Policy (1985). Their publications, and others from the Brookings Institution, the Center for Strategic and International Studies, and elsewhere, repeatedly called for a more assertive U.S. foreign policy in defending energy assets in the region. Calls were typically underscored by an implicit Orientalism and tied in with appeals for U.S. leadership in safeguarding 'global economic health' (Record 1981b; McNaugher 1985; J. M. Epstein 1987). The latter objective, of course, had long been shared by the major industrial powers, particularly with the decline of Europe's imperial reach in the aftermath of World War II (the Trilateral Commission, for example, had been expressly established in 1973 to foster closer economic cooperation between the United States, Europe, and Japan).

The 1980s ultimately witnessed the rise in government circles in Washington of what Bradley Klein (1988) has termed a hegemonic "strategic culture"—in which the use of force is seen as the exclusive instrument for effecting U.S. foreign policy. For Klein (1994, 5), this strategic culture was relentlessly advanced by the discipline of strategic studies, which "assigns to violence a regulative function in the international system," which in turn has a "generative nature," "generative of states, of state systems, of world orders." As he reasons, the "ability of strategic violence to reconcile itself with liberal discourse and modern civil society is possible only because that violence draws upon a variety of discursive resources that are themselves widely construed as rational, plausible and acceptable" (B. S. Klein 1994, 5). Such resources include a well-established imperial register of cultural binaries whose rhetorical power depends on simplified imaginative geographies: us/them, good/evil, civilized/barbarous, order/anarchy, and so on. As Klein (1994, 5–6) usefully shows, what strategic studies does is "provide a map for the negotiating of these dichotomies in such a way that Western society always winds up on the 'good' . . . side of the equation":

> Our putative enemy, whatever the form assumed by its postulated Otherness—variously the Soviet Union, or Communism, guerrilla insurgents, terrorism, Orientals, Fidel Castro, Nicaragua, Qaddafi, Noriega or Saddam Hussein—simultaneously is

endowed with all of these dialectically opposed qualities. Strategic violence is then called in to mediate the relationship, patrol the border, surveil the opponent and punish its aggression.

The aftermath of the attacks on the United States in 2001 saw strategic studies well positioned to make even more reductive arguments about 'strategic violence' and 'interventionary necessity', especially so in the Othered spaces of the Middle East and Central Asia. And such soundings were responsively heard by the wider U.S. military-political establishment (Morrissey 2011a). In the post-9/11 period, Klein's 'strategic culture' was discernibly superseded by what could be best described as a 'securitization culture', in which the use of force is advocated through the compelling language of 'security'. This culture is evident in the plethora of foreign policy declarations in which necessary U.S. intervention is conceived via registers of security that bind a range of elements—'national', 'global', 'military', and 'economic'—into a grand strategy for the long haul.

Washington's current securitization culture has an extensive array of actors across overlapping academic, military, and political circles. A host of DoD-affiliated higher education institutions, for instance, have variously contributed to the enactment of U.S. foreign policy in the name of 'national security' (Bacevich 2005); the late Chalmers Johnson (2004) put a conservative figure of 150 such institutions across the United States. Leading defense think tanks such as RAND, along with military journals such as *Joint Force Quarterly*, have also been prominent at the nexus of securitization discourse and foreign policy formulation. In the first ever issue of *Joint Force Quarterly* in 1993, the then chairman of the Joint Chiefs of Staff, Colin Powell, presented the journal as "the most recent addition" to what the U.S. military calls "jointness": that "all men and women in uniform, each service, and every one of our great civilian employees understand that we must fight as a team" (Powell 1993, 5). At this juncture, strategic studies was an integral part of that team, and the establishment of official DoD strategic studies centers was the natural progression for the ever-growing securitization culture of Washington and the Pentagon. From 1993 to 2000, five such DoD centers were established (figure 3.2). They are a direct strategic advisory support to the now six regional unified commands of the DoD (figure 3.3).[7] For example, the Near East South Asia Center for Strategic Studies (NESA), established at the National Defense University in Washington, coordinates closely with CENTCOM in effecting national security objectives in the Middle East and Central Asia. Since NESA's inception, its staff members have produced a prolific selection of strategic geopolitical and geoeconomic national security writings through a full gamut of publications ranging from monographs, book chapters, and journal articles to military briefing papers and mainstream op-eds and commentaries (Lawrence 2008).

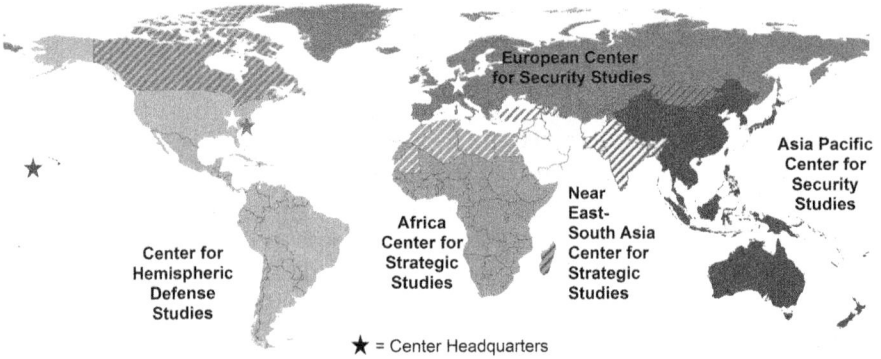

FIGURE 3.2. U.S. Department of Defense Regional Centers for Strategic Studies. Adapted from Africa Center for Strategic Studies 2008.

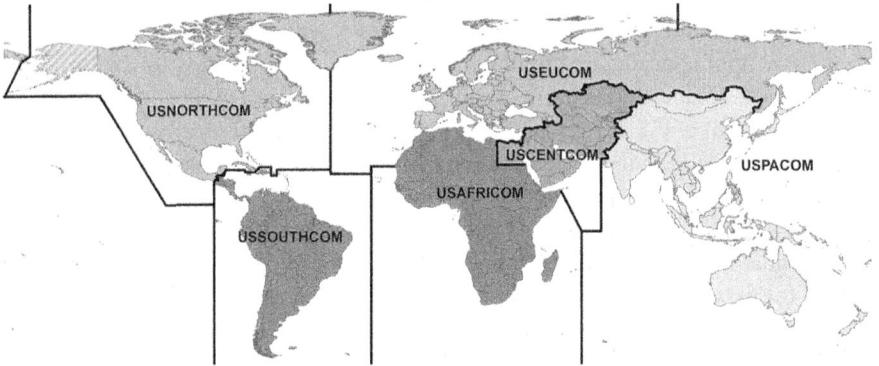

FIGURE 3.3. "The World with Commanders' Areas of Responsibility." Adapted from U.S. Department of Defense 2016a.

The Geopolitical Work of Strategic Studies

Bradley Thayer's writing on international relations is a good example of the prevailing world vision discernible in strategic studies:

> The war on terrorism and the condition of the international system at the present time—American hegemony—provide the United States with great opportunities. The American Empire may be expanded as it never has before into the Middle East with the result that anti-American regimes are replaced by pro-American ones, WMD programs are stopped, the terrorist threats of al Qaeda and Hizbullah are reduced, liberal political ideals are advanced, oil continues to flow to world markets, allies are supported, and the economies of states in the region are woven into the tapestry of the global economy. (Thayer 2003, 47)

For Thayer (2003, 4, 15, 19), the war on terrorism provided "the opportunity to increase significantly American military and economic power in the Middle East": it was "only by invading Iraq" that the United States could "reach its strategic objectives in the region," and since the United States is "an imperial power," it should "exert its influence in the region to bring about regional change." Thayer is one of numerous national security experts within an influential 'military–strategic studies complex' in the United States today. This complex is a well-funded assemblage of policy institutes, military colleges, and university departments, many with close links to the DoD and specializing in strategic studies research, teaching, and policy publications (Bacevich 2005). In the aftermath of the September 11 attacks in New York and Washington in 2001, the military–strategic studies complex quickly generated a dominant aggressive national security rationale for renewed U.S. interventions in the Middle East and Central Asia. A number of publicly prominent national security experts, furthermore, weighed in on the notion that U.S. commitment to a long war against radical Islam was necessary: Thomas Barnett (2004) conceived a binary world of 'functioning core' and 'non-integrating gap'; Robert Kagan (2008) envisioned a bipolar geopolitical world divided into 'liberal' zones and 'autocratic' zones; while Robert Kaplan (2012) imagined a Mackinder-inspired world defined by geographical determinism and necessitating control by military force (cf. Morrissey et al. 2009).

The reductive geographies of strategic studies, and especially those of its most popular enunciators, not only support U.S. military-economic grand strategy in the Middle East and Central Asia but also contribute to an enduring Orientalist discourse (Little 2002; Said 2003; Gregory 2004). As Stephen Graham (2005, 6, 8) notes, the result of the "combined vitriol of a whole legion of U.S. military 'commentators' who enjoy huge coverage, exposure, and influence in the U.S. media" is a world in which entire populations are decreed unworthy of "political or human rights": "[i]n the construction of people as inhuman 'terrorist' barbarians understanding little but force, and urban places as animalistic labyrinths or 'nests' demanding massive military assault, Islamic cities, and their inhabitants, are, in turn, cast out beyond any philosophical, legal, or humanitarian definitions of humankind or 'civilisation.'" A continuum of Orientalist representations of the Middle East and Central Asia extends back to at least the late 1970s, when the military–strategic studies complex began to increasingly assert U.S. geopolitical and geoeconomic designs for securing the region's volatility. Of course, the region *is* deeply volatile, but what Orientalist discourse does is to reinforce a powerful geographical imaginary that denies any effects of prior Western interventionary violence and eschews any sense that 'Westerners' might be implicated in the production of the volatility and terror that they see. Crucial to our reading of this work, furthermore, is the recognition that it typically circulates in government circles, as I have shown in relation to the Center for Strategic and Budgetary Assessments in Washington, for example (Morrissey 2011a). In addition, many of the leading research analysts in strategic studies institutes are often also prominent advisors to the Pentagon and the U.S. Congress. Thomas Barnett, for instance, worked as the assistant for strategic futures in the Office of Force Transformation at the DoD from the end of 2001 to mid-2003 while simultaneously holding a professorship in strategic studies at the Warfare Analysis and Research Department at the U.S. Naval War College in Newport, Rhode Island.

Strategic studies scriptings of U.S. national security have also been instrumental in advancing rationales for a widening of the role of the U.S. military in its global interventions (Jones and Smith 2015). As I have documented elsewhere, the U.S. military's recent embracing of the discourse of 'stability operations' mirrors an entwining of development and security concerns in the reimagining of an interventionary toolkit to secure the most broadly understood 'instability' (Morrissey 2015). Much of the reimagined remit envisions military-economic reconstruction, effective counterinsurgency, and 'culture-centric warfare', and there are numerous examples of embedded strategic studies support for such visions. Consider, for example, Sheila Jager's *On the Uses of Cultural Knowledge*, which set out a 'strategic' demarcation of the role of 'culture' in more successfully waging and ultimately winning the Iraq War: "[f]aced with a brutal war and insurgency in Iraq, the many complex political and social issues confronted by U.S. military commanders on the ground have given rise to a new awareness that a cultural understanding of an adversary society is imperative" (Jager 2007). Jager is a professor of East Asian studies at Oberlin College in Ohio, but at the time of writing she was a visiting fellow in national security studies at the Strategic Studies Institute of the U.S. Army War College. She concluded her analysis of the U.S. military's "uses of cultural knowledge" by submitting that it was "not too late" for "culture" to "rescue the United States from the strategic failures of the Bush Doctrine" (Jager 2007, 24). As Derek Gregory (2008, 8) has shown, the development of culture-centric warfare "does not dispense with killing" but rather is "a prerequisite for its refinement." That the U.S. military has reached such a dangerously clinical appreciation of culture, and why knowledge of it matters on the battlefield, should not surprise us. Arguably more troubling, however, is that the intellectual academy—from anthropology to East Asian studies, from geography to psychology—is being increasingly mobilized in the service of the military. Reflecting the extent of the neoliberalization of war, a new "model for institutions" has even emerged that uncritically links arms sales and "defense offsets" to university rankings and "benefits for all"—as in the case of the recent multimillion-dollar deal between the University of Massachusetts Lowell and defense contractor Raytheon (Bender 2014).

In U.S. strategic studies, there have been some important alternative articulations of U.S. foreign policy in the face of the pervasive aggressive and abstracted geopolitics typically advanced. Notable exceptions in Washington's policy institutes include Ted Carpenter at the Cato Institute and Charles Peña at the Independent Institute, both of whom were consistently critical of the national security strategy of George W. Bush (Peña 2003; Carpenter 2007). Carpenter, especially, has long argued for regional-led security strategies in the Middle East, not involving aggressive U.S. military action (Carpenter 2000). 'Realist' international relations critics such as Michael O'Hanlon at the Brookings Institution have variously offered defense policy critique too, but their critiques are usually centered on the question of how the United States can be more strategically effective in projecting overseas power. O'Hanlon's (2008) take on the transformation of the DoD's *Global Defense Posture Review*, for example, offers a more efficient approach to what he believes is "unfinished business" for the U.S. military presence in the Middle East in the twenty-first century.

Some former 'insiders' have had critical epiphanies upon exiting the military–strategic studies complex. In recent years, for example, Stephen Pelletiere has argued that U.S. involvement in both the Gulf War and Iraq War was driven by a neoconservative, pro-Zionist, military-industrial cabal whose endgame was the control of Persian Gulf oil and its political economy (Pelletiere 2004, 2007). When Pelletiere was a senior CIA policy analyst on Iraq and professor of national security affairs at the U.S. Army War College's Strategic Studies Institute, however, he enunciated a different reading of U.S. regional geopolitics. In the aforementioned 1992 strategy report commissioned by CENTCOM and cowritten by a colleague at the U.S. Army War College, Pelletiere strongly advised focusing "all of CENTCOM's efforts on the Gulf," centering strategy on "guarding Gulf oil," and "abandoning practically all other responsibilities" (Pelletiere and Johnson 1992, v). Another example of an academic speaking differently while inside the military–strategic studies complex is John Esposito at Georgetown University's School of Foreign Service. Esposito is one of the most quoted critics of the Orientalist notion of Islamic irrationality and inherent violence (Esposito 2000a). Yet when writing for one of the U.S. military's most widely read journals, *Joint Force Quarterly*, he gave readers the choice of "Islamic Threat" or "Clash of Civilizations" in conceptualizing East-West relations, thus echoing Bernard Lewis's 'crisis in Islam' thesis (Esposito 2000b, 51; cf. Lewis 2004). It seems difficult, then, to escape the perception that academics tend to speak and write more uncritically when 'enlisted to the cause'—and geography sadly is no exception. The introduction to the American Association of Geographers' 2003 publication *The Geographical Dimensions of Terrorism*, for example, sets out the discipline's indispensable utility in the war on terror—in providing "the knowledge, tools, techniques, and trained scientists that are needed if we are to be prepared to understand, prevent, mitigate and intervene where required" (Rubin 2003, xix; cf. Koopman 2016). "Collusion between 'knowledge' and 'power' must be forcefully exposed," Henri Lefebvre (1991, 415) once wrote, as must "the purposes to which bureaucracy bends knowledge's specialization." As Lefebvre (1991, 415) dolefully observed, "when institutional (academic) knowledge sets itself up above lived experience," "catastrophe is in the offing."

Conclusion

In 2008, the U.S. Army published a new version (the first since the September 11 attacks of 2001) of its capstone doctrine, *Field Manual 3-0: Operations*. It begins by declaring that not only is "America at war" but "it should remain fully engaged for the next several decades in a persistent conflict against an enemy dedicated to U.S. defeat as a nation and eradication as a society" (U.S. Department of the Army 2008a, viii). Having established this doomsday dystopia, it then presents a 'full spectrum operations' global security mission for the U.S. military. Soon after this publication, the army produced a follow-up manual, *Field Manual 3-07: Stability Operations*, which opens with a similarly bleak global geopolitical vision and proceeds to set out a necessary long war against radical Islam "in an epic struggle unlike any other in our history" (U.S. Department of the Army 2008b, C2). A world replete with "societal abysses," "precipitous divides," and a "fundamental clash of ideologies and cultures" is proclaimed for "an uncertain future" of "persistent conflict against enemies intent on limiting American access and influence throughout the world" (U.S. Department of the Army 2008b, vi).

The interventionary rationales above echo with multiple Malthusian and Orientalist geographical visions. They continue the use of a long-standing discursive mechanism at the heart of Western imperialism: the identification of threat coupled with the heralding of necessary correction. The interventionary mission appears not only necessary but indeed therapeutic to the liberal urge to improve (Morrissey 2016). As Mona Domosh remarks, formulations of U.S. national security concerns on a global scale have historically been based on "a way of seeing the world" in which strategies of intervention "come to be seen as plausible and desirable" (2013, 945). This liberal worldview remains and is seen most pointedly in political preferences for humanitarian uses of the 'military instrument' in contemporary U.S. foreign policy (Taw 2012)—preferences, of course, that commonly fail to acknowledge the broadened U.S. military understanding of what counts as war and security, a point I take up in chapter 6. Sadly, in all of this, in the face of ubiquitous scriptings of insecurity and necessary Western interventionary violence, the task of insisting on real places with real people seems as urgent as ever.

CHAPTER FOUR

Posturing for Global Security

Territory, Lawfare, and Biopolitics

Law and force flow into one another. We make war in the shadow of law, and law in the shadow of force.

David Kennedy, *Of War and Law*

Law and geography have long been deeply entwined. As Lauren Benton (2010, 9) observes, at the heart of imperialism since at least the early modern period, law has "formed an important epistemological framework for the production and dissemination of geographic knowledge, while geographic descriptions encoded ideas about law and sovereignty." A key concern in this chapter lies in teasing out the legal-territorial modalities of intervention we are witnessing in late modern imperialism, or what Jones and Smith (2015) usefully describe as the 'war-law-space nexus' of late modern war. In documenting the U.S. military's legal-territorial grand strategy, my aim is to illuminate how territorial access is governed by legal specification and conditioning. In focusing on the centerpiece of its global security posture, CENTCOM, I illuminate the 'mechanisms of security', including Status of Forces Agreements, which legally and biopolitically enable its spaces of intervention (Foucault 2007). This enabling is achieved through practices of 'lawfare' and more broadly by what I term 'full spectrum law'. I want to signal why the law and its specificities matter for CENTCOM—from its territorial security strategies to facilitate access and occupation to its overlapping biopolitical security strategies to regulate and safeguard the lives of its military personnel.

The 'Milieu' of Security: Geography, Territory, and the Law

At the heart of war, as Walter Benjamin (1978, 283) memorably noted, lies a "law-making character." The law underscores war's battlespaces, its territorial, naval, and aerial occupations, its extraterritoriality, and indeed any and all of its military operations (Morrissey 2015). For the U.S. military today, Judge Advocate General's Corps military lawyers (JAGs) work to prescribe all forms of military intervention through the adapted deployment of a range of legal armatures. JAGs play a vital role in the juridification of military actions, from legally conditioning the battlefield and sanctioning the privilege to kill, to regulating the circulation of troops and optimizing their operational capacities. Adapting an effective legal strategy is one of the defining features of late modern war (Weizman 2009; Gregory 2010; Braverman et al. 2014; Ohlin 2015; C. Jones 2016)—and such a strategy can be best described as 'lawfare'.[1] Lawfare is commonly understood to mean "the use of law as a weapon of war" by nonstate actors attempting to impose "reputational costs" on state actors by "alleging violations" (Dill 2014). In my account below of CENTCOM's framing and mobilization of the law, I reverse this conservative understanding by considering *state* lawfare, which typically comprises a highly coordinated form of 'offensive' lawfare that legally protects forward-deployed forces and the states that put them there (Morrissey 2011b). On one level, as Jeff Halper (2014) reasons, state lawfare frames the actions of "non-state actors" as *illegitimate violence*—those actors are "terrorists" and are "deprived of any legitimacy." However, this framing forms part of a wider, calculated legal strategy that simultaneously uses the law to wage *sanctioned violence* against whole populations, as laid bare by Israel's recent assaults on Gaza. Here is Halper again on the plight of Gazans facing Israel's offensive lawfare: "when they seek the protection of international law [. . .] and take steps to hold state actors accountable for their illegal actions, they are engaging in what Israel defines as 'lawfare' [. . .] but 'lawfare' best describes Israel's own efforts to bend IHL [international humanitarian law] to its needs—a kind of asymmetrical lawfare to remove all constraints on states in their attempts to pursue wars against peoples."

In critically conceiving the confluence of law, geography, and security, the works of Michel Foucault and especially his translated lectures at the Collège de France in 1978 and 1979 have been a source of inspiration for many (Foucault 2007, 2008). In *Security, Territory, Population*, Foucault (2007, 7, 11) sketches modernity's birth of a "society of security" in which new regulatory "apparatuses" or "mechanisms of security" emerged that reflected a shift in the sovereign's externally oriented concerns of 'territorial security' to internally oriented concerns of 'population security'. A core concept Foucault (2007, 108) developed in his analysis of how populations are secured is 'governmentality', which he theorized as having "the population as its target, political economy as its major form of knowledge, and apparatuses of security as its essential technical instrument." This envisioning speaks on a number of levels to the interventionary practices of U.S. Central Command in our contemporary moment, but I want to underline three in particular. First, in its interventions across the Middle East and Central Asia, CENTCOM is primarily interested in managing the 'circulation' and 'conduct' of one specific target population: its own forces. This may not be commonly recognized in biopolitical critiques of the war on terror, but the JAG Corps has increasingly adapted practices of lawfare that envisage all military personnel as subjects of "management and government" whose operational capacity must be legally optimized (Foucault 2007, 70). Second, as I explore in more detail in chapter 5, CENTCOM's grand strategy of security has been consistently justified by a power-knowledge assemblage that has successfully scripted a neoliberal political economy argument for its global forward presence. Securing economic volatility and regulating a neoliberal world order for the good of the global economy are powerful interventionary rationales repeatedly registered by CENTCOM and through multiple forums of the broader U.S. national security establishment. Third, Foucault's (2007, 11) conceptualization of a 'society of security' is one marked by an urge to govern by contingency, to anticipate what he calls "the aleatory." CENTCOM's Area of Responsibility equates in essence to what Foucault (2007, 20) terms a "milieu," a "space in which a series of uncertain elements unfold," and the command's preemptive lawfare is precisely oriented to anticipate uncertainty and plan for "possible events" therein.

CENTCOM's interventionary capabilities across its Area of Responsibility ultimately rely on a dual legal-territorial grand strategy comprising forward-operating bases and other security and logistics sites developed in tandem with a legal architecture allowing for, and governing, land access, troop circulation, and conduct. It is here that law becomes the conduit between geopolitical and biopolitical power. For Michael Dillon, the "geopolitics of security" revolve around "territory," while the "biopolitics of security" revolve around "population" (Dillon 2007a, 46). Both are indelibly intertwined, of course. As Derek Gregory (2008, 19) notes, "biopolitics is not pursued outside the domain of sovereign power but is instead part of a protracted struggle over the right to claim, define and exercise sovereign power." Geopolitics has always centrally involved biopolitics; the challenge lies in teasing out their complex interrelations and avoiding what Kolson Schlosser (2008, 1631) calls "dualistic notions of bio-political and sovereign power." For CENTCOM commanders and the other five regional commanders across the globe, geopolitics and biopolitics converge on the legal-territorial management of the forward-deployed military personnel in their respective Areas of Responsibility. This is their primary population security challenge, and Foucault's (2007, 20–21) "problem of circulation and causality" must be both anticipated and regulated "within a multivalent and transformable framework." Military JAGs provide the legally transformable frameworks; they work to "fabricate, organize, and plan a milieu" even before ground forces are deployed (as in the case of the first action in the war on terror, which I return to later, the negotiation by CENTCOM JAGs of a Status of Forces Agreement with Uzbekistan in early October 2001) (Foucault 2007, 21). A JAG's milieu is ultimately a "field of intervention" in which the objective is to "affect, precisely, a population," and, to this end, securing the uncertain is pivotal (Foucault 2007, 21). As Dillon (2007a, 46) argues, central to the securing of populations are the "sciences of the aleatory or the contingent" in which the "government of population" is realized through "statistics and probability"; or "rule by numbers," as U. Kalpagam (2014) has detailed so well for colonial India. As Dillon (2007b, 12) argues elsewhere, you "cannot secure anything unless you know what it is," and therefore effective governmentality demands that "people, territory, and things are transformed into epistemic objects." In planning the milieu of forward-deployed U.S. military personnel, JAGs translate Areas of Responsibility into legally enabled grids upon which the broadest range of actions and events can take place. Such legally transformable frameworks are put in place to anticipate uncertainty in interventionary missions where the security of 'certain lives' is in fact the most important security endgame. As CENTCOM commander General Lloyd Austin concluded in his 2015 posture statement, U.S. forces in the frontlines "are and will remain our foremost priority" (U.S. Central Command 2015a).[2]

Life and the Biopolitical Project of Security

In recent years, we have witnessed a gradual mission creep of military jurisdiction over the governance of life. Roger Stahl (2014) conceives this as "biomimetic war," where war is ubiquitous in a biosphere requiring permanent intervention. In such a war, the 'project of security' is "life's patrol, maintenance, and production"; it is a war waged by "a military that concerns itself with the biopolitical in Foucault's sense of the word" (Stahl 2014, 122). Such a move within Western militaries mirrors a prevailing discourse of liberal interventionism that scripts the necessity of waging war for the securitization of life, what Michael Dillon and Julian Reid (2009) term "killing to make live" (cf. Shaw 2013). Deconstructing what liberal interventionism has historically entailed, Mark Neocleous (2008, 13) shows how 'life' and 'security' have long been conflated in a liberal "project of liberty" that can in fact be more appositely termed a liberal "project of security." By drawing on a range of examples from twentieth-century governments in the United States and the UK, Neocleous dissects the pursuit of security in Western liberal democracies and shows how it has consistently been centered on the governmentality of life. Neocleous prompts us to question where the law lies in this project of security, arguing that its application has at all times been contingent on periodic episodes of 'emergency' in otherwise 'normal' times. This is part of Andrew Neal's (2010, 2) point about the intrinsic ability of Western democracies to invoke the language and powers of emergency to make "exceptions to liberty in the name of liberty, or exceptions to the law in the name of the law" (cf. Paye 2007). CENTCOM is a key appendage of the national security apparatus of one such democracy. Its interventions are activated by selective and tactical uses of the law and underpinned by a securitization discourse that is shot through with recurring registers of emergency, threat, and inevitable conflict for the long haul. In this sense, the long-term U.S. military footprint in the Middle East and Central Asia is presented as a necessary response to a 'permanent emergency'.

A wide range of critique across the social sciences and humanities in recent years has considered how discourses of emergency, precarity, and risk are discursively mobilized and function centrally in the governing modalities of our contemporary world (Beck 1992; Dean 1999; O'Malley 2004; Mythen and Walklate 2006; Anderson 2010; Neal 2010). In a society interminably scripted as insecure, such discourses have a profound power to invoke danger as "requiring extraordinary action" (Dalby 2009, 47). Registers of emergency play pivotal roles in justifying military grand strategy, where 'risk' has become permanently bound to 'securitization'. As Claudia Aradau and Rens van Munster (2007, 108) point out, the "perspective of risk management" elevates military interventions to be seen as expected, legitimate, and even therapeutic (cf. Heng 2006). Military securitization discourses are further emboldened by the mobilization of visions of the future featuring 'evental' registers. Randy Martin (2007) has underlined, for example, how U.S. military strategy in the war on terror uses the risk of dystopian future events to justify preemption as the tactic of their securitization.[3]

The U.S. military's preemptive grand strategy in the war on terror has prompted a number of reflections on the work of Italian social theorist Giorgio Agamben on the 'state of exception' to consider the war's 'spaces of exception' (Agamben 2005). Claudio Minca (2007), for example, has drawn on Agamben to interrogate the reprisal of the role of the 'camp' in politically and legally stripping individuals to the status of 'bare life'—opening them up to an "unthinkable range" of sovereign violence (Minca 2007, 92; cf. Agamben 1998). In the U.S. military's milieu of camps and prisons in the Middle East and elsewhere, 'spatial exceptionalism' in managing detainees is undoubtedly an important element. As General John Abizaid made clear to the Senate Armed Services Committee in 2006, "an essential part" of CENTCOM combat operations in both Iraq and Afghanistan entailed "detaining enemy combatants and terrorists," and this detention typically took place in specifically designated facilities such as Abu Ghraib Prison and Bagram Air Base (U.S. Central Command 2006a). However, it would be a mistake to characterize CENTCOM's broader biopolitical security strategy as exceptional. Both Agamben's and Minca's emphases on the notion of 'exception' are useful in accounting for how CENTCOM has *defensively* managed the threat of enemy combatants; it does not account, however, for how it has *offensively* managed the conduct of its own armed forces in its long war against them. Across the Central Region, CENTCOM has pursued a preemptive legal strategy, focused on the securing of Status of Forces Agreements with host nations, which has rigorously protected its armed personnel from both local and international prosecution. This form of lawfare establishes for CENTCOM normative parameters in exercising legally sanctioned violence—thus maximizing its operational capacity throughout its Area of Responsibility. Maximizing operational capacity on a *global* scale has increasingly occupied the wider U.S. military in recent years, and their efforts have centrally involved a proactive legal strategy, as I explore more broadly below.

The American "Leasehold Empire" and Global Security

The extensive overseas military presence of the United States today has been aptly termed the American "leasehold empire" (Sandars 2000). David Vine (2015) puts the U.S. military's current global footprint at a staggering eight hundred bases in over seventy countries. This coverage has been made possible by a sustained legal strategy since World War II to secure strategic access points via long-term leases, and has been rationalized by a well-versed national security discourse that, as Matt Farish (2016) notes, is "endlessly flexible" in inflating "a variety of threats." The DoD's contemporary overseas basing structure equates to a dispersed geography of vital interventionary spaces throughout the world, where territorial access, rather than territorial control, is key. This strategy is perhaps less of a departure from imperial history than our common understanding of empire would allow. As Lauren Benton (2010, 2) discerns, territorial control was frequently an "incidental aim" of imperial interventions, even at the height of high colonialism, and empires never covered spaces "evenly" but rather "composed a fabric that was full of holes," "politically fragmented," and "legally differentiated." The historical workings of imperialism, and how their contexts differ from the imperial grand strategy of the contemporary United States, have in fact been considered in some detail by the defense think tank community in Washington. Andrew Krepinevich and Robert Work, for example, at the influential Center for Strategic and Budgetary Assessments,[4] have reflected on the historical imperial lessons for the contemporary American 'leasehold empire':

> unlike Imperial Britain or Rome, the United States has traditionally enjoyed far less unfettered operational access to many of its exterior bases, or complete freedom of action for the forces stationed at them. However, despite the constraints on its operational freedom of action—a circumstance that would not have been tolerated by earlier empires—the U.S. legally negotiated "leasehold" overseas basing structure has proven to be one of the most remarkably effective, flexible, and durable in history. (Krepinevich and Work 2007, iii)

Historically, securing territorial access and networks was essential to imperial ambition, as Robert Young (2001) and others have shown (cf. Lester 2001). This imperative endures for U.S. global ambition today, where the territorial endgame is a "legally negotiated 'leasehold' overseas basing structure" (Krepinevich and Work 2007, iii). In developing the current leasehold basing structure, 'land power'—defined by 'land access'—has been a requirement consistently cited by military strategists in Washington since the early 1980s. At this juncture, heightened tensions in the Cold War saw a prevailing discourse emerge in strategic studies that was centered on the 'problem of access' in the Middle East and Central Asia in countering Soviet threat (J. M. Epstein 1981; Waltz 1981). Jeffrey Record (1981a, 112), for example (then senior fellow at the Institute for Foreign Policy Analysis and professional staff member of the Senate Armed Services Committee), made the case for "[s]ecure military access ashore in the Persian Gulf," which he argued was "essential" for an effective U.S. foreign policy to be enacted in the region. The two principal interventionary rationales were "[d]eterrence of overt Soviet aggression" and "uninterrupted access to Persian Gulf oil" (Record 1981a, 109). For Record, both rationales prompted the need for land access and the development of a Rapid Deployment Force. As explored in chapter 2, CENTCOM began to intensify efforts at this point to secure access rights for its forces with a range of countries across the Persian Gulf and Horn of Africa. These efforts continued throughout the 1980s, with a particular focus on Saudi Arabia, and subsequent to the Gulf War a new U.S. deterrence strategy prompted the command to secure more permanent access rights and extend its basing structure across the region. By 1994, it had forged close relationships with all six GCC countries, signing bilateral defense and access agreements with each state (Hajjar 2002).

The land access acquired in the Gulf War's aftermath was key to projecting CENTCOM's deterrence strategy in the 1990s, a strategy whose success hinged on the imperative of 'forward presence'. As Stephen Pelletiere and Douglas Johnson II (1992, 18) explain, the United States had "sought forward presence in the Gulf since the Soviet invasion of Afghanistan and the enunciation of the Carter Doctrine"; the Gulf War secured it and facilitated "the option of forward positioning heavy ground forces." In considering the argument that there may be "no need to station large forces or preposition heavy equipment in the region since air power will be the primary instrument of intimidation," Pelletiere and Johnson (1992, 18, 19) reason that this has never "proved a satisfactory argument" and that "there is a continuing requirement for the United States to be able to place large forces on the ground, quickly." They ask why could CENTCOM not "protect the Gulf on the cheap, as it were" by patrolling it "with ships" and staging "regular flyovers" but deploying "no land forces" (Pelletiere and Johnson 1992, 12)? Their answer is unambiguous in insisting on the import of a "land component" in projecting an effective deterrence grand strategy: "the enemies we oppose will not be impressed by a force that lacks a land component[; . . .] the United States is trying to intimidate them and they will not be coerced if we lack a force which, ultimately, can engage them on the ground" (Pelletiere and Johnson 1992, 12).

Since the 1990s, the long-term requirement of territorial access for CENTCOM's overseas mission has been repeatedly affirmed by its military commanders. In 1999, for example, General Anthony Zinni outlined to the Senate Armed Services Committee how its continuous ground presence was the "key" to "CENTCOM's theater strategy" and its "ability to project overwhelming and decisive military power" (U.S. Central Command 1999b). The command's extensive forward-operating sites, coupled with its pre-positioning of fighting materials and supplies, were crucial throughout the 1990s in its major deterrence operations, including Operation Southern Watch and Operation Vigilant Warrior. The command's forward presence later facilitated the attacks on Afghanistan in 2001 and Iraq in 2003. In 2005, the U.S. Overseas Basing Commission reaffirmed the importance of land access and insisted on an aleatory and preemptive logic to secure it:

> The U.S. overseas basing structure must serve both in the near term and for decades to come [. . .] Any base structuring cannot be designed to deal only with the threats of today. The base structure we develop in the near future must enable us to meet the threats that will emerge over the next quarter century and beyond. (U.S. Overseas Basing Commission 2005, iii, 6–7)

The commission stressed a particular urgency of "maintaining a forward presence" for CENTCOM's long-term mission, whose objectives it summed up thus: "uninterrupted flow of Arabian Gulf oil, security of coalition partners and allies, regional peace and security and access to commercial markets" (U.S. Overseas Basing Commission 2005, G2). The enduring import of 'land power' for U.S. overseas missions continues to be flagged in all the main doctrinal and operational policy documents emanating from within the U.S. military. For example, the current iteration of the U.S. Army's primary field manual, *Field Manual 3-0: Operations*, underlines how "landpower will remain important to the military effort and essential to victory" (U.S. Department of the Army 2008a, viii).

In 2006, the then CENTCOM director of logistics, Major General Brian Geehan, outlined how the command supported 128 operating bases across its Area of Responsibility (see figure 4.1)[5] (U.S. Central Command 2006b). Their locations mirrored the principal nodes in the region's network of energy production. By 2010, the bulk of CENTCOM's military facilities could be found in the energy-rich GCC countries of the Arabian Peninsula (see table 4.1). At this point, CENTCOM had over 225,000 armed services personnel forward deployed across its Area of Responsibility (U.S. Department of Defense 2010); and although after the cessations of Operation Iraqi Freedom and Operation Enduring Freedom this number has been scaled down, tens of thousands of U.S. forces remain deployed, particularly in the GCC countries of the Persian Gulf (U.S. Department of Defense 2015a). The U.S. global overseas ground presence is even more extensive, of course. Data artist Josh Begley has produced a base map with the aid of aerial photography and satellite imagery depicting more than 640 U.S. military bases around the world (Begley 2015). This may, in fact, understate the fuller picture (as noted earlier, David Vine sets the figure at approximately 800), as the map does not include secret installations or those of a 'nonpermanent' nature. However, the map, along with the critical work of others including Mark Gillem (2007), Trevor Paglen (2009), and David Vine (2009, 2015), gives us a "vivid reminder" of how U.S. boots are "firmly planted on other people's ground" (Gregory 2013).

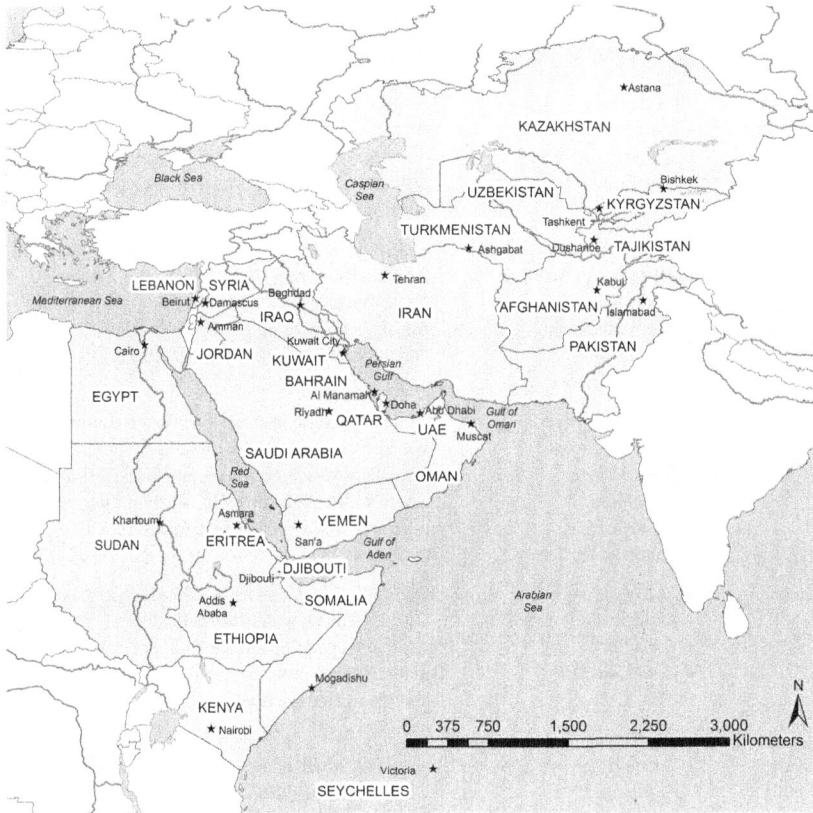

FIGURE 4.1. CENTCOM 'Area of Responsibility', 2006.

In terms of rationales for maintaining 'boots on the ground', CENTCOM has a particular consciousness of 'ungoverned spaces'. In identifying spaces of insecurity across its Area of Responsibility, it sees countering 'nonstate malign actors' in ungoverned spaces as a critical challenge. David Dawson (2014) explains: "for us, national borders are a barrier; for them, national borders are a gap they can exploit—they can cross them easily to conduct attacks or malign activities in one country, then cross back into de facto sanctuaries; which is why we see ungoverned space as one of our main strategic problems." An additional problem for CENTCOM posed by ungoverned space is piracy. As Dawson (2014) vividly recalls, former commander General John Abizaid cited its elimination as vital to the command's security mission:

Back in 2005, the commander asked "what eliminated piracy in the past?" Answer one: "what makes you think it was eliminated?" Answer two: "the establishment of governance ashore." As long as there were ungoverned/lightly governed places pirates could use as bases, piracy existed. Once government extends control to the

TABLE 4.1 Major U.S. military facilities in GCC countries in the Persian Gulf, 2010

Country	Major Facilities*	Description
Bahrain	• Isa Air Base • Mina Salman Port • Muharraq Airfield • Naval Support Activity Bahrain	Bahrain is home to the U.S. Navy's HQ in the Persian Gulf and to the Fifth Fleet at Naval Support Activity Bahrain; access is also granted at Mina Salman Port and Muharraq Airfield, and pre-positioned equipment is sited at Isa Air Base.
Kuwait	• Ahmed Al Jaber Air Base • Ali Al Salem Air Base • Camp Arifjan • Camp Buehring • Camp Doha • Camp Patriot	Kuwait hosted thousands of U.S. military personnel for Operation Iraqi Freedom at Camp Arifjan, Camp Buehring, Camp Doha, Camp Patriot, and Ali Al Salem Air Base; it also grants the U.S. Air Force access to Ahmed Al Jaber Air Base.
Oman	• Khasab Air Base • Masirah Air Base • Muscat Port • Salalah Port • Seeb Air Base • Thumrait Air Base	Oman accommodates pre-positioned equipment and gives access rights to the U.S. Air Force at Khasab, Masirah, Thumrait, and Seeb Air Bases, where it also hosts some U.S. Air Force personnel; the ports of Muscat and Salalah also provide facilities.
Qatar	• Al Udeid Air Base • As Sayliyah Army Base • Doha Port • Umm Said Port	Qatar is home to CENTCOM's forward HQ at Al Udeid Air Base, which also is the hub of U.S. Air Force operations in the Gulf; pre-positioned materials are housed at As Sayliyah, while Doha and Umm Said are used for fuel storage and port facilities.
Saudi Arabia	• Eskan Village Air Force Compound • Jeddah Air Base • King Abdulaziz Air Base • King Abdulaziz Naval Base • King Fahad Air Base • King Khalid Air Base	After the launch of Operation Iraqi Freedom, the United States withdrew and relocated most of its Saudi-based forces to Qatar by September 2003; U.S. military personnel are still deployed, however, at various bases directing the ongoing 'United States Military Training Mission to Saudi Arabia' initiated in 1953.
United Arab Emirates	• Al Dhafra Air Base • Jebel Ali Port • Fujairah International Airport	The UAE hosts military personnel and refuelling facilities for the U.S. Air Force and U.S. Navy at Al Dhafra Air Base; Jebel Ali Port and Fujairah International Airport also provide logistical support.

*This 2010 list is based on an earlier publication (Morrissey 2011b) in which I draw on official government sources only. Various other sources identify a far greater number of bases and access facilities for each GCC country, then and now; see, for example, Global Security 2010, Begley 2015, and Vine 2015. On the long struggle against the U.S. military's overseas presence and the effects of its militarization in spaces throughout the globe, see the excellent work of Catherine Lutz (2009) and David Vine (2009).

base areas, piracy effectively disappears. Naval action can reduce or displace piracy (we have seen this off Somalia) but it cannot eliminate it.

The corollary here is that territorial access is ultimately required for CENTCOM not only to eliminate piracy but to effect the "establishment of governance ashore." It is a case for 'troops on the ground' well versed by CENTCOM commanders in their annual posture statements to Congress (U.S. Central Command 1990, 1995, 2000, 2005, 2010, 2015a). Such envisionings typically negate any declared territorial interest in the interiors of CENTCOM's Area of Responsibility per se, but at the same time map a clear territorial concern for securing the region's pivotal nodes and access points in terms of the wider global economy.

Visions of Rapid Deployment and the Emergence of the SOFA Concept

CENTCOM is part of a U.S. global security grand strategy in which "The World" is divided into "Commanders' Areas of Responsibility" (figure 3.3). In this global milieu of security, forward-operating bases are vital. Much of the current U.S. overseas basing structure was established during and immediately after World War II. With the onset of the Cold War, "global security relationships and legal agreements" came to the fore in what Krepinevich and Work (2007, 134) term the U.S. lead in "the global ideological struggle between free nations and communist totalitarianism." By the 1960s, the United States had entered into bilateral defense agreements with a host of countries, from Central and South America to Australasia and Japan, and this ensured a U.S. military presence on every continent—a "leasehold empire that literally spanned the globe" (Krepinevich and Work 2007, 134, 136). In this expansion of global reach, Status of Forces Agreements (SOFAs) were key, allowing the United States to extend its Cold War defensive perimeter to the frontiers of the Soviet Empire, as Krepinevich and Work (2007, 134) explain:

> in return for its pledge to protect countries from Soviet aggression or other outside attack, the United States gained powerful leverage to negotiate forward basing access, which resulted in a rapid expansion of the number of foreign exterior bases in the U.S. global basing network. In the process, Status of Forces Agreements between the United States and host basing states—which outlined the rights of U.S. personnel living or operating in a foreign country—became very important.

The Cold War's "era of entangling alliances" saw "an explosion of SOFAs"; by its end in the late 1980s, the United States had "standing Status of Forces Agreements of some kind with approximately 40 countries" (Krepinevich and Work 2007, 134, 135). In the 1990s, CENTCOM merely continued the use of SOFAs, by which point they had become obligatory legal instruments in securing the wider U.S. military's global expeditionary posture.

A SOFA is outlined by the DoD as "an agreement that defines the legal position of a visiting military force deployed in the territory of a friendly state" (U.S. Department of Defense 2007a, 512). Although always classified, the agreements' fundamental components serve to legally protect forward-deployed military personnel from accountability to both national and international law. SOFAS also serve to legally secure facilities access and lethal and nonlethal equipment prepositioning, and they commonly set out too the financial trade-offs for participating countries, as well as commitments to joint training exercises and arms sales (Katzman 2006; cf. U.S. Department of Defense 2003b). All of this is done a priori, of course, and in this sense SOFAS are exactly the kinds of mechanisms of security that Michel Foucault (2007, 21) conceived as necessary to anticipate the 'aleatory', plan for the 'evental', and ultimately "fabricate, organize, and plan a milieu." In planning the interventionary 'milieus' of the U.S. military, SOFAS fulfill multiple security goals:[6] "SOFAS govern mission-critical and mundane matters including base access and security; provision or purchase of food, fuel, electricity and other supplies; taxes, visas and customs regulations; and criminal jurisdiction over U.S. personnel" (W. C. Smith 2003, 14). The final security imperative above is arguably the chief governmental concern for the U.S. military's overseas interventions. As one assistant staff judge advocate at U.S. Southern Command underlined in *The Army Lawyer*, the basic JAG responsibility is to "keep military personnel from going to jail for doing the right thing" (Stafford 2000, 1)—or perhaps more precisely for 'doing what is legally enabled'.

The use of SOFAS in the legal-territorial grand strategy of the U.S. military has long been linked to the idea of rapid deployment. Cold War ambitions for global deterrence against the threat of the Soviet Union led to increased efforts to create a U.S. overseas basing structure specifically for rapid deployment. As outlined in chapter 2, by the early 1980s the Rapid Deployment Force concept was officially adopted as the U.S. military identified new interventionary requirements to effect a global security role. This led to a gradual refocusing of its global posturing, prompted in part by a perceived need to move beyond inherited and static Cold War basing arrangements. By the 1990s, CENTCOM forces were repeatedly drilled in rapid deployment and readiness to fight via a series of regular war-gaming and training exercises. Forward-deployed troops at Prince Sultan Air Base in Saudi Arabia, for example, periodically war-gamed logistical plans to defend the Persian Gulf. In 1995, U.S. secretary of defense William Perry outlined to the Council on Foreign Relations CENTCOM's operational plan to protect U.S. interests in the Gulf, a plan that did not just "sit on the shelf gathering dust": "[w]e war-game it, we exercise it, and we modify it to meet challenging circumstances" (U.S. Department of Defense 1995b). These plans were operationalized a year earlier for Operation Vigilant Warrior, a successful and subsequently much-heralded

CENTCOM rapid deterrence operation against Iraq along its border with Saudi Arabia.

In 2003, the DoD began a formal transformation of the U.S. global defense posture, and from the outset a core element of planning centered on the construction of an effective legal-territorial strategy to facilitate rapid deployability.[7] To this end, SOFAs that eschew the jurisdiction of international law were identified as crucial. Speaking in Washington in December 2003, the then undersecretary of defense for policy, Douglas Feith, set out the transformation in the context of "longer-term thinking about U.S. defense strategy," which revolved around developing "rapidly deployable capabilities" worldwide—capabilities that necessitated specific legal codifications sanctioning interventionary force (U.S. Department of Defense 2003b). Feith proceeded to outline the obligatory lawfare:

> For this deployability concept to work, U.S. forces must be able to move smoothly into, through, and out of host nations, which puts a premium on establishing legal and support arrangements with many friendly countries. We are negotiating or planning to negotiate with many countries legal protections for U.S. personnel, through Status of Forces Agreements and agreements (known as Article 98 agreements) limiting the jurisdiction of the International Criminal Court with respect to our forces' activities. (U.S. Department of Defense 2003b)[8]

The rapid deployability concept was officially codified with the publication and report to Congress of the *Global Defense Posture Review* in 2004. Therein "bilateral and multilateral legal arrangements" are underlined as critical components of the U.S. "global defense posture," allowing for the "necessary flexibility and freedom of action to meet 21st-century security challenges" (U.S. Department of Defense 2004b, 8). The review also details Defense Under Secretary Feith's previously announced plans to bypass international law and the International Criminal Court (which the United States does not participate in) in all future access agreements (U.S. Department of Defense 2004b, 15). Subsequently, the 2005 U.S. *National Defense Strategy* further underscored this expressly 'exceptionalist' U.S. position, in remarkably listing 'international fora' and 'judicial processes' to be opposed alongside 'terrorism': "our strength as a nation will continue to be challenged by those who employ a strategy of the weak using international fora, judicial processes, and terrorism" (U.S. Department of Defense 2005a, 5; cf. Bacevich 2008).

To meet the "21st-century security challenges" of U.S. grand strategy, technological advancements as part of the so-called Revolution in Military Affairs (RMA) also coalesced in the ambition toward rapid deployability.[9] Just prior to the launch of Operation Iraqi Freedom, for example, CENTCOM initiated a new technical instrument to further augment rapid deployment to the front lines of its Area of Responsibility. In February 2003, while the UN Security Council was still in the throes of resisting the U.S./UK plans to attack Iraq, the military defense company Raytheon announced that it had delivered a deployable command and control headquarters to CENTCOM and that it had already been set up in As Sayliyah, Qatar. Raytheon introduced the new CENTCOM Deployable Headquarters (CDHQ) as "the first deployable command post for unified combatant commanders" and heralded how it "provides full command and control capabilities," "supports rapid forward deployment of essential personnel," and, crucially, can be "operated anywhere within CENTCOM's Area of Responsibility" (Raytheon 2003). The then CENTCOM commander,[10] General Tommy Franks, proclaimed the initiation of CDHQ as fulfilling urgently needed rapid deployment capabilities (Raytheon 2003).[11] Franks's commander in chief, President George W. Bush, declared a year later that the "world has changed a great deal, and our posture must change with it [. . .] so we can be more effective at projecting our strength and spreading freedom and peace"—in the face of "today's threats," "emerging threats," and "unexpected threats" (U.S. Department of Defense 2004a). Anticipating the fullest possible range of threat underpins the discursive rationale for rapid global deployability, placing a premium on flexible legal and support arrangements and ultimately using the law as an integral weapon of war.

Lawfare, and Law as Communication

Writing nearly two centuries ago, in the aftermath of the Napoleonic Wars, Prussian military strategist Carl von Clausewitz (1989, 87) observed how war is not "merely an act of policy but a true political instrument, a continuation of political intercourse, carried on with other means." Today, lawfare is a continuation of war by legal means. For former deputy judge advocate general Charles Dunlap (2007), it "has become a key aspect of modern war."[12] Dunlap retired from military service in 2010 to take up the positions of professor of the practice of law and executive director of the Center on Law, Ethics and National Security at Duke University in North Carolina. During his time as deputy judge advocate general at the U.S. Air Force Headquarters in the Pentagon, Dunlap was an influential figure in designing and implementing the evolving legal strategy of the U.S. military in the war on terror (he testified as a cited expert before the U.S. House of Representatives regarding the Military Commissions Act of 2006, for example). Dunlap has repeatedly outlined a core concern facing the JAG Corps and forward-deployed U.S. military personnel: the imposition of legal restraints on the battlefield as "a matter of policy"—a practice, he argues, that "plays into the hands of those who would use [international law] to wage lawfare against us" (Dunlap 2007). On the contrary, he implores a recognition that "sometimes the legitimate pursuit of military objectives will foreseeably—and inevitably—cause the death of noncombatants" and asks that "this tenet of international law be thoroughly understood" (Dunlap 2007). The international law that Dunlap has in mind is, in actuality, a selective and malleable set of legal conventions that legitimate military violence. As the

war on terror was launched, for instance, one primary reference of military inter
national law, the Geneva Conventions, was quickly identified as restrictive for the
new paradigm of late modern warfare. In January 2002, Attorney General Alberto
Gonzales, as White House chief legal counsel, advised President George W. Bush
that the war on terrorism "render[ed] obsolete Geneva's strict limitations on questioning enemy prisoners" (Center for American Progress 2004).

Since the September 11 attacks in 2001, winning the discursive battle for the
legality, ethics, and appropriateness of military practices has been a focal goal of
the U.S. national security establishment. Harvey Rishikof (2008, 11), former chair
of national security strategy at the National War College in Washington, proclaims
that since the war on terror began, "juridical warfare" (his preferred label to lawfare) has emerged as a distinct legal strategy of the enemies of the United States.
For Rishikof, juridical warfare equates to a legal strategy of the 'weak' *against* the
United States, not a legal strategy ever deployed *by* the United States. However, juridical warfare, or lawfare, is neither new nor a tactic adopted only by the enemies
of the U.S. military in late modern war. As the legal scholar David Kennedy (2006,
12) reasons, in "today's asymmetric wars," law can be "weaponized quite differently
by our own [U.S.] technologically sophisticated forces and by dispersed groups of
terrorists and insurgents against whom they [find] themselves in combat." Historically, furthermore, lawfare has been a staple component of U.S. military grand
strategy since World War II, when, as detailed above, it began using SOFAs to
expand its global basing structure and interventionary operations; and in the case
of CENTCOM, legal advisors have participated in every aspect of CENTCOM's operations from the beginning.[13] Since the 9/11 attacks, however, we have undoubtedly
witnessed a further expansion of the weaponization of the law: on the front lines
of the war on terror, from Uzbekistan to Iraq, CENTCOM JAGs have spearheaded
efforts to reform, prioritize, and mobilize the law as a key instrument in the U.S.
military's interventionary arsenal. The proliferation of lawfare in times of disorder
does prompt the question of its actual significance. As Jean and John Comaroff
(2006) pondered, does a fixation on governing legalities in times of disorder simply overcompensate for, and perhaps even mask, interventionary impotence? This
impotence is evident to a certain extent in colonial history;[14] but I think there is
a danger in overstating it, both historically and in our contemporary moment.
Throughout colonial history, imperial violence, dispossession, and accumulation
were secured successfully and extensively through the law. Today, U.S. JAGs activate the law as an indispensable modality of interventionary power. The law acts
as a legitimating communication of security necessity and right, and lawfare is
ultimately about "managing law and war together" in such a manner as to always
"frame the situation to their advantage" (Kennedy 2006, 125).

Legally framing the situation for CENTCOM has long featured SOFAs at the
heart of interventionary grand strategy. As the war on terror was launched, their
importance was elevated even further. The administration of George W. Bush

steadily signaled its intentions to use SOFAS to exempt forward-deployed U.S. forces from accountability to the jurisdiction of both host governments and international law—as underlined in the 2005 U.S. *National Defense Strategy*:

> Many of the current legal arrangements that govern overseas posture date from an earlier era. Today, challenges are more diverse and complex, our prospective contingencies are more widely dispersed, and our international partners are more numerous. International agreements relevant to our posture must reflect these circumstances and support greater operational flexibility. (U.S. Department of Defense 2005a, 19)

The strategy's conclusion completes the scripting of a necessary customized "global force management" framework for "surge capabilities" and reaffirms the vital security mechanism required: "legal protections for our personnel through Status of Forces Agreements" (U.S. Department of Defense 2005a, 20). Across CENTCOM's Area of Responsibility, such protection shields U.S. military personnel from local prosecution, as happened in the case of Airman Zachary Hatfield, for example, who fatally shot a civilian at a checkpoint at Manas Air Base in Kyrgyzstan in late 2006 (Morrissey 2011b).[15] More broadly, the heightened American exceptionalism at the heart of the post-9/11 Bush administration showed itself to be particularly averse to any international legal jurisdiction in the governing or regulation of its military forces (Ohlin 2015). Checks on U.S. violations of international law were especially resisted as the U.S.-led war on terror progressed. In 2005, for instance, just a few days after DePaul University professor of international law Cherif Bassiouni released a UN report criticizing the U.S. military for committing human rights abuses in Afghanistan, intense U.S. pressure saw him removed as UN independent expert on human rights in the country (Goodman and Bassiouni 2005).

From the outset of the war on terror, CENTCOM accelerated negotiations with various states in its Area of Responsibility to formalize military ties and secure interventionary SOFAS. The lawyer and legal journalist William Smith (2003, 14) notes that "[b]efore the first American bomb fell on Afghanistan, an advance battalion of State Department lawyers and JAGs descended on nearby nations to negotiate or update 'status-of-forces agreements.'" Uzbekistan was one of those nations. Just three weeks after the 9/11 attacks, "concerted negotiations involving teams of CENTCOM JAGS and State Department lawyers" culminated in the Uzbeks signing a crucial SOFA for the U.S. military, which permitted U.S. forces access to Uzbekistani territory and airspace in preparation for the then imminent attack on Afghanistan (Robbins 2004, 180). Conditioning this legal geography was the first salvo in the war on terror, and soon thereafter CENTCOM signed SOFAS with other key allies in its Area of Responsibility, including Kuwait, Bahrain, and Qatar (U.S. Overseas Basing Commission 2005).

In CENTCOM's spearheading of the war on terror, law has demonstrably been an integral element of grand strategy. Its heightened strategic use over the last ten years or more is not unique and mirrors a wider trend in Western military interventions, as David Kennedy (2006, 37) observes: "Military action has become legal action—just as legal acts have become weapons." In setting out how Western militaries have increasingly "weaponized the law," Kennedy (2006, 37, 167) shows how the law "privileges, channels, structures, legitimates, and facilitates acts of war" (cf. McMahan 2009). The law, in other words, is commonly used to enable the proliferation of violence rather than contain it, as Eyal Weizman has instructively shown in the case of recent Israeli incursions into Gaza. Weizman (2009) concludes that instead of "moderation and restraint, the violence and destruction of Gaza might be the true face of international law," and he urges anyone "concerned with the interests and rights of people affected by war" to employ a "double, even paradoxical strategy" that "uses international humanitarian law" but also recognizes the "dangers implied in it" and the import of challenging its "truth claims" and "the basis of its authority" (cf. Weizman 2011). More recently, Jeff Halper (2014) has shown how Israel's latest attack on Gaza, Operation Protective Edge, was not "merely a military assault on a primarily civilian population" but also, as in previous operations, "part of an ongoing assault on international humanitarian law by a highly coordinated team of Israeli lawyers, military officers, PR people and politicians, led by (no less) a philosopher of ethics." As Halper (2014) makes clear, this coordinated effort works to "not only get Israel off the hook for massive violations of human rights and international law, but to help other governments overcome similar constraints when they embark as well on 'asymmetrical warfare,' 'counterinsurgency' and 'counter-terrorism' against peoples resisting domination."

Weizman's and Halper's concerns echo Kennedy's (2006, 8) fears for how Western militaries have increasingly appropriated and mobilized the law as part of a concerted *communication strategy* involving "a powerful legal vocabulary for articulating humanitarian ethics" in justifying interventions and the use of force: "What does it mean [. . .] to find the humanist vocabulary of international law mobilized by the military as a strategic asset[, and how] should we feel when the military 'legally conditions the battlefield' by informing the public that they *are entitled* to kill civilians?" This is where lawfare becomes a crucial communication tool. Alex Jeffrey and Michaelina Jakala (2015, 46) note that both "military and developmental interventions" today are commonly legally and ethically justified "on the basis of protecting rights through the notion of humanitarianism" (frequently underscored with reference to the 1995 United Nations initiative Responsibility to Protect; see Hyndman 2000). As they point out, however, there is also an "allied set of legal manoeuvres" wherein "claims to legality and illegality are flexibly appropriated" (Jeffrey and Jakala 2015, 46; cf. Douzinas 2007; see also McMahan 2009 for a critique of just war theory). This is especially evident in CENTCOM press releases on civilian casualty assessments, in which statements typically acknowledge that "civilian casualties unfortunately did occur" while insisting that "strikes complied with the law of armed conflict" and that "all appropriate precautions were taken" (U.S. Central Command 2016d). In press releases of the most high-profile airstrike investigations, such as the strike on the Médecins Sans Frontières Trauma Center in Kunduz, Afghanistan, in 2015, CENTCOM pronouncements often include denying "war crimes" and setting out arguments that such "labels" are "reserved for intentional acts" (U.S. Central Command 2016e). As David Kennedy (2006, 122) observes, in these kinds of military knowledge forums, the public is effectively rendered passive as an audience via rhetorical declarations of legal compliance: "Defining the battlefield is not only a matter of deployed force, or privileging killing; it is also a rhetorical claim." In recent years, the U.S. military has increasingly sought to both *define* and *communicate* the legality of its interventionary violence through the conceptualization of lawfare. As the aforementioned Charles Dunlap (2009, 35) notes, "lawfare conceptualization in the national security context is to provide a vehicle that resonates readily with nonlegal audiences." For successful U.S. interventions overseas today, conceptualizing and communicating lawfare is ultimately essential.

War by Other Means: Military Interventions and 'Full Spectrum Law'

In *Of War and Law*, Kennedy (2006, 8) captures brilliantly what many fail to acknowledge when it comes to invocations of international law, its communicative, legitimating power:

> We need to remember what it means to say that compliance with international law "legitimates." It means, of course, that killing, maiming, humiliating, wounding people is legally privileged, authorized, permitted, and justified.

International law does not simply restrict, it also enables, and this malleability is understood best by military JAGs. A forum on 'juridical warfare' in 2008 in the U.S. military's flagship journal *Joint Force Quarterly* is especially indicative of this. The forum brought together a range of leading judge advocates, specialists in military law, and former legal counsels to the chairman of the Joint Chiefs of Staff. All contributions addressed the question of "[w]hich international conventions govern the confinement and interrogation of terrorists and how" (Rishikof 2008, 12).[16] The use of the term 'terrorists' sets the tone for the ensuing debate. In an impatient defense of practices of detention, Colonel James Terry (2008a, 18) bemoans the "limitations inherent in the Detainee Treatment Act of 2005 and the Military Commissions Act of 2006" (which, he underlines, only address detainees at Guantanamo) and asserts that "requirements inherent in the war on terror will likely warrant expansion of habeas corpus limitations." Assessing the policy of rendition, Colonel Kevin Cieply (2008, 20) asks if it is "simply recourse to the beast at a necessary time." Colonel Peter Cullen (2008, 22) argues for the necessity of the "role of targeted killing in the campaign against terror." Commander Brian Hoyt (2008, 34) contends that any assessment of U.S. policy toward the International Criminal Court "should be done through a strategic lens." And to conclude the special issue, Colonel Terry (2008b) furnishes an additional essay with the instructive title "The International Criminal Court: A Concept Whose Time Has *Not* Come." These commentary pieces from the highest-ranking officers tasked with the legal stewardship of the various armed services of the U.S. military reflect a prevailing preoccupation of the JAG Corps and the broader military-political executive at the Pentagon: the possibility of "real, perceived, or even orchestrated incidents of law-of-war violations being employed as an unconventional means of confronting American military power" (Dunlap 2007). The polemical arguments above mirror the rise in the post-9/11 period of an influential cohort of U.S. law professors hostile to international law and international institutions—the so-called New Realists—whose assault on international law has been documented by Jens David Ohlin (2015). They echo too, of course, official U.S. foreign policy. The 2005 U.S. *National Defense Strategy*, for example, defiantly signaled the spatiotemporal dimensions of winning the war on terror thus: "we will defeat adversaries at the time, place, and in the manner of our choosing" (U.S. Department of Defense 2005a, 9).

When military intervention is scripted in a 'manner of our choosing' language of contingency, this prompts an especially proactive legal strategy to capacitate, regulate, and maximize any and all military operations. On the first page of the U.S. military's *Operational Law Handbook*, we get a clear signaling of the import of *jus ad bellum*, the law governing a state's resort to force: "Any decision to employ force must rest upon the existence of a viable legal basis" (U.S. Army Judge Advocate General's Legal Center 2016, 1). The execution of military force, in other words, must always work *through* the law. The *Operational Law Handbook* is the primary reference point for the legal framing of all U.S. military operations—it is updated annually by the International and Operational Law Department at the JAG Corps's Legal Center in Charlottesville, Virginia. The handbook outlines a key concept in the framing of military conduct in today's war-law-space nexus: what JAGs instructively call the 'notional legal spectrum'. All military interventions are legally enabled somewhere along this spectrum, with JAGs being instructed as follows:

> Judge Advocates should understand that U.S. forces enter other nations with a legal status that exists anywhere along a notional legal spectrum. The right end of that spectrum is represented by invasion followed by occupation. The left end of the spectrum is represented by the utter lack of any legal protection [in previous annual handbooks, 'tourism' is exemplified here]. When the entrance can be described as invasion, the legal obligations and privileges of the invading force are based upon the list of straightforward rules found within LOAC [Law of Armed Conflict]. As

the analysis moves to the left end of the spectrum and the entrance begins to look more like tourism, host nation law becomes increasingly important. (U.S. Army Judge Advocate General's Legal Center 2016, 72–73)

The idea of a 'notional legal spectrum' captures perfectly the malleability of the law in terms of both its selective identification and prioritized utilization by the U.S. military. It echoes too the designed ambiguities integral to biopolitical management practices in our contemporary moment, practices that operate extraterritorially and at the "geographical margins of the nation-state" (Mountz 2011, 118; see also Mountz 2012). For the U.S. military, a notional legal spectrum can be referenced for a wide range of legal modalities underpinning the broadest array of interventionary practices. It allows for contingencies and anticipates any and all operational missions to secure the most approximately conceived instability.[17] It reflects, ultimately, a blurring of what counts as war (the legal distinction between 'War' and 'Military Operations Other Than War' had been dropped in 2006—U.S. Joint Chiefs of Staff 2006, iii), and it facilitates the operation of what I have conceived elsewhere as 'full spectrum law' (Morrissey 2015). In blurring distinctions between war and peace, military operations and stability operations, full spectrum law operates in an interventionary milieu that allows what Derek Gregory (2011, 238) calls an "everywhere war" or what the U.S. Army terms "full spectrum operations" (U.S. Department of the Army 2009).

Conclusion

When Walter Benjamin (1978, 283) remarked nearly a century ago that at the heart of military violence lies a "lawmaking character," he was in a sense observing how lawfare works—through the legal enabling of military force. Today, as the DoD's most recent *Law of War Manual* makes clear, the law has been fully incorporated into military tactics; it has become "part of who we are" (U.S. Department of Defense 2015b, ii), and its strategic deployment through proactive lawfare has become indispensable in military interventions. As David Kennedy (2006, 170) reflects, the military lawyer who "carries the briefcase of rules and restrictions" has been replaced by the military lawyer who "participate[s] in discussions of strategy and tactics." What lawfare does, in effect, as Kennedy (2006, 167) discerns, is to focus "the attention of the world on this or that excess" while simultaneously arming "the most heinous human suffering in legal privilege," redefining horrific violence as "collateral damage, self-defense, proportionality, or necessity." It mobilizes the law "as a tactic of statecraft and war" that on the one hand is channeled toward "evasion" in securing classified SOFAs, while on the other is oriented toward "careful pragmatic assessment" in "parcelling out responsibility" (Kennedy 2006, 169). Since the inception of the war on terror, the U.S. military has waged incessant lawfare to enable its operations throughout the globe. Lawfare legally conditions the various milieus of its military commanders on the ground and in doing so facilitates the interventionary capacity of U.S. overseas power. It activates, in essence, the biopolitical security focus of U.S. interventions, sanctioning violence against illiberal threats to the Western way of life and legally protecting those carrying it out. This echoes, of course, what Foucault (2003, 247) called the "power of regularization": simultaneously "making live and letting die."

U.S. global ambition today is primarily advanced by a legal-territorial grand strategy enacted by the U.S. military. CENTCOM, arguably its most important and globally pivotal command, enacts a core mission that is sustained by the legal conditioning of territorial, naval, and aerial access. CENTCOM's presence in the Middle East and Central Asia ultimately depends on an amalgam of geographically specific legal agreements, secured bilaterally with host states. As the war on terror began, the U.S. military's focus on legal strategy was matched by a simultaneous commitment to reorganize the type and extent of its territorial strategy to more effectively posture for a renewed global security ambition. To this end, visions of rapid deployability prompted a shift toward a new global expeditionary posture, a posture that relies on a legal framework based on negotiated SOFAS and transit right agreements with allies and friendly states across the globe. The legal-territorial modalities of the U.S. global forward presence today tell us much about the forms of intervention we are witnessing in late modern imperialism and its ongoing wars. For CENTCOM's Long War, lawfare and the functioning of 'full spectrum law' are vital operational instruments. CENTCOM JAGS play a key role in legally framing and communicating their command's interventions. Theirs is an expressly biopolitical project of security that works in tandem with a wider geopolitical and geoeconomic project of security, which I take up further in chapter 5. That broad interventionary mission is ultimately oriented to advance U.S. liberal imperial reach, and it works through the law.

CHAPTER FIVE

Military-Economic Securitization

Closing the Neoliberal Gap

CENTCOM forces ensure the flow of global resources and deter hostile powers throughout the region. These activities are mutually reinforcing. Progress in one spurs momentum in others.

CENTCOM commander General John Abizaid, 2006

The military-economic conflation of CENTCOM's global security mission is neatly captured above by former commander General John Abizaid. As Abizaid made clear in his posture statement to the U.S. Congress in 2006, the command's success revolves around its ability to 'shape' its Area of Responsibility, both militarily and economically (U.S. Central Command 2006a). From the first major deployment of CENTCOM forces in the Tanker War in the Persian Gulf in 1987, the command has fashioned itself as the 'Guardians of the Gulf', tasked with securing the free-market global economy. This chapter traces the establishment of this universalist neoliberal register, which forms part of a persuasive securitization discourse that has consistently acquired U.S. congressional support for the command's grand strategy. I focus especially on the notion of 'geoeconomic deterrence', which lies at the heart of this strategy. My aim is to demonstrate how deterring regional rivals and enabling markets and commercial openings were integral to CENTCOM's mission from the beginning. In more recent years, this fused military-economic brief has been further cemented by calls for the U.S. military to take a more active lead in overseeing what some commentators have called "messy capitalism" (Schramm 2010). Framed in the economic language of business and free markets, yet operationalized via force of arms, such a regulatory role echoes CENTCOM's long-standing interventionary rationale in safeguarding open global trade in a neoliberal capitalist economy. The accrued *global* benefits are impossible to disaggregate and chart, of course, and hence CENTCOM's reliance on vaguer but promissory logics about 'keeping the global economy open'. I demonstrate the abstracted formulation of this key discursive touchstone and ask questions of simplified and nebulous visions of military-economic relations in an era marked by globalization and new forms of capitalist accumulation.

Military and Economic Security Logics

Former CENTCOM commander General Lloyd Austin opened his 2015 posture statement to the U.S. Congress with the following overview of his command's Area of Responsibility.

> We are in the midst of one of the most tumultuous periods in history. There is growing unrest throughout much of the world, while a vast array of malevolent actors seek to capitalize on the increasing instability to promote their own interests. This trend is especially pronounced in the Central Region, where state and non-state actors are in conflict, and the resulting turmoil impacts the affected countries and also directly affects the global economy and the security of the United States. (U.S. Central Command 2015a)

Austin's use of the language of emergency, replete with registers of "tumultuous" "unrest," "instability," "conflict," and "turmoil," sets up an overlapping argument for necessary intervention—to protect the ostensibly interchangeable "global economy" and "security of the United States." He continues: "the U.S. must continue to exert strong leadership and act vigorously to protect our core national interests in this strategically important region[; . . .] if we hope to achieve improved security which provides for greater stability and prosperity around the globe, then the Central Region must remain a foremost priority" (U.S. Central Command 2015a). In his 2016 posture statement the following year, he repeated his scripting of the resource-rich strategic geography of the Central Region—abounding in "proven oil reserves and plentiful natural gas deposits"—and emphasized once again CENTCOM's vital role in securing the "free flow of resources through key shipping lanes" and safeguarding the "global energy market" (U.S. Central Command 2016a; cf. U.S. Central Command 2014a). The idea of the Central Region as a global security pivot had been firmly established at this point, of course—Austin was simply referencing an accepted military-economic geography. As former commander General David Petraeus remarked in his 2009 posture statement, CENTCOM's Area of Responsibility encompassed the most strategically 'critical' space on earth:

> United States Central Command (CENTCOM) is now in its eighth consecutive year of combat operations in an area of the world critical to the interests of the United States, its allies and partners. (U.S. Central Command 2009b)

The United States has variously projected economic interests in the Middle East from the early nineteenth century (Said 1993; Pease 2000). Since then, the region gradually became what Michael Palmer (1992, 1) calls "an open field for American capital and industry," despite British colonial hegemony. As Palmer (1992, 18) has shown, by the 1930s, "American corporations fueled the region's development," and to secure its economic interests therein, the United States increasingly assumed Western geopolitical and military leadership as Britain declined as a colonial power. This leadership came to the fore in the late 1970s following a range of regional political and economic crises, as explored in chapter 2, and drew on a securitization discourse that framed the Middle East as a pivotal yet insecure space in the global economy, requiring military-economic safeguarding and regulation. This interventionary rationale was solidified politically with the enunciation of the Carter Doctrine in 1980. President Jimmy Carter's (1980) State of the Union Address that year confirmed U.S. commitment to the security of the Persian Gulf region, whose escalating volatility demanded "resolute action, not only for this year but for many years to come." The idea of the Long War for global security has its origins here and builds on an existing conflation of military and economic security logics that prompted the establishment of the Rapid Deployment Joint Task Force and subsequently CENTCOM.

With CENTCOM's initiation and with increasing financial and political support from the Reagan administration, the United States assumed the role of "guardian of the Persian Gulf" (Palmer 1992, viii; cf. U.S. Central Command 1985, 10–17). This did not happen unilaterally with support from the Global North, however: from the 1970s, the major industrial powers issued growing calls for greater U.S. military leadership in the Middle East, especially after the formation of the Trilateral Commission in 1973 to foster closer economic cooperation between the United States, Europe, and Japan (Gold 1988); British and French warships were rushed to the Indian Ocean in the late 1970s in support of a potential U.S. naval intervention in the Persian Gulf (Morrissey 2017); CENTCOM's reflagging of Kuwaiti oil tankers with U.S. ensigns was unanimously endorsed at the G7 Summit in Venice in 1987 (Gamlen 1993); and less than a month after the September 11 attacks in 2001, military forces from France, Germany, Greece, Italy, Spain, and the United Kingdom joined up with twenty-three thousand of CENTCOM's Army, Air Force, Navy, Marine Corps, and Special Operations components in Egypt for Exercise Bright Star, a coalition military exercise conducted in CENTCOM's Area of Responsibility since the early 1980s (U.S. Department of Defense 2001b). It is important to remember too that this broad international alliance of military support for CENTCOM's mission continues today. Much of this support and liaising is physically accommodated at the CENTCOM Coalition Village, adjacent to CENTCOM Headquarters in MacDill Air Force Base in Tampa (see figure 5.1).[1]

CENTCOM extended its 'guardianship' of the Persian Gulf after its first major operational mission during the Tanker War. Its naval presence in the region remained in the later 1980s, and its ground presence was gradually built up as a key component of the U.S. military's overseas basing structure. By the early 1990s, CENTCOM CINC general Norman Schwarzkopf was regularly reminding the U.S. Senate Armed Services Committee of the importance of the command's forward presence and readiness to intervene—for both regional and global economic security (U.S. Central Command 1990). When the Schwarzkopf-led Gulf War

FIGURE 5.1. CENTCOM Coalition Village, MacDill Air Force Base. Source: Paul Courtnage.

came to pass, it was a war entirely consistent with CENTCOM's regional military-economic security mandate.

In the aftermath of the Gulf War, a number of CENTCOM-commissioned studies advocated an even more focused military-economic security brief for the command. Such a brief was set out in *Oil, the Persian Gulf, and Grand Strategy*, which was part of a larger 1991 RAND project sponsored by CENTCOM and the Joint Chiefs of Staff examining U.S. oil security interests across the command's Area of Responsibility (Lesser 1991). The following year, the aforementioned *Oil and the New World System: CENTCOM Rethinks Its Mission* was published as part of the CENTCOM 2000 project run by the Strategy, Plans and Policy Directorate of the command at MacDill Air Force Base. The grand strategy presented therein emphatically establishes CENTCOM's indispensable regional security role and confidently discards the very idea of the region's states taking responsibility for their own security: "the study rejects the argument that Saudi Arabia and the other Gulf Cooperation Council states can defend themselves—only CENTCOM can do that" (Pelletiere and Johnson 1992, v). CENTCOM's unilateral mandate is then expounded: "in effect, CENTCOM must become the Gulf's policeman, a function it will perform by mounting constant patrols" (Pelletiere and Johnson 1992, v). The report's delineation of CENTCOM's 'policing function' fascinatingly reveals how deterrence and the always imminent use of force are formulated and projected in its grand strategy. That grand strategy may well be aggressive in its military forward presence, yet dialectically it also exudes all the liberal hallmarks of ruling from a distance via the 'benign panopticon' (Foucault 1977; Joyce 2003; cf. Dean and Villadsen 2016). As the authors reason, "whenever nonviolent coercion fails, CENTCOM will have to apply more forceful means" to "compel compliance" via "a policing function"; and this, they feel, is "a perfect way to describe what CENTCOM will be doing throughout the decade—it will be policing the Gulf" (Pelletiere and Johnson 1992, 17, 18).[2] The report concludes with a reminder of CENTCOM's core mission and how its policing function will most efficiently achieve it:

> CENTCOM has a crucial mission to perform—guarding the flow of oil [. . .] Hence we repeat our earlier injunction, that the command adopt the role of policeman. A policeman keeps the peace by applying a minimum of force. He does not seek to expose himself unnecessarily. In a word, he is not pro-active. It is enough that he regulates matters. (Pelletiere and Johnson 1992, 26)

'Regulating Matters'

'Regulating matters' through 'military policing' captures precisely CENTCOM's assigned deterrence mission in the aftermath of the Gulf War. Enacting it entailed a range of elements, from the development of a more permanent basing structure to the signing of bilateral treaties confirming access and logistics sites with host states. In 1997, CENTCOM CINC general James Peay explained his command's deterrence policy to the House Appropriations Committee's Subcommittee on National Security: "we know from experience that [Middle Eastern] leaders are intimidated by military strength [and] consequently we deter these individuals by continuing to organize, equip, and exercise premier joint and combined forces; positioning a credible mix of those forces forward in the region; maintaining the national will to use them; and communicating our resolve to our opponents" (U.S. Central Command 1997b). So what does deterrence look like in practice? Here is General Peay elaborating on the command's day-to-day theater strategy of "enforcing freedom" through the modus operandi of police power:

> Sailors and marines [. . .] show the flag daily, conducting frequent naval exercises to demonstrate American naval prowess to friend and foe, enforcing freedom of navigation in narrow channels and vital choke points, and rappeling in the middle of the night onto rolling decks of merchant ships to enforce U.N. economic sanctions against Iraq. Over 12,000 such boardings have been carried out since August 1990. The sailors and marines are joined by airmen secur[ing] the skies over southern Iraq, carrying out operations to prevent the wholesale slaughter of Iraqi Shiites by Saddam Hussein's marauding bands. More than 48,000 sorties have flown over southern Iraq since August 1992. (Peay 1995a, 6)[3]

In addition to naval and air deterrence, ground deterrence has been a constant element of the command's operations since the Gulf War. Ground deterrence has, in fact, been the primary mechanism of CENTCOM's security operations from the beginning, and in its early years this was achieved by gradually building up a wide range of forward-deployed military exercises and operations across the command's Area of Responsibility (U.S. Central Command 1985, 82–99; U.S. Central Command 1986a, 73, 106, 318; U.S. Central Command 1987, 15–16). In the aftermath of the Gulf War, ground deterrence was extended via large-scale military maneuvers such as Operation Vigilant Warrior, Operation Desert Spring, and war-game exercise Internal Look. This last exercise regularly mobilized tens of thousands of ground troops and military arsenal, resulting in a "near continuous presence" to "deter conflict, promote stability, and facilitate a seamless transition to war, if required" (U.S. Central Command 1997a, 5). Both the universalist legitimacy and the unilateral constitution of this deterrence strategy have been repeatedly claimed and affirmed by CENTCOM commanders in their annual reports to Congress. Echoing the then emergent 'shock and awe' concept and underpinned by an unproblematic geopolitical imaginary of U.S. hegemony in the Middle East, General Anthony Zinni asserted in 1999, for example, that the "ability to project overwhelming and decisive military power is key to CENTCOM's theater strategy" (U.S. Central Command 1999b; cf. Ullman et al. 1996; Blanke 2001). Its chief strategy document from that year further underlined deterrence as the central means of carrying out its security mission, documenting the success of air, ground, and naval maneuvers, joint military exercises, war gaming, and the enhancement of pre-positional programs and logistic sites (U.S. Central Command 1999a, 9–13).

CENTCOM's post–Gulf War regional military hegemony further enabled its grand strategy of deterrence, in which forward operations were seen as vital in projecting "deterrent credibility":

> in the eyes of the deterree, the deterrer must demonstrate his capability to perform. Of the elements of deterrence over which CENTCOM has control, the ability to project real combat power is the most important. Exercises fulfill the dual purpose of providing training for the force and demonstrating, to friend and potential foe, America's commitment to the region [. . .] If the United States is to have any deterrent credibility, we must be able to undertake operations of whatever scale necessary. (Pelletiere and Johnson 1992, 19, 21)

Directing CENTCOM's deterrence strategy involves a number of everyday activities for command personnel, including "monitoring and analyzing significant military, political and economic events"; "planning and conducting unit and combined (foreign) military exercises and operations"; and "refining deployment and contingency plans for the region" (U.S. Central Command 2007b). The last concern, refining deployment and contingency procedures, wholly depends on CENTCOM's basing strategy, which comprises a range of "Forward Operating Sites," "Cooperative Security Locations," and the "contingency use of ports and airfields throughout its AOR"—all systematically developed "to assure U.S. access to enable the projection and sustainment of forces" (Global Security 2016b). All of these mechanisms to enable force projection are guided by the goal of 'rapid deployability'. As explored earlier, this ambition had been actively pursued since the early 1980s in efforts to reorganize the U.S. military to achieve optimum global interventionary power.

In the 1990s, CENTCOM's deterrence "mission and vision" were "clear" according to former CINC general James Peay: "CENTCOM supports U.S. and free-world interests by assuring access to Mid-east oil resources" (Peay 1995a, 8, 10). To this seemingly universalist end, CENTCOM adopted a military posture with all the hallmarks of liberal police power. It implemented a strategy that rested on "five pillars of peace"—"power projection, forward presence, combined exercises, security assistance, and readiness to fight"—and involved an international policing and regulatory role: "Our nation has several vital interests in the region: maintaining the free flow of oil at stable and reasonable prices; ensuring freedom of navigation and access to commercial markets; assuring the security of American citizens and property abroad; and promoting the security of regional friends" (Peay 1995a, 1, 2, 5; cf. Peay 1995b). At this point, CENTCOM's military strategy was being systematically directed to deter, patrol, and wage war if necessary in the name of both U.S. and global economic security. Peay's successor at CENTCOM, General Anthony Zinni, unequivocally affirmed the economic basis for continued military intervention, noting the "growing commercial significance of the area" and the pattern of global investments "flowing into the region because of its geostrategic position" (Joint Force Quarterly Forum 2000a, 26; see also Joint Force Quarterly Forum 2000b). This specific geoeconomic interventionary rationale has always received bipartisan political support in Washington, where CENTCOM's securitization discourse is proclaimed annually.

Through the first decade of the new millennium, the military-economic import of CENTCOM's Central Region remained the focal element of presentations to Congress (U.S. Central Command 2005, 2006a, 2007c). Here is General John Abizaid presenting the region's geostrategic importance to the U.S. Senate Armed Services Committee in 2005:

> the Central Region has continued to grow in importance and is the overseas area where U.S. interests are most likely to be directly threatened. Maintaining stability in this volatile region is key to the free flow of oil and other commerce essential to the world economy. Through continued attention to the legitimate defense needs of our friends, and by maintaining appropriate military presence and access, we can promote regional security while protecting our own vital interests. (U.S. Central Command 2005)

David Dawson (2014) sees Abizaid as CENTCOM's most capable visionary in recent years in terms of communicating the command's 'strategic' remit, in addition to its 'operational' goals. As commander, Abizaid, who holds a master's degree in Middle Eastern studies from Harvard, seemed especially conscious of articulating an interventionary rationale comprising a liberal reconstructive urge, reflecting a more widely held American ambition to "engineer" liberal political and economic subjects in the Middle East (Mitchell 2011, 3). As he remarked in an interview in 2006, he considered it "imperative" to communicate this vision and for all U.S. commanders on the ground to "educate the world about their work" (De la Garza 2006). A year later, CENTCOM set out its mission vision plainly with the following primary objective: "FOCUS SHAPING in the Central Region through integrated engagement and forward presence that enhances regional security and stability, promotes peace, and deters aggression" (U.S. Central Command 2007b; emphasis as in the original).

In the mission statement above, CENTCOM registers once more the most enduring element of its securitization discourse: necessary 'shaping' of the Central Region through forward presence. Its military-economic shaping is achieved primarily via an operational strategy of deterrence that has dialectically entailed both coercion and consent, and this strategy has mirrored more broadly global capitalism's shifting and expanding logics of extraction in its "endless accumulation of capital" (Harvey 2003, 183; cf. Sassen 2010). As elsewhere in today's globalized world, the Central Region (especially the GCC countries) is marked by the territorial presence of transnational global capitalism, and undoubtedly many of the companies availing of the commercial opportunities enabled by CENTCOM's security architectures have a distinctly multinational hue. Any global economic benefits are impossible to chart, of course, and hence CENTCOM's securitization discourse relies on more nebulous logics about open global trade and free markets. Certainly, I do not see any straightforward national correlation of military-economic relations being facilitated by CENTCOM, but below I explore further the command's agency in opening up access to commercial markets by doing what it says it does: 'shaping' and 'closing the gaps' of global economic security (Simmons, Manuel, and Arquilla 2003; Morrissey 2011c). In a period marked by new forms of capitalist accumulation, CENTCOM has nonetheless consistently fashioned itself in a neoliberal 'world policeman' role. To fulfill that function, it has employed a strategy that can be best described as one of 'geoeconomic deterrence'.

Geoeconomic Deterrence

In effecting U.S. foreign policy, CENTCOM's grand strategy incorporates both geoeconomic and geopolitical calculations that are "bound together and cogenerative in complex ways" (Essex 2013, 130).[4] Matt Sparke (2013, 289–290) has helpfully considered this entanglement as a "double vision" that serves to sanction "territorial fixing and geographical expansion" as the means to militarily secure global capitalism in a world that is divided into "distinct zones."[5] Sparke draws on the influential writings of Thomas Barnett (2004) on the 'functioning core' and 'non-integrating gap' to point out the overlapping visions between Barnett's geoeconomic gaze (and those of so many other exponents of strategic studies) and "business views on globalization" that "remain widely shared" in U.S. foreign policy circles (Sparke 2013, 294; cf. Luttwak 1990). Such abstracted visions herald "the benefits of economic globalization" for all (Sparke 2013, 294; cf. Schwartz 2008; Glück 2015), and the responsibility for enacting them eventually wings its way to the U.S. military, where commands such as CENTCOM are tasked, in effect, with 'closing the neoliberal gap'. It is in this capacity that I conceive CENTCOM's primary interventionary tactic of 'geoeconomic deterrence'. My use of the term 'geoeconomic' here is twofold.[6] First, I want to emphasize how CENTCOM's interventionary rationale continues and extends what Mona Domosh (2013, 962) calls the "geoeconomic imagination" at the heart of liberal thinking on "America's benevolent role" in global affairs for over a century. I consider CENTCOM's contemporary security mission as predicated by a particular geoeconomic imagination that is shot through with universalist claims about guarding the free-market global economy. Second, I show how CENTCOM's envisaged security mission seeks to support 'geoeconomics in practice' on the ground (Palmer 1992; Cowen and Smith 2009). I outline how the command anticipates the burgeoning of private-sector enterprise by providing a military policing and regulatory security blanket through deterrence operations.

Disaggregating the various attendant interests of CENTCOM's deterrence operations is a considerable challenge, but there is no doubt that multiple commercial and other interests have a stake in the command's mission.[7] Successive CENTCOM commanders have persistently affirmed the command's geoeconomic vision in its policing of "stability and security" in a region pivotal to the "economic wellbeing of the international community" (Peay 1995b, 32). Crucially, they have also shown a firm awareness of the pivotal role CENTCOM plays in facilitating commercial activities (despite never detailing the far-from-straightforward relationship between militarization and markets, which a range of critical work on war economies has emphasized: Prashad 2002; Chatterjee 2004; Boal et al. 2005; Glassman and Choi 2014). In 1995, CENTCOM CINC general James Peay delivered the keynote address at the Fourth Annual U.S. Mideast Policymakers Conference. His paper "Five Pillars of Peace: A Blueprint for Achieving Peace and Stability in the Central Region" was subsequently published by the US-GCC Corporate Cooperation Committee, a prominent Washington-based committee comprised of some of the world's biggest multinational corporations and focused on developing private-sector economics in the Persian Gulf (Peay 1995a).[8] In the foreword, the committee's secretary, John Duke Anthony—himself an influential commentator since the 1970s on U.S. commercial markets in the Persian Gulf—enthusiastically celebrated CENTCOM's "front and center" role in securing "regional and global well-being" (Peay 1995a, iv). Subsequently, General Peay (1995a, 2) elaborated on the "vibrant economic relationship between the U.S. and Middle Eastern states" that is facilitated by CENTCOM's territorial presence—a presence that supports "an array of commercial activities" and is "integral to the economic well-being and political stability of the entire world." Peay (1995a, 2) went on to identify some tangible, material specifics: "sixty-five percent of the world's proven oil reserves are located in the region, from which the U.S. imports 22% of its energy resources, Western Europe imports 43%, and Japan imports 68%"; and highlighted how this oil trade in turn facilitates "commercial activities ranging from military hardware to construction, health services, and consumer goods." Securing the kinds of commercial activities General Peay identifies encompasses a series of contradictions, of course, which lie at the heart of interventionary capitalism (Harvey 2003). CENTCOM's geoeconomic deterrence mission is about "*enforcing* freedom of navigation" and "*overseeing* economic sanctions" (Peay 1995a, 6) while simultaneously being part of a broader U.S. national security strategy that is about "*ensuring* freedom of action" and "*protecting* the integrity of the international economic system" (U.S. Department of Defense 2005a, 6; my emphases).

Despite the degree of contradiction and illogic present in much of CENTCOM's securitization discourse, its commanders have shown themselves to be particularly proficient in presenting the success of its military-economic mission to the U.S. government. Arguably the most important reason for this has to do with the rubrics of effective rhetorical communication. Each year, commanders present a 'statement' that is self-justificatory, budget driven, and rhetorically performed for a commonly passive Senate Armed Services Committee. That evolving committee, furthermore, has long held links to a military-industrial complex with a stake in the budget requests of CENTCOM and the wider DoD each year. Crucially too, CENTCOM posture statements typically repeat well-versed mantras about enabling free markets, safeguarding freedom of movement, and securing the global economy. All of these registers activate powerful liberal political imaginaries in the United States, and CENTCOM commanders always have the capacity to showcase specific operational successes, such as ensuring the flow of oil to U.S. shores, to signify tangible, quantifiable mission 'deliverables' to Congress and the U.S. public. This discursively works to negate any precise questioning of the success of wider operations. In the translation from interventionary imaginings and promissory hopes to the 'reality' of operations, CENTCOM's grand strategy may well get muddied on the shores and lands of the Middle East and Central Asia, but repeatedly emphasizing longer-term strategic interests and global security responsibility is the core communication goal at the nexus of military-political power in Washington.

Enabling Expeditionary Economics

At the heart of CENTCOM's interventionary rationale lies a geoeconomic imagination that promises the securing of "economic well-being" and the enabling of "commercial activities" (Peay 1995a, 2). This economic security role for the broader U.S. military has been increasingly advocated in recent years, with many calling for the widening of the military's interventionary toolkit accordingly, especially in the context of 'stability operations' (Taw 2012). In 2010, U.S. economist Carl Schramm published an indicative article in *Foreign Affairs* titled "Expeditionary Economics: Spurring Growth after Conflicts and Disasters." In it, Schramm (2010, 90) ardently pleas for the United States to take seriously the import of postconflict economic reconstruction and to task the military with what he sees as a global economic responsibility: "It is imperative that the U.S. military develop its competence in economics [and treat] economic reconstruction as part of any successful three-legged strategy of invasion, stabilization or pacification, and economic reconstruction." For Schramm (2010, 91), although the U.S. record of what he terms "expeditionary economics" was poor in Afghanistan and Iraq, its military is nonetheless "well placed to play a leading role in bringing economic growth to devastated countries" because "it has both an active presence and an active interest in places where economic growth is sorely needed." Schramm (2010, 98) sees capitalism as inevitably "messy" and appears oblivious to, or uninterested in, its human geographical effects: "a successful entrepreneurial system requires a willingness to accept messy capitalism even when it appears chaotic, trusting that the process will eventually bring sustained growth." He is a leading champion of entrepreneurship (and former president of the Kauffman Foundation), and although he acknowledges that entrepreneurial capitalism is disorderly and unstable, he argues that an econocentric approach to U.S. military interventionism would be the "most potent way of projecting soft power" (Schramm 2010, 99).[9] Schramm is far from alone, of course, in setting forth an expanded project of economic security for the U.S. military, and his argument is not especially new (J. M. Carter 2008). From Jeffrey Record's (1981b) writing on expeditionary rapid deployment in the 1980s through to the current abstracted visions of Robert Kaplan (2012), one can trace a now familiar arc of U.S. military-economic securitization discourse, advanced especially by strategic studies.

Visions of military-led expeditionary economics formed part of CENTCOM's grand strategy long before Schramm's piece in *Foreign Affairs*. A good exemplar of how such visions fed into the command's actions was the incorporation of the five former Soviet Central Asian states of Kazakhstan, Kyrgyzstan, Tajikistan, Turkmenistan, and Uzbekistan into the Central Region in 1999. The move territorially extended CENTCOM's mission to secure energy and economic enterprise in a pivotal region of the global economy, as CENTCOM CINC general Anthony Zinni explained to the Senate Armed Services Committee in 1998: "when the Central Asian states are added to CENTCOM's AOR in 1999, the addition of their energy resources, currently estimated at 15–25 billion dollars of oil, will only increase the importance of the region to economies worldwide" (U.S. Central Command 1998). The backdrop of national security thinking in the then Clinton administration is important here too: its efforts to support the extension of CENTCOM's AOR to the oil-, gas-, and mineral-rich countries of Central Asia mirrored a foreign policy of advancing a dominant global military posture in tandem with a strategy of global economic liberalization. Clinton's national security strategy was centrally inflected by the ambition of neoliberal economic "enlargement and engagement"—for a "new century" and for a "global age."[10]

After the USSR's breakup in the early 1990s, the independence of the Central Asian states opened up a range of new markets for the United States. Tailored strategy studies soon followed (e.g., Blank 1995), and the Central Asia–Caucasus Institute, set up at Johns Hopkins University in 1996, quickly became the "primary institution" and "forum for policymakers" for "the study of the Caucasus, Central Asia and the Caspian Region" (Central Asia–Caucasus Institute 2008). These developments were not marked by any sustained critical reflection on how "neoliberal globalization and its associated geoeconomic discourse" might create the potential for "rampant crisis" or exacerbate "social, political, and economic inequality" in Central Asia (Essex 2013, 131). Rather, the region's resources were designated "a matter of national security" by President Clinton, who, as Michael Klare (2004, 133) notes, was a "vigorous advocate for American companies seeking drilling rights in the Caspian basin." In 1997, Clinton sent a high-level delegation including deputy assistant secretary of defense Catherine Kelleher to Kazakhstan to attend the inaugural joint military exercise, CENTRAZBAT (Central Asian Battalion), in which U.S. troops took part with forces from Kazakhstan, Kyrgyzstan, and Uzbekistan. The Clinton administration subsequently touted the combined military and diplomatic expedition as a major success in efforts to integrate post-Soviet states into the global economy. It was a strategy driven by the administration's ambition to extend the Carter Doctrine into Central Asia.[11] In subsequent CENTRAZBAT exercises in 1998 and 2000, CENTCOM solidified U.S. ties to the region, and all of these efforts mirrored how "American policymakers" were increasingly viewing the region's energy assets as representing "very substantial new opportunities" for U.S. commercial interests (U.S. Senate 1997, S4207). CENTCOM's military extension into Central Asia was scripted as "necessary"—so that U.S. companies could "operate effectively with the governments of those nations in developing energy resources"—and the broader geoeconomic sensibility of U.S.-global energy security could not be more evident in government circles: "as a consumer nation, the United States is interested in enhancing and diversifying global energy supplies [. . .] to reinforce Western energy security" (U.S. Senate 1997, S4207–S4208).

Three years after CENTCOM's extension into Central Asia in 1999, then U.S. secretary of defense Donald Rumsfeld championed the success of the command's military connections in the region that had secured the opening of bases and access for U.S. forces in the war on terror (U.S. Department of Defense 2002). What Rumsfeld failed to acknowledge, however, was the extent of economic connections also enabled by CENTCOM's expedition to Central Asia and how these continued to be pursued in conjunction with military operations (Nichol 2003). On March 21, 2003, just as the Iraq War was beginning, Kazakhstan's deputy prime minister Karim Masimov declared that over the next fifteen years U.S. investments in Kazakhstan would exceed $80 billion and would target connecting the Aktau-Baku oil pipeline with the Baku-Tbilisi-Ceyhan pipeline (Caspian News Agency 2003). Earlier that month, Steven Mann, special adviser to the U.S. secretary of state on Caspian Sea energy issues, had met with Kazakhstan's foreign minister, Qasymzhomart Toqaev, in Astana to discuss "the investment climate in Kazakhstan's energy sector for American firms interested in developing newly discovered oil and natural-gas deposits and how to make that climate more attractive" (EurasiaNet 2003).

CENTCOM's fused military-economic mission to Central Asia in the late 1990s provides a useful historicization of current calls to expand the U.S. military's lead in economic interventionism and stability operations, which have been wide ranging in recent years (Taw 2012). For example, Alexander Benard (2012), managing director of Gryphon Partners, an investment firm focused on the Middle East and Central Asia, laments the reluctance of the United States to embrace "business promotion" as "a strong pillar of its foreign policy": "for too long now, Washington has almost entirely neglected commercial diplomacy, ceding too many economic battles." Other examples include Jason Thomas (2012), director of Majorca Partners, a human terrain specialist company, who calls for "a strategic partnership between multi-national corporations and the U.S. military" in future interventions, citing the "extractive industries" as the ideal partners (see also Majorca Partners 2014). He elaborates: "given the attractive return on investment from oil, gold, copper and other commodities, resource companies such as ExxonMobil, BHP Billiton, Rio Tinto, AngloGold Ashanti and Chevron are prepared to embark on major projects in conflict or postconflict environments" (Thomas 2012). Thomas (2012) proceeds to ask if U.S. military planners could "benefit from working more closely with corporations such as Shell," arguing that "multi-national corporations, particularly those from the extractive sector, could act as a force multiplier for U.S. military and foreign policy planners." Interestingly, Thomas heralds the emergence of a more focused U.S. military-economic gaze on Africa, with the establishment of U.S. Africa Command (AFRICOM) in 2008, as an exemplar of the U.S. military's entrepreneurial vision. And certainly the DoD's envisioning of the need for AFRICOM (prior to it being initiated) was dominated by setting out the continent's "strategic and economic importance" (U.S. Department of Defense 2007b). Subsequently, its first operational posture statement made clear the command's core objectives in overseeing "stability and economic growth," helping manage the continent's "abundant natural resources," and aiding projects of "reconstruction and economic development" (U.S. Africa Command 2009). Such visions, of course, sit firmly on and extend the colonial history of exploitative resource extraction in Africa (Lubeck, Watts, and Lipschutz 2007; Watts 2008; Bridge and Le Billon 2013).

The economic dimensions of the U.S. military's interventionary mission overseas have been supported for many years by an amalgam of expertise in strategic planning and operational infrastructure. Defense Acquisition University (DAU), for instance, set up in 1992 at Fort Belvoir, Virginia, in close proximity to the Pentagon, houses an Acquisition Community Connection Practice Center that provides a wide range of operational expertise on "business and enterprise systems" and "joint rapid acquisition" among other topics (Defense Acquisition University 2016). DAU forms part of an assemblage of military expertise typically emphasizing speed, innovation, and flexibility in the rapid securitization of ground operations for both the U.S. military and its attendant industries. Rapid security support is a key objective, for example, for the U.S. Office of the Assistant Secretary of Defense for Logistics and Materiel Readiness, which hosts an annual three-day conference that engages with "government officials, industry executives, and academia on integrating government and industry for improved product support processes and procedures" (2015). A recurring conference narrative in recent years has celebrated the success, in particular, of 'rapid acquisition' in activating efficient and accelerated battle-space operations (cf. Romero 2012; Vinch 2012).

Validations of accelerated U.S. interventionary power are part of a technological discourse that binds rapidity with flexible force deployment for more efficient military and economic security. Retired U.S. Army colonel Douglas Macgregor (2011, 22), who advised CENTCOM commander General Tommy Franks prior to the Iraq War in 2003, urges "American political and military leaders" to finally break with "the industrial age paradigm of warfare" by building a "21st-century scalable 'Lego-like' force design" that would ensure "a more efficient and integrative [use of] manpower and resources" in the orientation of a more broadly conceived interventionary mission.[12] This would then open up new commercial opportunities for companies like Burke-Macgregor Group (where Macgregor is now executive vice-president), which is "[d]edicated to developing cost effective solutions supporting national security and economic prosperity objectives" by partnering with "federal and state governments" and working with "select domestic and international commercial partners" to "capture the resulting evolving market opportunities" (Burke-Macgregor Group 2016a). In anticipating that market, they see future conflicts as revolving "around the competition for energy, water, food, mineral resources and the wealth they create" and advocate that in "this volatile setting, the alternative to direct American military intervention must include the use of commercial partnerships to resolve conflicts and disputes through economic development" (Burke-Macgregor Group 2016b).

Enabling commercial partnerships for Burke-Macgregor is about building "new engines of prosperity that will support international cooperation" (Burke-

Macgregor Group 2016b). These kinds of aspirational rationales for 'refocused', 'smarter', and more 'innovative' U.S. military intervention can often be heard emanating from former military personnel who, post–military service, find themselves part of the defense industry's private sector (Singer 2003; Leander 2005). The broad link between the U.S. military and defense contractors has long been known, but what has been less clear until recently is the degree of employment overlap of former high-ranking officers such as Douglas Macgregor. In 2012, Citizens for Responsibility and Ethics in Washington (CREW) published a detailed examination of this so-called revolving door phenomenon. They interrogated the top one hundred federal defense contractors in the United States and uncovered that 70 percent of three- and four-star generals and admirals who retired between 2009 and 2011 took up positions as defense consultants (frequently with one of the five largest defense contractors, Boeing, General Dynamics, Lockheed Martin, Northrop Grumman, and Raytheon) and that in many cases they also continued to "advise the Pentagon" (CREW 2012, 1–2). CREW's research ultimately reveals the extent of the 'revolving door'. The aforementioned former commanders of CENTCOM, John Abizaid, James Peay, and Anthony Zinni, are all cases in point. Abizaid is on the board of directors at Defense Venture Group, a portfolio company of J. F. Lehman and Company, a leading private equity investment firm in the defense, aerospace, and maritime industries, while Peay and Zinni are directors at BAE Systems, Inc., the U.S. component of one of world's largest defense contractors. Even the briefest perusal of the posture statements of Abizaid, Peay, and Zinni for CENTCOM over the last twenty years divulges how they have been consistently conscious of the dual military-economic remit of the command's mission. Who better, then, to advise private-sector defense companies on the operational delivery of military-economic security in the Long War?

Conclusion

Visitors to the U.S. Department of Defense's website are welcomed with an introductory overview titled *DoD 101*, which opens with a striking pronouncement of the history and vision of the DoD:

> With our military units tracing their roots to pre-Revolutionary times, you might say that we are America's oldest company. And if you look at us in business terms, many would say we are not only America's largest company, but its busiest and most successful. (U.S. Department of Defense 2016b)

Reflecting this long history of 'business' consciousness, CENTCOM's security project in the Middle East and Central Asia has entailed from the beginning a distinct geoeconomic rationale in safeguarding U.S. interests and ensuring access to regional resources and markets. Its current mission statement is set forth thus: "U.S.

Central Command promotes cooperation among nations, responds to crises, deters or defeats state and non-state aggression, and supports development and when necessary reconstruction to establish the conditions for regional security, stability and prosperity" (U.S. Central Command 2016b). Critically considering how CENTCOM's mission involves a focal geoeconomic imagination prompts us to see how the U.S. military is being deployed today as a key appendage of U.S. efforts to orchestrate the conditions for global economic 'security, stability and prosperity'. CENTCOM's primary operational strategy of deterrence depends on specific legal-territorial arrangements as explored in chapter 4, and these work to enable access and freedom of movement to militarily police and secure the regional and global economy. In a neoliberal global security vision, the quickening of commercial opportunities is promised in a long war of military-economic deterrence, which requires "21st-century scalable 'Lego-like' force design," "rapid acquisition," "rapid deployment," and "a willingness to accept messy capitalism" to "capture the evolving market opportunities" (U.S. Department of Defense 2004b; Schramm 2010; Macgregor 2011; Vinch 2012; Burke-Macgregor Group 2016a). How much of these goals are actually new is debatable, of course. Such recent calls merely mirror a long-established CENTCOM military strategy to geoeconomically shape the most energy-rich region on earth. But the question remains: What is the geoeconomic endgame? What kind of capitalism, in essence, is CENTCOM supporting through its forward presence and deterrence practices? And in whose interests is deterrence enacted at such an enormous annual human and financial cost? This cost is one that we sometimes forget is being paid for maintaining a standing overseas military force far vaster than any nation in the era of high colonialism.

CENTCOM's Long War has involved from the outset a commitment to neoliberal capitalism on a global stage that combines the inherent contradictions of "narrow national self-interest" with universalist values of "global good" (N. Smith 2003a, xii). The command has successfully fashioned itself a neoliberal 'world policeman' role in a period of dynamic globalization and to that end has employed an operational strategy that is ostensibly about safeguarding the global economy. CENTCOM's mission implements a military strategy to regulate 'geographical pivots', control 'choke points', and facilitate 'commercial opportunities' in a global economic network. The strategy depends on specific legal-territorial constellations enabling intervention, as well as a persuasive rationale for a long war to secure free markets, access to energy assets, and open transportation routes. This rationale is perennially presented to Congress as CENTCOM's long-haul grand strategy, and politically the logic is rarely if ever challenged on Capitol Hill. Indeed, as Asli Bâli and Aziz Rana (2010, 233) remark, both the Republicans and the Democrats "continue to take as given the centrality of pacification and global omnipresence for the promotion of American interests, despite the extent to which the experience of the last decade underscores the counter-productivity of these policies."

For over thirty years, a period palpably marked by globally rapacious forms of capitalist accumulation, extending further excesses of uneven development, CENTCOM's operational mission has nonetheless consistently held fast to a belief in an ostensibly free-market, neoliberal global economy (cf. Harcourt 2012; Piketty 2014). Loïc Wacquant (2009) makes the point that neoliberalism today typically manifests itself in a centaur-like form, comprising a liberal head and authoritarian body. He has in mind the confines of the state here and draws extensively on the United States as an example. However, his analogy seems equally as useful in considering the extension of U.S. state power in efforts to secure neoliberalism on a global scale—appealing to neoliberal open markets and the common good on the one hand, yet involving on the other the same devastating use of interventionary violence familiar to any reader of colonial history. There are multiple contradictions in this neoliberal interventionist project, of course: national interventions on a global stage, in the name of national vital interests and global common good, yet ultimately for the securitization of transnational capital (N. Smith 2003b, 2005; Sparke 2013). CENTCOM appears to intrinsically trust the notion of so-called free markets, and it seems oblivious to the contradictions and failures of its self-declared universalist mission to secure them—in part perhaps because such failures, and ongoing failed states, necessitate new cycles of military intervention and economic correction in a seemingly never-ending Western imperial moment (Chomsky 2003). It appears particularly unmindful of how the expansion of Western corporate interests in the Middle East could be seen as invasive, exploitative, and destabilizing (cf. Prados 2001).

Mary Kaldor and Joseph Stiglitz (2013, 5) argue that there is "no longer confidence in the ability of free and unfettered markets to assure economic security," and moreover that there is "no longer confidence in the ability of the United States to assure the world of its military security, let alone the rest of the world's security." I doubt CENTCOM military strategists see it this way. They would point to military deterrence continuing to provide a crucial security blanket in enabling markets in, and through, the Middle East and Central Asia. They would possibly point too to other levels of interventionary power that are vital in the relationship between militarization and market provision, and certainly the signing of free trade agreements (with attached joint security commitments), SOFAs (typically including arms sales), and other bilateral agreements with host states across CENTCOM's Area of Responsibility are key modalities of geoeconomic grand strategy, serving to legally frame and shape market relations. And of course it is important to remember too that the U.S. military's function is not simply to secure an overseas capitalist accumulation architecture that the military itself is not an integral part of. It has long been a special kind of national and global economic actor in its own right—through its enormous oil consumption, for example, or via its defense supply contracts whose domestic procurement strategy spreads DoD spending across congressional districts throughout the United States. As the DoD notes, the U.S. military is, in fact, "not only America's largest company, but its busiest and most successful" (U.S. Department of Defense 2016b). In CENTCOM's long-haul military-economic mission, it employs grand narrative to signal a broad geoeconomic raison d'être: the guardianship of the global economy and free markets. And although this narrative is unambiguously and unrelentingly scripted in its annual posture statements to the U.S. Congress, what is less clear is how well its geoeconomic imagination matches with evidence of geoeconomic enterprise on the ground. There is certainly a danger of abstracting too much from its grand imperial projections, but that should not detract from our analysis of the deeply entwined military and economic security logics of CENTCOM's grand strategy that have resulted in the Middle East and Central Asia being repeatedly conditioned as requiring corrective military-economic intervention.

CHAPTER SIX

No Endgame

The Long War for Global Security

The end is in the beginning and yet you go on.

Samuel Beckett, *Endgame*

CENTCOM's rationale for its very existence captures perfectly the seemingly never-ending Western imperial urge: the command is the "practical solution to the challenge of projecting U.S. military power to the Central Region from halfway around the world"; its mission is to "deter aggression" and any regional ambition to "control" key spaces in the global economy; and in the aftermath of the September 11 attacks in 2001 it was "tasked with taking the fight to the enemy" (U.S. Central Command 2008, 9). In its assumption of global security responsibility, CENTCOM's gaze has increasingly exhibited a temporal consciousness of the future—an uncertain future replete with visions of geopolitical and geoeconomic volatility. In its discursive production of ongoing necessary intervention, the command successfully binds imaginings of future uncertainty to practices of securitization in the present—thereby securing what Foucault (2007) termed the 'aleatory'. In reflecting on a prevailing discourse of future insecurity, I explore in this final chapter the temporality of CENTCOM's Long War and the broader U.S. military's envisioning of what it calls 'full spectrum operations', which sanctions the perpetual use of U.S. forward-deployed forces in an era of persistent conflict with no endgame in sight.

CENTCOM's 'Area of Responsibility'

Too often with military euphemism, we lose sight of meaning. Acronyms seduce us more than most, and AOR is a perfect exemplar. CENTCOM's AOR, or Area of Responsibility, is meant primarily in terms of 'geographic responsibility'. As explored in chapter 3, CENTCOM has been assigned a geographic responsibility to militarily patrol, police, and intervene in a specified region of the earth as part

of a wider U.S. global security project whose ambition is cartographically announced in a map titled "The World with Commanders' Areas of Responsibility" (figure 3.3). Such mappings involve a profound reductionism, freeze-framing
imperial constellations of power, knowledge, and geography and reinforcing a
global security vision that naturalizes the U.S. military's carving up of the world.
CENTCOM's Area of Responsibility has been framed as a militarily and economically pivotal global space, which it terms the 'Central Region', and therein it in-
tervenes. In intervening, of course, it also assumes 'ideological responsibility' for
something, and that responsibility has consistently been the lofty goal of capitalist global economic security. The command's 1997 posture statement began
with the following predication: "[t]he unrestricted flow of petroleum resources
from friendly Gulf states to refineries and processing facilities around the world
drives the global economic engine" (U.S. Central Command 1997c, 1). For then
CENTCOM CINC general James Peay, the message was simple: "America's vital
interests" in the region were "compelling" (U.S. Central Command 1997c, 1). Not
shy of asserting global interventionary responsibility, he subsequently declared to
the House Appropriations Committee's Subcommittee on National Security that
his command's mission was critical for a successfully functioning global economy, as any disruption to the flow of oil from the Persian Gulf would trigger
"economic calamity for developed and developing nations alike" (U.S. Central
Command 1997b). His successor, General Anthony Zinni, located in more detail CENTCOM's global security mission in outlining four core military-economic
objectives:

> The first is obvious—providing access to the energy resources of the region, which
> is a vital national interest. The second element is something often overlooked—the
> growing commercial significance of the area. The pattern of global trade is shifting
> from east to west. Investments are flowing into the region because of its geostrate-
> gic position. The third is the number of maritime choke points in the region, such
> as the Suez Canal and Strait of Hormuz. We must ensure these passages remain
> open to communication and trade. Fourth, there are issues of stability—the Middle
> East peace process, extremism, and other concerns. (Joint Force Quarterly Forum
> 2000a, 26)

Today, all of these merged U.S.-global security objectives remain for CENTCOM. In
one of his last pronouncements as commander, General Lloyd Austin seamlessly
conflated U.S. and global security interests in speaking of "growing unrest" that
"directly affects the global economy and the security of the United States" before
registering yet again CENTCOM's mission: "to achieve improved security which
provides for greater stability and prosperity around the globe" (U.S. Central Command 2015a). At the ceremonial handover of command leadership to General Joseph Votel at MacDill AFB in March 2016, the chairman of the Joint Chiefs of Staff,
General Joseph Dunford, expressed particular appreciation to Austin for "the ser-

vice and sacrifices of the CENTCOM team" in overseeing a vital military-economic security mission: "when you're *responsible* for a part of the world that consists of places like Iraq, Syria, Iran, Yemen, Egypt, Pakistan, Afghanistan and Lebanon, you never know what kind of crisis or challenge you are going to wake up to in the morning" (U.S. Central Command 2016c; my emphasis).

A fused military-economic interventionary responsibility has long been assigned to the broader U.S. military, but there is no doubt that it has been more explicitly signaled in recent years. Dichotomous representations of security and insecurity, involving powerful geoeconomic registers, are present in many of the key U.S. national security documents. The *National Military Strategic Plan for the War on Terrorism*, for example, asserts that extremists use terrorism to "impede and undermine political progress, economic prosperity, and the security and stability of the international state system," while the United States promotes "freedom, democracy, and economic prosperity around the world to mitigate those conditions that terrorists seek to exploit" (U.S. Department of Defense 2006, 11, 21).[1] Similar scriptings of military responsibility to ensure free-market capitalism are predominant in each of the major national security and defense documents of successive U.S. administrations over the last ten years (U.S. Department of Defense 2005a, 2008, 2012; U.S. National Security Council 2006, 2010, 2015). Running through much of these is an emphasis on maintaining freedom of global movement and global capital into and through each regional commander's Area of Responsibility. This was a core rationale for CENTCOM's deterrence strategy from the beginning;[2] and its Gulf War in 1991 was not just to free Kuwait but also to secure the functioning of a capitalist global economy by becoming "the Gulf's policeman" and "mounting constant patrols" (Pelletiere and Johnson 1992, v). Global economic security has steadfastly remained a focal objective of U.S. foreign policy in recent years (Dalby 2007). For instance, four of the nine chapters in the Bush administration's 2006 U.S. *National Security Strategy* set out a grand strategy of "economic integration and globalization" (U.S. National Security Council 2006; see also Katzman 2006).[3] The Obama administration, furthermore, did not deviate from Bush's entwined military-economic U.S. foreign policy; it simply solidified the policy in an even more persuasive and universalist neoliberal language: "The success of free nations, open markets, and social progress in recent decades has accelerated globalization on an unprecedented scale[, and this] has opened the doors of opportunity around the globe, extended democracy to hundreds of millions of people, and made peace possible among the major powers" (U.S. National Security Council 2010, i).[4] President Obama's preface to the most recent U.S. *National Security Strategy* further declares that "sustained American leadership is essential to a rules-based international order that promotes global security and prosperity" (U.S. National Security Council 2015, i). For contemporary U.S. foreign policy, 'global security' and 'global prosperity' are the repeatedly stated goals of grand strategy, and CENTCOM is the spearhead. As David Dawson (2014) notes, such a universalist interventionary urge lies at the heart of the command's foundation and ongoing mission:

> From its founding, CENTCOM has conceived of the free flow of commercial traffic through the Strait of Hormuz and indeed worldwide as an international issue. Freedom of navigation and the free flow of international commerce is also a vital U.S. interest. Very little of the oil going through the Strait of Hormuz goes to the U.S., but the oil market is a global market and any disruption in the flow of oil will invariably affect the U.S.

In spearheading U.S. efforts for global security, CENTCOM has deployed various legal-territorial tactics, as explored in chapter 4, that enable intervention within its Area of Responsibility. Getting to and from its Area of Responsibility also requires carefully negotiated transit rights agreements with allies and friendly states across the globe, including so-called neutral countries like Ireland, which has seen hundreds of thousands of U.S. troops in transit to, and from, the front lines of the U.S.-led war on terror (see figure 6.1). All of this coalesces into a global interventionary posture that facilitates an imperial reach unprecedented for any imperial age (cf. U.S. Central Command 2006b; Krepinevich and Work 2007). Late in his first term of office, U.S. president George W. Bush announced that the United States would "redistribute forces now stationed at overseas locations where the wars of the last century ended" (U.S. Department of Defense 2004a). "The

FIGURE 6.1. U.S. troops, Shannon Airport, Ireland, June 2005. Photo by the author.

world has changed a great deal," Bush declared, and "our posture must change with it" so that "we can be more effective at projecting our strength and spreading freedom and peace." He went on to emphasize that it was not just "today's threats" that needed to be secured but also "emerging" and "unexpected" threats and that "a more agile and flexible force" would enable the power to "surge quickly" (U.S. Department of Defense 2004a). This objective of rapid deployability continues to be underscored in U.S. national security circles as vital to global interventionary capability (Scahill 2013). It promises a more efficient use of taxpayers' money in fiscally restricted times, and it also registers a seductive *technological* fix for security challenges on a global scale. Leon Panetta, for example, before retiring as U.S. secretary of defense, heralded a "Joint Force for the future" that would be "smaller and leaner" but "ready and technologically advanced" (U.S. Department of Defense 2012, v). The key register in the DoD's current envisioning of global rapid deployability, however, is a *temporal* one. Its repeated assertions of necessary rapid intervention centrally feature a 'temporality of preemption' that, in effect, assumes responsibility for 'future global security'.

Securing against Future Risk

A wide range of work in the humanities and social sciences in recent years has explored how discourses of future insecurity and risk feature constitutively in everyday governmentalities of the state (cf. Bernstein 1996; Lupton 1999; Mythen and Walklate 2006). The late Ulrich Beck's (1992, 1999) formulation of a 'risk society' has been particularly influential (cf. Dean 1999; O'Malley 2004). In the specific context of the war on terror, the goal of averting 'future risk' has played an instrumental role in the legitimization of military intervention. It is through the "perspective of risk management" that "securitization" is seductively seen to function by the "deployment of technologies to manage dangerous irruptions in the future" (Aradau and van Munster 2007, 108). President George W. Bush's declaration of the war on terror in 2001 was substantially based on a war strategy of risk management. This preemptive war had already begun, of course, several years earlier when his predecessor, President Bill Clinton, dispatched bombing raids on Afghanistan and Iraq. In setting out those attacks in 1998, Clinton used the phrase "the risks of inaction outweigh the risks of action," which subsequently became a "catch-all phrase for action" that was "repeated verbatim" by Bush in launching the preemptive strikes on Iraq in 2003 (Heng 2006, 147). Five years later, Bush's 2008 *National Defense Strategy* concluded with a specific segment titled "Managing Risk." Therein, securing "future challenges risk" is underlined as critical for effective U.S. foreign policy (U.S. Department of Defense 2008, 20–23).

U.S. grand strategy to manage 'future challenges risk' is underpinned by neoliberal beliefs that long-term practices of military-economic intervention can function to variously 'correct', 'reboot', and 'close the gap' of the global economy (Simmons, Manuel, and Arquilla 2003; Barnett 2004; Knights 2006). In all this grand strategizing, temporality is a vital discursive register: economic reconstruction is always envisaged for the long term, and the very language of the 'long term' is drawn on to persuasively signify 'vision', 'hope', 'improvement', 'progress', and so on. Such visions of the future have an entirely nebulous endgame, of course, but that does not prevent them from underscoring a wide array of appeals for ongoing interventions, from across the U.S. military–strategic studies complex: Michael O'Hanlon, for example, sets out "unfinished business" for the U.S. overseas presence to secure in the "21st Century"; while CENTCOM speaks of its perpetual project of "shaping" the most pivotal space on earth for the "21st Century" (U.S. Central Command 1999a; O'Hanlon 2008). CENTCOM's temporal gaze has always been directed decades ahead:[5] it has consistently looked to the future in strategically initiating infrastructural, pre-positioning, and programmatic developments to secure its Area of Responsibility; its Long War has focally entailed a primary tactic of deterrence; and ultimately preemptive intervention has been the security logic that has directed grand strategy from the beginning (U.S. Central Command 1985, 1986a, 1987).

Preemptive interventionary security logics have acquired proliferated governmental utility in our contemporary moment, as various authors have detailed (Dillon 2007a; Anderson 2010). In the context of the war on terror, Randy Martin (2007) has shown how a preemptive political economic calculus of risk aversion has featured centrally in U.S. military interventions. Martin (2007, 18) sketches a logic of preemption fearfully driving U.S. foreign policy in which an aleatory future is "made present" and potential threats are "actualized as demonstrations of the need for further intervention." Melinda Cooper (2007) too has argued that the U.S. war on terror is based on a "mode of intervention that is curiously indifferent to its own 'success' or 'failure', since both eventualities open up a market of future risk opportunities"—or, more precisely, further interventionary requirements to secure such risks. And of course the U.S. military's various attendant industries and beneficiaries of its overseas mission also acquire new fields of intervention in the project of securing against future risk. As Deborah Cowen and Neil Smith (2009, 42) note, the U.S.-led wars in Iraq and Afghanistan were in many ways "market war[s] par excellence" in which hundreds of corporations "feasted at the trough" of billion-dollar contracts "committed to destruction and failed reconstruction" (cf. Scahill 2007). In all of this, an aleatory future remains, as does the goal of its securitization.

The United States' mission to secure the aleatory future of the Middle East can be traced back to the signing of the Roosevelt-Abdulaziz pact in 1945 (Palmer 1992; Vitalis 2006; T. C. Jones 2010). The pact can be read as a fusing of military and economic interests at the heart of emerging U.S. national security interests as the Second World War came to a close (Painter 1986). In the 1970s, a series of political and economic crises in the Middle East and Central Asia solidified this link and served to refocus U.S. foreign policy. CENTCOM's forerunner, the Rapid Deployment Joint Task Force, was created in late 1979 with crisis management as its foundational remit. Soon thereafter, U.S. president Jimmy Carter (1980) politically established the idea of preemptive U.S. military action in the Middle East and Central Asia and the necessity of "resolute action, not only for this year but for many years to come." Carter's State of the Union Address in 1980 was the first key political moment in charting CENTCOM's subsequent Long War. The Middle East and Central Asia's uncertain future has since been a staple discursive touchstone of CENTCOM geopolitical and geoeconomic discourse. The command's strategy papers, mission statements, and annual reports to Congress have repeatedly foregrounded geopolitically and geoeconomically charged senses of future risk in articulating grand strategy. As Jennifer Hyndman (2007, 361) reasons, discourses of risk management have a particularly potent power because they neatly combine an "expression of vulnerability" with a "rationale for security measures." CENTCOM's core deterrence strategy is underpinned thus. Its fundamental logic of preemption entails envisioning long-term insecurity and therefore necessary ongoing intervention. In the early 1980s, Joshua Epstein (1981, 126), an international affairs consultant working at RAND Corporation, remarked that it was "difficult to imagine a region at once so vital economically and so volatile politically" as the Middle East and Central Asia. Over a generation later, CENTCOM commander General James Mattis declared to the Senate Armed Services Committee that in "over 30 years of supporting U.S. forces in the Central Command Area of Responsibility" he had "never witnessed it so tumultuous" (U.S. Central Command 2012). Those thirty years coincided with the institutional lifespan of Central Command, during which time the idea of its necessary interventions has become a given.

CENTCOM's mission has undoubtedly been compellingly advanced by signifying a responsibility to secure against future risk—risk primarily from global economic instability. In such rhetoric, one wonders, however, if there is ever a pause for thought about the kind of future being envisaged, and whether sensibilities other than military and economic ones can productively inflect risk management practices. In the summer of 2015, the former senior intelligence officer with Joint Special Operations Command (JSOC), retired U.S. Army lieutenant general Michael Flynn, was interviewed by *Al Jazeera English*'s Mehdi Hasan on his reflections on the war on terror during his time as head of the Pentagon's Defense Intelligence Agency. He was asked about its success and more broadly how efficacious U.S. grand strategy over the course of the previous fifteen years had been. His reply captured an essential truth so rarely acknowledged: "what we have is this continued investment in conflict" (Al Jazeera 2015). During the course of the interview, Flynn referred in particular to the strategic failure of intervention in Iraq during the Bush years and the counterproductive extension of the drone program under the Obama administration. He is retired, of course, and so is out of the chain of command, both militarily and politically, but within such a bare-bones admission from a man described as the "father of the modern JSOC" (Ackerman 2012) lies a profound sadness for the people of the Middle East and Central Asia today and the acutely precarious geographies they inhabit.

Broadening the Military Toolkit: 'Full Spectrum Operations'

The objective of securing against future risk has in recent years fed into a broader re-envisioning of the U.S. military's interventionary remit, a re-envisioning that has been reinforced by a combination of political calls and defense policy writings stressing the urgency of greater military involvement in postconflict reconstruction and stability operations (Patrick and Brown 2007; Bachman 2010; Taw 2012). The result has ostensibly been a "doctrinal renaissance" within the U.S. military that "acknowledges and codifies a dramatic change in thinking: no longer does the mission of the military stop at winning wars; now it must also help 'win the peace'" (Kem 2008). In 2008, the U.S. Army published a new version of its core field manual, *Field Manual 3-0: Operations*. It began by declaring that America must "remain fully engaged for the next several decades in a persistent conflict against an enemy dedicated to U.S. defeat" (U.S. Department of the Army 2008a, viii; cf. Filkins 2009). To do so effectively, it outlined a new doctrinal concept, 'full spectrum operations' (first coined in the manual's 2001 version), which moves from "an 'either-or' view of combat and other operations" to a new vision that emphasizes the "essentiality of nonlethal actions with combat actions" (U.S. Department of the Army 2008a, viii; see also U.S. Department of the Army 2009). In a follow-up field manual on 'stability operations', the U.S. Army further set out its postconflict responsibility to secure an "uncertain future" of "persistent conflict" (U.S. Department of the Army 2008b, vi, C2). Such visions of future uncertainty and how the U.S. military can, and must, respond have been prompted in part by the military's difficulties and failures in its reconstruction efforts and counterinsurgency campaigns in Afghanistan and Iraq. As a result, doctrinally at least, an augmented military strategy reflecting the goal of 'full spectrum operations' has to some degree emerged (Taw 2012; cf. Morrissey 2015). In all of this, however, and despite the underscoring of the "vital importance of nonlethal action to change the civil situation," the Army's basic field manual continues to recognize that "the Army's primary purpose is deterrence" (U.S. Department of the Army 2008a, viii). Moreover, old-fashioned military force in "decisively winning the Nation's wars by fighting" remains as the centerpiece of an interventionary doctrine that "seeks nothing less than victory for the United States" (U.S. Department of the Army 2008a, viii; cf. Bacevich 2005). As Emily Gilbert (2015, 215) observes, although military operations have increasingly been justified in terms of "democratization, humanitarianism, and the rule of (Western) law," their execution in practice "undermines these state-oriented principles in favour of a militarized neoliberalism where military might is right" (cf. Douzinas 2007; Weizman 2011).[6]

The objective of 'full spectrum operations' resonates with a long-standing U.S. liberal imperial sensibility that stretches back to the early twentieth century (Domosh 2013). It echoes too a broader and older Western interventionary "will to improve" (Li 2007). The modern-day orientation of full spectrum operations in the U.S. military acquired momentum in 2004 when the Office of the Coordinator for Reconstruction and Stabilization was set up in the U.S. State Department (U.S. Department of State 2004). Soon thereafter, the DoD issued Directive 3000.05 (Military Support for Stability, Security, Transition and Reconstruction Operations), which outlined how the U.S. armed forces would proactively respond to a new vision of overseas intervention containing an explicit focus on fostering postconflict economic development, stability, and security (U.S. Department of Defense 2005b). U.S. president George W. Bush subsequently issued National Security Presidential Directive 44 (Management of Interagency Efforts Concerning Reconstruction and Stabilization), which solidified the U.S. government's commitment to the new vision: "The United States has a significant stake in enhancing the capacity to assist in stabilizing and reconstructing countries or regions, especially those at risk of, in, or in transition from conflict or civil strife, and to help them establish a sustainable path toward peaceful societies, democracies, and market economies" (The White House 2005, 1). A few years later, the U.S. Army detailed how the new interventionary objective of 'stability operations' would target an economic endgame of "infrastructure development" and "enterprise creation"—in a military-economic grand strategy comprising a familiar imperial language of 'improvement':

> peace and stability endure when follow-on efforts succeed. Such efforts aim to restore order and rebuild infrastructure, governance, and civil society institutions [. . .] This governance capacity is critical to establishing rule of law and a market economy that ensure lasting stability and prosperity. (U.S. Department of the Army 2008b, 1–12)

The rule of law and a functioning market economy feature centrally in the contemporary U.S. military's envisioning of its responsibility to perform postinterventionary stability operations. DoD Directive 3000.05 declared that stability operations should be "conducted to help establish order that advances U.S. interests and values," with a long-term goal to "develop indigenous capacity" for "a viable market economy" and "the rule of law" (U.S. Department of Defense 2005b). In a subsequent joint publication of the U.S. Department of State and Joint Warfighting Center on the emergent framework of reconstruction and stabilization strategy, the following economic mechanisms are highlighted as "essential components" of "American military power": "bilateral and multilateral economic relations," the "commercial sector," "trade," "foreign direct investment," "sanctions," "regulatory frameworks," and "policy towards international financial institutions" (U.S. Department of State and U.S. Joint Warfighting Center 2005, 33–34). This devising of expressly economic interventionary mechanisms divulges how the U.S. military is being directed to engage in late modern war's ostensibly wider theater of operations. Its commitment to 'full spectrum operations' attests mostly to a broadening of an already well-established military-economic logic of security involving mechanisms of legal and economic correction and regulation for a neoliberal global economy.

Military-Economic 'Stability Operations'

In deconstructing the official policy framing of 'full spectrum operations', it becomes clear that the kind of 'stability operations' the U.S. military is primarily concerned with are in fact 'military-economic stability operations'. It is this vision and version of security that the U.S. military can offer in enabling 'expeditionary economics' (Schramm 2010); and citations of historical successes to this end (such as the "Marshall Plan in Europe" and the "postwar rebuilding of Japan") have buttressed calls for increased "military–private sector partnerships" in postconflict development today (Patterson and Stangler 2010, 15–16). Such calls have been made by an extensive array of popular U.S. strategic studies experts who have eagerly anticipated both geostrategic and geoeconomic opportunities in the war on terror (Byman and Wise 2002; Thayer 2003; Barnett 2004; Friedman 2005; Kaplan 2012). Not everyone agrees that the U.S. military should take the lead on expeditionary economics or trusts in its capacity to oversee postconflict economic reconstruction. For example, responding to Schramm's (2010) article, the then chair of the House Committee on Foreign Affairs, Congressman Howard Berman, argued that it is "civilian, not military, forces" that "should lead in this regard": "What is needed, instead of a military doctrine of 'expeditionary economics' is a civilian-led peacebuilding corps that can operate in conflict zones and help local communities lay the foundations for robust economic growth" (Kaufman and Berman 2010, 175–176).[7] Here too, however, neoliberal notions of activating 'robust economic growth' in the fragile worlds of conflict and postconflict remain at the heart of the interventionary vision; and, as Mark Duffield has shown so well, the conjoining of 'development' and 'security' concerns in late modern war has opened up multiple new markets (Duffield 2001, 2007; cf. Schwartz 2008; Mac Ginty 2012).

Neoliberal global security is the declared goal of the Obama administration's latest expression of U.S. grand strategy. In *Sustaining U.S. Global Leadership: Priorities for 21st Century Defense*, it proclaims that the United States will increasingly "emphasize non-military means" to "address instability" (U.S. Department of Defense 2012, 6). Yet addressing instability will still primarily involve *militarily* protecting U.S. economic interests, and especially so in CENTCOM's Central Region:

> U.S. economic and security interests are inextricably linked to developments in the arc extending from the Western Pacific and East Asia into the Indian Ocean region and South Asia [. . .] The maintenance of peace, stability, the free flow of commerce, and of U.S. influence in this dynamic region will depend in part on an underlying balance of military capability and presence [. . .] The United States will continue to make the necessary investments to ensure that we maintain regional access and the ability to operate freely in [. . .] a rules-based international order that ensures underlying stability. (U.S. Department of Defense 2012, 2)

Militarily policing the "global commons" and enabling "economic growth and commerce" are also laid out as key elements of a stability operations strategy defined in military-economic terms: "America, working in conjunction with allies and partners around the world, will seek to protect freedom of access throughout the global commons—those areas beyond national jurisdiction that constitute the vital connective tissue of the international system" (U.S. Department of Defense 2012, 3). A commitment to securing the stability of global commerce evidently lies at the heart of the Obama administration's framing of U.S. overseas interventionary responsibility, and this commitment extends the long-established military-economic grand strategy of U.S. foreign policy. An additional 2012 national security document, *National Strategy for Global Supply Chain Security*, is underscored with an unambiguous binding of 'economy' and 'security' in which "America's future economic growth" is firmly intermeshed with national security interests (The White House 2012, 6). The strategy calls for partnerships "with state, local, and tribal governments, the private sector, and the international community"—to realize "our shared goal of building a new framework to strengthen and protect this vital [global economic] system" (The White House 2012, C3, 6).[8] Envisioning such partnerships is partly about communicating 'whole of government' approaches to addressing instability, but such approaches always rely on militarily enforced security. In CENTCOM's 2013 posture statement, General James Mattis briefly referred to a 'whole of government' approach to security operations, prompted no doubt by pressure to demonstrate value and utility for the command's massive military arsenal in a time of budget cuts across the U.S. government: "U.S. Central Command's approach—working in tandem with the State Department and other agencies through a whole of government approach—is to protect our interests using fewer military resources in an era of fiscal restraint" (U.S. Central Command 2013b). CENTCOM's primary role, however, in militarily policing and protecting the regional and global economy was the overwhelmingly dominant message, as in previous posture statements. Signaling a 'whole of government' approach to this objective can be read as merely an additional rhetorical justification for its ongoing military-economic security mission.[9]

In what is now a proliferated discourse of military-economic securitization, CENTCOM's ground presence in the Middle East and Central Asia assumes both an ostensibly regulative and generative function in the international economic system. For 'generative' economic interventionism, the concept of 'stability operations' can, of course, be usefully incorporated. The JAG Corps, for instance, advises its judge advocates in the field that stability operations primarily entail establishing "essential services, economic and infrastructure development, and governance" (U.S. Department of the Army 2013, 5-4). In all of this, it is striking how malleable and enabling the discourse of 'stability operations' is. In 2007, CENTCOM set out its grand strategy for the future around the following three objectives:

> [1] FOCUS SHAPING in the Central Region through integrated engagement and forward presence that enhances regional security and stability, promotes peace, and deters aggression; [2] remain ready to SELECTIVELY RESPOND to the full spectrum of military operations and, when necessary, fight and win our nation's war; and [3] PREPARE our command and families for the challenges and opportunities of an uncertain future through modernization and transformation throughout the Central Region in order to promote and protect United States' interests. (U.S. Central Command 2007b; emphases as in the original)

The command is particularly adept here in discursively mapping out a broad mission rationale that not only envisages continual preemptive interventions as security imperatives but also manages to chart flexible selectivity and prioritization in mission operations. It registers a license for 'selective intervention' by invoking the necessity of adaptable preparation for an 'uncertain future'. This interventionary flexibility, furthermore, is crucially mirrored in a legal conditioning that equally exhibits a strategic malleability for any and all operations. The thoughts of former U.S. deputy judge advocate general Charles Dunlap are especially revealing of the legal flexibility at the heart of contemporary U.S. grand strategy. In citing von Clausewitz, Dunlap pinpoints how selective lawfare is strategically enabling: "by anchoring lawfare in Clausewitzean logic, military personnel—and especially commanders of the militaries of democracies—are able to recognize and internalize the importance of adherence to the rule of law as a practical and necessary element of mission accomplishment[; they] need not particularly embrace its philosophical, ethical, or moral foundations; they can be Machiavellian in their attitude toward law because adherence to it serves wholly pragmatic needs" (Dunlap 2009, 35). This is lawfare's inherent strategic flexibility. It is vital in conditioning and communicating a wider yet selective interventionary remit for Western militaries today, and it forms part too of the political corollary: taking 'responsibility' for military actions yet eschewing 'culpability' for any of the consequences (BBC News 2016; The Iraq Inquiry 2016).

Conclusion: Global Security and Imperial Promise

In introducing his administration's final *National Security Strategy*, U.S. president Barack Obama began with the following pronouncement: "any successful strategy to ensure the safety of the American people and advance our national security interests must begin with an undeniable truth—America must lead" (U.S. National Security Council 2015, i). This belief in American global leadership is found centrally in one of the key appendages of the U.S. national security state enacting U.S. foreign policy today: CENTCOM. Its commanders have consistently divulged a deeply embedded liberal imperial 'will to improve' at the heart of their ongoing interventions. In his 2007 posture statement to the U.S. House Armed Services Committee, former commander Admiral William Fallon underlined how the command's mission is about facilitating "stability and security," helping "people manage social, political, and economic change," and furthering the "interests of peace and representative Government" (U.S. Central Command 2007c). More recently, General James Mattis echoed this promise specifically on Afghanistan: "In Afghanistan, U.S. forces continue to support the largest coalition campaign in modern history to ensure it will not again become a haven from which violent extremist organizations can plan, rehearse and execute terrorist attacks[; we] posture our forces to inhibit the spread of these radical and violent organizations and rapidly respond to protect U.S. interests" (U.S. Central Command 2013b). Mattis's interventionary vision intermeshes U.S. and global security interests, an envisioning that has become one of the core hallmarks of CENTCOM's communications strategy. Evident too is an implicit certainty in the superiority of Western political, economic, and social values and a responsibility to extend them to the Central Region. Former commander General John Abizaid declared in 2005 that "the people of the region do not want the future" that "extremists desire": the "enemy's vision of the future is unappealing and a backward step in time" (U.S. Central Command 2005). Yet in all of these pronouncements of liberal grand strategy, CENTCOM commanders seem entirely oblivious to the effects of prior U.S. and Western interventions.

In much of the grand strategizing in support of CENTCOM's mission, we find echoes of familiar historical senses of imperial calculation and geostrategy, where the "name of the game" is "control" (Pelletiere and Johnson 1992, 17). But there is a palpable sense too of imperial delusion and historical amnesia: "The aim of any operation CENTCOM undertakes must be to get it over with quickly, with no complications—at least none that could cause us to become bogged down[; and the] necessity of this should be readily apparent—any action that roils the waters of the Gulf causes extraordinary commotion to world financial centers" (Pelletiere and Johnson 1992, 22). Promissory envisionings of 'quick' military successes with 'no complications' captures well a recurring feature of contemporary Western interventions: their ahistorical reasoning. For CENTCOM and more broadly U.S. grand strategy, the absence of any significant historicization is by no means an accident. It facilitates an always present-centered securitization discourse that enables new and cyclical fields of intervention. For this reason alone, documenting and insisting on the imperial 'blowback' of interventionary violence, occupation, and expropriation remains an enduring challenge (Johnson 2000; Sparke 2013).[10]

In its key grand strategy document at the turn of the century, *Shaping the Central Region for the 21st Century*, CENTCOM proclaimed its Area of Responsibility as occupying "a pivotal role in world events," as containing "more than 70 percent of the world's proven oil reserves," and as spanning "the major trade routes that link the Middle East, Europe, Asia and the Western Hemisphere" (U.S. Central Command 1999a, 4). Signaling an imperial role long into the new century, it outlined a globally oriented strategy of military deterrence for a straightforward geoeconomic rationale: "Access to the region's petroleum resources is vital to the stability of the global economy" (U.S. Central Command 1999a, 4). This is CENTCOM's Long War. Only CENTCOM can secure the Central Region, as command advisors opined in the early 1990s (Pelletiere and Johnson 1992); only CENTCOM can shape it "for the 21st century" (U.S. Central Command 1999a). But are the stakes in this 'shaping' sufficiently high to explain the extraordinary commitment of U.S. money, military hardware, and ground troops annually to the region over the last thirty years? For a nation whose declared foreign policy endgame is "global security and prosperity," the answer is an emphatic yes (U.S. National Security Council 2015, i). Securing the region's oil production and distribution has been endlessly cited by CENTCOM as a global security responsibility, and over the course of CENTCOM's existence, oil has become even more critical to the U.S. economy, the U.S. military, and Western economies and militaries more widely. The late Milton Copulos, former president of the National Defense Council Foundation, outlined to the U.S. Senate Foreign Relations Committee in 2006 that the supply disruptions of the late 1970s cost the U.S. economy "between $2.3 trillion and $2.5 trillion" and that such a repeat event would cost "$8 trillion, 62.5 percent of U.S. GDP" (Copulos 2006). He underlined an equally dystopic vision for the U.S. military's capacity to defend the nation without access to an oil supply that it increasingly, rather than decreasingly, depends on.[11] Such visions of a risk-laden, aleatory future centrally feed into a compelling rationale for a preemptive grand strategy to secure global energy, and the U.S. military has undoubtedly honed its energy security expertise in recent years (U.S. Department of the Army 2015b).[12] In late 2013, the Strategic Studies Institute, the research arm of the U.S. Army War College, organized a conference on the "new realities of energy security in the 2010s" and the "implications for the U.S. military." In the foreword to the subsequent edited conference proceedings, the institute's director, Douglas Lovelace, outlined how the U.S. military's future overseas missions will increasingly be driven by "evolving energy-based U.S. national interests" and how this priority will even "shape the degree to which the U.S. military becomes involved in political or humanitarian crises" (Deni 2015, x).

In his preface to the 2015 U.S. *National Security Strategy*, President Barack Obama proclaimed that "[t]oday, the United States is stronger and better positioned to seize the opportunities of a still new century and safeguard our interests against the risks of an insecure world" (U.S. National Security Council 2015, i). How to do this is through "sustained American leadership" in "a rules-based international order that promotes global security and prosperity," because U.S. "economic strength" is "the foundation" of U.S. "national security" (U.S. National Security Council 2015, i). This is the same entwined military-economic security logic that has resulted in the Middle East and Central Asia being repeatedly scripted as requiring regulative military intervention. For CENTCOM, the 'Central Region' has long needed securitization from itself. Its energy resources and global geographical position, coupled with its seemingly perpetual political instability and irregular military threats, present CENTCOM with an enduring mission. In this mission, securing resources has often been theorized as the primary objective—Michael Klare (2004), for example, has considered the Iraq conflict as yet another illustration of the contemporary world's 'resource wars' (cf. Klare 2002; Le Billon 2004; T. C. Jones 2012; Bacevich 2016). This is part of the story, of course, but CENTCOM's intervention in Iraq was never just about resources; rather, it forms part of a much longer U.S. regional grand strategy combining military and economic security interests in maintaining a neoliberal global economy. From its first major forward deployment in reflagging Kuwaiti oil tankers with American ensigns in the Persian Gulf in the 1980s, CENTCOM's mission involved what Mona Domosh (2013, 945) calls a "geoeconomic imagination" and served elite economic interests. In more recent times, those elite interests include defense companies such as Raytheon, who have posted unprecedented global sales on the back of securing large-scale contracts to supply CENTCOM with various electronic and information technology services (Raytheon 2003). The innumerable defense think tanks and policy institutes in Washington and elsewhere, which serve the DoD in multiple ways, are also an elite interest. And, of course, the interested parties served by CENTCOM's Long War are not just those in, or directly related to, the military. Operating as 'Guardians of the Gulf', by patrolling assets, access points, and transportation networks, CENTCOM provides a security blanket for a raft of multinational companies in the region, where territorial access remains important (Gillem 2007; N. Klein 2007).

Has CENTCOM's grand strategy ultimately been successful? Answering this question depends entirely on what version of success is the endgame, and by whose standards we measure success. The Middle East and Central Asia today can hardly be said to be secure; the rise of ISIS shows that this is a period of intense turmoil and interventionary blowback (Prashad 2014; Greenwald 2015).

Of course, the goal of securitization is never full security, but in crucial senses—namely its major interventions in Iraq and Afghanistan—U.S. efforts at regime change and state-building have decidedly failed.[13] Through all of this, however, CENTCOM commanders have managed to square the circle on presenting a version of mission success to the U.S. Congress each year—primarily because CENTCOM measures its success 'strategically'. This in turn allows commanders to highlight mission accomplishments of 'geoeconomic securitization' that have long been held up as the 'big picture' of security. Consider, for example, General John Abizaid's posture statement from 2005. He acknowledged the then "security challenges" in Iraq and Afghanistan but quickly shifted emphasis to his command's success during the previous year in a mission seldom acknowledged as integral to the broader war on terror: "we patrolled key air space and waterways in the region to ensure the free flow of commerce" (U.S. Central Command 2005). Success measured in this way reflects an overtly geoeconomic framing of CENTCOM's mission, which is difficult to challenge given that the command's prime interventionary remit has long been delineated thus. As noted earlier, humanitarian concerns, human rights, and the lives of 'Others' have never been CENTCOM's top priority (Pelletier and Johnson 1992; Robbins 2004); and, of course, one could argue that the absence of successful 'human security' outcomes merely adds to an instability that further requires new cycles of intervention, new rounds of corrective violence (Boal et al. 2005; Cooper 2007). The real tragedy in the midst of such abstracted geostrategic calculations is that the human geographies of Western interventions continue to be erased, hidden, or forgotten. Indeed, they were never really acknowledged. For millions across the Middle East and Central Asia, their fate is to repeatedly pick up the pieces of unremitting military violence (Gopal 2014). Families, homes, lives: shattered and lost. Yet there appears no pause in how the United States militarily seeks the lofty goal of global security.

Dennis Crow (2015) observes that "we are at a watershed of needing a new vocabulary to address the fluid and liquid and transient movement of politics, administration, economics, and war." Certainly, our contemporary moment exhibits a complexity of global spatial organization and intricacy of legal-territorial interventions. But imperial interventions have long been heterogeneous in mobilizing mechanisms of security and tactics of law. From at least the early modern period, imperial administrations depended on "a fluid legal politics" that worked to produce myriad "territorial variations" (Benton 2010, 3). Today, the "incompleteness and contingency" of "territorial control" endures (Essex 2013, 6), and a key challenge lies in teasing out the specificities of law, geography, and security that encompass and enable interventionary power, which in essence has been the core concern of this book. CENTCOM's story over the last thirty years critically informs our reading of U.S. global ambition today. Its Long War has been enabled by careful legal specification and conditioning of territorial, naval, and aerial access in a pivotal strategic space of global security in the Middle East and Central Asia. In this ongoing war, the law and lawfare are vital in coalescing both geopolitical and biopolitical power and in communicating the legitimacy of interventionary rationales. CENTCOM's scripting of necessary intervention in the present has been successfully mobilized in tandem with a discursive identification of future economic risk, whose volatility must be preemptively guarded against for the broader global economy. This implicitly assigns the command an enduring mission, replete with universalist rhetoric, to effect a globally oriented U.S. foreign policy. "Our global responsibilities are significant, we cannot afford to fail," concludes a recent DoD pronouncement on global security (U.S. Department of Defense 2012, 8). For over thirty years, its key appendage, CENTCOM, has executed a military-economic security mission of forward presence and deterrence in the most energy-rich region on earth. It forms part of a grand strategy for global security that the DoD calls "shaping activities" (U.S. Department of Defense 2001a, 32). Imperialism has always been about shaping, and there is no endgame.

NOTES

CHAPTER 1. "Shaping the Central Region for the 21st Century"

1. Examples include former CENTCOM deputy commander Mike DeLong's *Inside Cent-Com* (2004) and CENTCOM senior intelligence analyst Jeffrey Hooker's *Shaping the Plan for Operation Iraqi Freedom* (2005). There has also been some examination of how U.S. military commanders implement U.S. foreign policy in the field of strategic studies; see, for example, Derek Reveron's interesting edited volume *America's Viceroys* (2004).

2. The only notable academic book examining the advent of CENTCOM has been Dore Gold's short, Israeli-focused monograph from 1988, *America, the Gulf and Israel*.

3. Dawson is a retired colonel with the U.S. Marine Corps Reserve, now serving as command historian at CENTCOM Headquarters, which houses approximately thirty-six hundred staff, including nine hundred or so personnel from each of the four military services: the U.S. Air Force, U.S. Army, U.S. Marine Corps, and U.S. Navy (Global Security 2016a). MacDill AFB also houses the headquarters of U.S. Special Operations Command, which was established in 1987.

4. Compared to other Western powers, where much material is classified or unpublished, the U.S. military produces an enormous range of publications. CENTCOM's own website houses an extensive archive of news articles and press releases dating back to December 2007 (http://www.centcom.mil/news/press-release-archives). Much of this material records summative military accounts of everyday CENTCOM operations, including reports of the almost daily military airstrikes in the command's Area of Responsibility. There is also a rich video and imagery archive (http://www.centcom.mil/media/images-and-video), and its substantial online social media presence is linked in too (http://www.centcom.mil/media/social-media).

5. The current U.S. military Unified Command Plan has its origins in World War II and the establishment of geographic theaters of operation (namely Europe and the Pacific) composed of forces from multiple service branches that reported to a single commander. Reflecting the newfound hegemony of the U.S. military on the global stage post–World War II, U.S. president Harry Truman approved the first Unified Command Plan in December 1946, which established the two oldest geographic commands, European Command (EUCOM) and Pacific Command (PACOM).

6. In chapter 3, I explore CENTCOM's geographical representation of its 'Central Region,'

which includes twenty nations, and how this fits into a distinctly imperial cartography of 'The World with Commanders' Areas of Responsibility'.

7. The broader DoD has been equally concerned with communication strategy. The National Military Strategic Plan for the War on Terrorism, for example, underlined the importance of "a sustained, proactive strategic communication effort" (U.S. Department of Defense 2006, 30). Communicating legality and legitimacy is especially important, as signaled in the U.S. Army's most recent legal field manual: "JAGC [Judge Advocate General's Corps] personnel are well versed in the relationship between legitimacy and operations[; . . . the law] connects the government to the people" (U.S. Department of the Army 2013, 9-2).

8. What also remains unseen is prior Western interventionism and regional grand strategy (Cockburn 2014). As Vijay Prashad reasons, an old CIA term 'blowback' best explains the advent of ISIS; for Prashad (2014), the "tinderbox of regional chaos was opened by the U.S. invasion of Iraq." Western geopolitical pragmatism has, of course, left a legacy of horrific human geographical consequences on every continent (Johnson 2000). As Glenn Greenwald (2015) reflects on the descent into chaos in post–NATO intervention Libya, "what we see here is what we have seen over and over: the West's wars creating and empowering an endless supply of enemies." None of this appears to have moved those who initiated the defining event in the recent violent history of the Middle East: the invasion and occupation of Iraq in 2003. Former UK prime minister Tony Blair, for instance, responded to the publication of the UK Government's Chilcot Inquiry into the Iraq War—and specifically to a key conclusion that "military action would increase the threat from Al Qaida to the UK and to UK interests" (The Iraq Inquiry 2016, 6)—by asserting that he still believed that "it was better to remove Saddam Hussein" and that he did not believe that doing so was "the cause of the terrorism we see today whether in the Middle East or elsewhere in the world" (BBC News 2016).

9. Elsewhere, Dawson has outlined in depth the shortcomings of CENTCOM in orienting a 'strategic' view across its AOR, comprising a "whole of government" approach in which "non-military elements of national power" are sufficiently resourced (Dawson 2010, 20, 22). For Dawson, the Long War briefs were, in military parlance, concerned with moving from 'operational' to 'strategic'.

10. The subsequent emergence of feminist geopolitics has crucially added to the scope and incisiveness of geographical perspectives on geopolitics by focusing particularly on its human geographies—its materiality, corporeality, and lived experience (Dowler and Sharp 2001; Hyndman 2007; for overviews of the evolving canon of work in critical geopolitics, see Dalby 2010, Dodds 2010, and Kuus 2010).

11. A rich tradition of historical and cultural geography has also addressed the complex and overlapping political, economic, and cultural dimensions of historical imperial networks (cf. Lester 2000; Blunt and McEwan 2002; Clayton 2004; Morrissey et al. 2014).

12. Rationales of border 'protecting' continue to underpin practices of security. Boundary 'making', indeed, remains as important as ever (Coleman 2003).

13. In outlining what he called "the law-space nexus," Nicholas Blomley (1989, 512–513) argued that "[g]eographically informed analyses" are "essential" in considering how the "enactment of law has a vital role in the structuring of social relations and their expression and mediation in space."

14. A group even "more dangerous than ISIS" is always potentially citable too, as the CBS news network showed in airing the "fake terror threat" quickly mobilized by the Obama administration to justify air strikes on Syria in September 2014—a familiar scripting of 'necessary intervention' in which "the corporate media went along" (Goodman and Hussain 2014; Greenwald and Hussain 2014).

15. As Derek Gregory (2015c) dolefully observes in his reading of the UK's political reaction to the second Paris attacks in 2015, "hawks on both right and left" have "learned nothing from the 100-odd years of the history of bombing, or even from its more recent effects."

CHAPTER 2. CENTCOM Activates

1. Although not facilitating U.S. military bases, Israel was and remains a strong regional military ally. Komer's statement speaks to the U.S.-Israeli relationship being so exceptional that it is often forgotten (see Gold 1988).

2. POMCUS was an "integral part of the NATO war plan" for countering the Soviet presence in Eastern Europe and was tested annually during the Return of Forces to Germany exercises that began in 1968 and formally ended in 1990; see U.S. Congressional Budget Office 1983, 37.

3. A wide range of pre-positioning programs across the globe continues to enable U.S. military capacity today.

4. As Ben Anderson (2012) and others have outlined, since the war on terror began, organizing for 'rapid response' occurs across "all domains of life at a time when disparate events and conditions are grouped under the category of emergency" (cf. Mythen and Walklate 2006; Gregory 2012). Transcending the now familiar critique inspired by Giorgio Agamben of how modern governments commonly respond to crises by declaring 'states of exceptions' and invoking emergency powers, Anderson (2012) reasons that 'rapid response' does not simply involve the "temporary 'suspension' of normal rights" but also the proactive initiation of "flexible, intersecting, protocols that govern how things should be done in response."

5. Key moments in 1979 included the Iranian Revolution and removal of the U.S.-backed Shah; escalating discord with the other U.S. 'pillar' in the region, Saudi Arabia, over ongoing crises in the Horn of Africa; the Tehran hostage crisis; and the Soviet invasion of Afghanistan.

6. At activation, the RDJTF Headquarters at MacDill AFB had a staff of approximately 250 (Rapid Deployment Joint Task Force 1981, I-3). This was increased to 336 in 1981 and 843 by 1982 (Rapid Deployment Joint Task Force 1982, II-2; Rapid Deployment Joint Task Force 1984, 25). In its own words, these staff over the "1036 days of the RDJTF's existence" were focused on interventionary planning for "the region of the world then considered most likely to require rapid deployment of American forces" (Rapid Deployment Joint Task Force 1984, 1). Former CENTCOM command historian Jay Hines (2000, 43) notes that the RDJTF's activation culminated U.S. efforts to "solve the vexing geostrategic problems of the previous three decades." As documented in the final command history of the RDJTF, two geostrategic problems immediately preceding its establishment "deeply affected the thinking of President Jimmy Carter": the Shah in Iran being "replaced by the fanatical theocrat Ayatollah Khomeni" and Afghanistan being "invaded and conquered by Soviet forces" (Rapid Deployment Joint Task Force 1984, 2–3). As the command history records,

"with the Shah gone, Iran was no longer a stabilizing force," and so the United States was compelled to "shore up its other allies in the region" by operationalizing the RDF concept (Rapid Deployment Joint Task Force 1984, 3).

7. For the RDJTF, Southwest Asia was defined thus: "all states on the Arabian Peninsula south of the northern borders of Saudi Arabia and Kuwait; the countries of Iraq, Iran, Afghanistan, and Pakistan on the Middle East landmass; Ethiopia, Djibouti, Somalia, and Kenya on the Horn of Africa; and the Red Sea and the Persian Gulf and adjacent waters" (Rapid Deployment Joint Task Force 1981, III-1).

8. On the cover of the three official command histories of the RDJTF is a seal with the words "Rapid Deployment Joint Task Force" encircling a partial map of the globe showing a lightning strike emanating from the eastern and southern seaboards of the United States and piercing the Persian Gulf (Rapid Deployment Joint Task Force 1981, 1982, 1984). For the first three command histories of CENTCOM (those declassified), the cover seal features the words "United States Central Command" encircling a similar map with a spotlight shining from Florida and centering on the Persian Gulf (U.S. Central Command 1985, 1986a, 1987).

9. Over the course of it first year, the RDJTF carried out rapid deployment 'field training exercises', 'communications exercises', and 'readiness operations', conducted mainly at MacDill AFB and elsewhere in the United States, including Fort Bragg in North Carolina. The command participated in its maiden overseas joint training exercise in the Middle East, Bright Star, in Egypt in November 1980. Fourteen hundred RDJTF troops, comprising both ground and air units, took part in a three-week readiness exercise held at Cairo West Air Base in conjunction with Egyptian forces (Rapid Deployment Joint Task Force 1981, V-26, V-67–V68). The second Bright Star a year later comprised a larger joint training exercise, again in Egypt but also including forces from Oman, Somalia, and Sudan (Rapid Deployment Joint Task Force 1982, II-6, II-36). The RDJTF also participated in the joint training exercise Accurate Test in Oman in February 1981 (Rapid Deployment Joint Task Force 1982, II-26, II-37). In 1982, RDJTF forces participated in the readiness war game and joint training exercise Jade Tiger, which took place in Oman, Somalia, Sudan, and the Red Sea and Gulf of Aden in November and December 1982 (Rapid Deployment Joint Task Force 1984, 115). And the RDJTF also oversaw a successful "Military Construction (MILCON) program for Southwest Asia," entailing facilities and logistics projects in Oman, Kenya, Somalia, and Diego Garcia (Rapid Deployment Joint Task Force 1984, 81).

10. CENTCOM Headquarters was also set up at MacDill AFB, with an initial staff of 843, growing to 893 by the end of its first year (U.S. Central Command 1985, 35, 45). This staffing level remained relatively consistent over its first three years (U.S. Central Command 1986a, 59–60; U.S. Central Command 1987, 4, 6).

11. The original nineteen countries in CENTCOM's AOR were Afghanistan, Bahrain, Djibouti, Egypt, Ethiopia, Iran, Iraq, Jordan, Kenya, Kuwait, Oman, Pakistan, Qatar, Saudi Arabia, Somalia, Sudan, United Arab Emirates, South Yemen, and North Yemen (U.S. Central Command 1985, 7–8). After Yemen's unification in 1990 and Eritrea's independence from Ethiopia in 1991, CENTCOM's AOR remained at nineteen countries until the Seychelles was added in 1996. The five Central Asian states of Kazakhstan, the Kyrgyz Republic, Tajikistan, Turkmenistan, and Uzbekistan were added in 1999 to bring the AOR to twenty-five countries, while in 2004 the addition of Lebanon and Syria brought that

number to twenty-seven. On October 1, 2008, seven former CENTCOM countries officially became part of a new U.S. Africa Command: Djibouti, Eritrea, Ethiopia, Kenya, Seychelles, Somalia, and Sudan. As a result, CENTCOM's AOR reduced to twenty nations in the Middle East and Central Asia, its current AOR, seen in figure 1.2.

12. In terms of war strategies, planning for war with the Soviet Union was a very real concern for CENTCOM in its early years. As the first command history notes, wartime strategies considered by CENTCOM "derived from two basic scenarios": the first "envisioned a local conflict without Soviet involvement, ranging from a low-intensity insurgency to a mid-intensity confrontation"; the second "assumed a medium-to-high-intensity direct confrontation with the Soviet Union" (U.S. Central Command 1985, 13).

13. Bright Star 1983 was a massive logistical endeavor, involving the deployment and support of approximately six thousand CENTCOM forces in Egypt, Oman, Somalia, and Sudan in August and September of that year. Costing hundreds of millions of dollars, the deployment comprised regular and Special Operations forces from across the full spectrum of the U.S. military, including air, ground, and naval units, and required the transportation of some thirty thousand metric tons of support cargo (U.S. Central Command 1985, 82–98). Other CENTCOM deployments in its AOR during its first three years included Exercise Black Rock in Kenya in 1983 (U.S. Central Command 1985, 98–99); Exercise Accurate Test, Exercise Iron Cobra, Exercise Shadow Hawk, and Operation Intense Look in Oman, Egypt, Jordan, the Gulf of Suez, and the Red Sea in 1984 (U.S. Central Command 1986a, 73, 106, 318); and Exercise Bright Star, Exercise Eagle Claw, Exercise Natural River, and Exercise Shadow Hawk in Egypt, Jordan, Oman, Somalia, Sudan, and Kenya in 1985 (U.S. Central Command 1987, 15–16). In addition to building up military contacts and interoperability with host nation forces, all these exercises and operations honed CENTCOM's capacity to fulfill its core mission: "to respond quickly and effectively to crises within its Area of Responsibility" (U.S. Central Command, 1986a, 1).

14. A key early military construction project for CENTCOM was developing landing and logistical facilities at Ras Banas Air Base in Egypt. After protracted negotiations with the Egyptian government and testimony heard in Washington from CENTCOM CINC Lieutenant General Robert Kingston, the Military Construction Subcommittee of the U.S. House Appropriations Committee endorsed the commitment of $49 million to the project (U.S. Central Command 1985, 109–110). Other important CENTCOM construction and engineering projects in its initial years included those at Mombasa Harbor in Kenya; Khasab Air Base, Masirah Air Base, Seeb Air Base, and Thumrait Air Base in Oman; and Berbera Airfield and Harbor, and Mogadishu Airport in Somalia (U.S. Central Command 1986a, 211–213; U.S. Central Command 1987, 57–59). Ammunition, petroleum, and water pre-positioning projects were extended too during CENTCOM's early years, as were various security assistance and communications projects in Bahrain, Djibouti, Egypt, Kenya, Kuwait, Pakistan, Saudi Arabia, Somalia, Sudan, and the United Arab Emirates (U.S. Central Command 1987, 63–67, 105–106).

15. These initiatives are detailed in CENTCOM's first command history (U.S. Central Command 1985, 86–87, 106, 109, 111, 113, 117, 119–121, 124–125, 162, 219).

16. At its outset, CENTCOM had 222,000 troops to call upon, a number that increased to 400,000 by 1986 (U.S. Congressional Budget Office 1983, xiii; U.S. Central Command 1986b).

17. See, for example, Ian Lesser's 1991 study, *Oil, the Persian Gulf, and Grand Strategy: Contemporary Issues in Historical Perspective*, which was part of a larger RAND project, sponsored by CENTCOM and the Joint Chiefs of Staff, calling for a U.S. grand strategy on the Middle East that was primarily focused on oil security. These kinds of calls were echoing appeals repeatedly made in the 1980s for a forward U.S. military regional presence in defense of vital U.S. interests (Record 1981b; cf. McNaugher 1985; J. M. Epstein 1987).

18. CENTCOM's current Area of Responsibility, similar to the Area of Concentration argued for in the report, no longer includes the Horn of Africa countries (see note 11 above) where military interventions would, according to the authors, only become "bogged down" in "non-essential operations" (Pelletiere and Johnson 1992, 26).

19. The official command histories reveal how conscious CENTCOM and its predecessor, the RDJTF, were of a "moribund" British Empire leaving a geostrategic vacuum in the Middle East, post–World War II, which the United States needed to occupy (Rapid Deployment Joint Task Force 1984, 2). As noted in the RDJTF's final command history, "traditionally western interests in the Middle East had been looked after by forces of the British Empire," but with the "independence of India from the British Raj in 1948 and the removal of British forces from east of Suez in the late 1960s, U.S. involvement in the area gradually began to increase" (Rapid Deployment Joint Task Force 1984, 2).

20. Charles Ferguson's (2007) film *No End in Sight* illuminates the CPA's ineptitude in various governmental capacities. The film fails, however, to critique its neoliberal agenda that was not so badly served.

CHAPTER 3. Envisioning the Middle East

1. GCC partners have long been the prime military cooperation targets: Eagle Resolve, for example, is one of more than a dozen exercises CENTCOM participates in with its GCC allies as part of its Cooperative Defense Program. Designed specifically to "increase communication and interoperability in the area of regional consequence management," CENTCOM calls Eagle Resolve its "premier multi-warfare exercise within the Arabian Peninsula" (U.S. Central Command 2011, 2013a). Kuwait hosted Eagle Resolve 2015, the thirteenth instance since the exercise started in 2000 in Bahrain (Kuwait News Agency 2014).

2. Dawson elaborates on CENTCOM's support of pragmatic, geopolitical cooperation: "A big factor has been the increasing belligerence of Iran—this has led the Arab countries in the Gulf to decide that their shared concern over Iran outweighs their differences. It is notable that the recent split in the GCC, in which Ambassadors from Saudi Arabia, UAE and Qatar were recalled, was about different approaches to the opposition in Syria; which is fundamentally about balancing the threat from Iran and its proxies against the threat from the Muslim Brotherhood and Sunni terrorist groups like al-Qaeda" (Dawson 2014).

3. Israel was also keen to stay under the protectorate of U.S. European Command (EUCOM) when CENTCOM was first established in 1983. Israel and the Occupied Territories remain in EUCOM today.

4. Derek Reveron and Michelle Gavin (2004) have documented how unified commanders have acted in various capacities as "America's Viceroys" overseas; and the U.S. military has considered the "lessons for the Pax Americana" offered by comparisons between U.S. CINCs and the Roman Republic's Proconsuls (Bradford 2001).

5. From 1983, unpublished 'Country Books' for all countries in CENTCOM's AOR were

produced, periodically updated, and disseminated to the CENTCOM Command Group—to "provide a single-source document" for "data on the countries" and an "overview of the history, people, military, and various geopolitical aspects" (U.S. Central Command 1985, 143–144). As discussed in the opening chapter, such reductive geographical abstractions have all the hallmarks of area studies, which presumes that regions generally have an 'essence', culturally, economically, and so on (Gibson-Graham 2004; Szanton 2004). It is this reductionism that enables the U.S. military to simplistically map the world into AORs.

6. Events such as the October 2000 al-Qaeda bombing of USS *Cole* in Aden, Yemen, in which seventeen U.S. sailors were killed, undoubtedly served to reinforce perceptions of volatility and threat.

7. There are nine unified commands in total in the U.S. military: six with geographic responsibilities (U.S. Africa Command, U.S. Central Command, U.S. European Command, U.S. Northern Command, U.S. Pacific Command, and U.S. Southern Command), and three with functional responsibilities (U.S. Special Operations Command, U.S. Strategic Command, and U.S. Transportation Command).

CHAPTER 4. Posturing for Global Security

1. For a succinct genealogy of the emergence and use of the term 'lawfare', see C. Jones 2016, which does an excellent job of tracing its selective employment by the U.S., Israeli, and other militaries from the early years of the twenty-first century.

2. This prioritization echoes elements of the broader U.S. military's 'leave no man behind' principle, and it mirrors too what former CENTCOM commander Tommy Franks conceded at the beginning of war on terror about the lives of non-U.S. personnel: "we don't do body counts" (E. Epstein 2002).

3. Naomi Klein (2007) has similarly laid bare the powerful event-based logic of 'disaster capitalism', while others have pointed out how a 'logic of premediation', in which possible future events are already "mediated," is a marked feature of the "post-9/11 cultural landscape" (Grusin 2004, 19; de Goede 2008, 158). It was Foucault who first underlined the import of the 'event' in the biopolitical focus of governmentality. He cites the "anti-scarcity system" of seventeenth-century Europe as an early exemplar of a new 'evental' biopolitics in which "an event that could take place" is prevented before it "becomes a reality" (Foucault 2007, 33; cf. Butler 1997).

4. Established in Washington in 1983 in the same year that CENTCOM was initiated, the Center for Strategic and Budgetary Assessments offers annual analyses of DoD policy and budgeting, frequently focusing on U.S. foreign policy in the Middle East. In February 2016, it hosted its thirty-third annual prebudget press briefing on the DoD's fiscal year budget request (Center for Strategic and Budgetary Assessments 2016). It has developed an especially influential position as a knowledge producer and conduit between strategic studies and senior decision makers in the executive and legislative branches of the U.S. national security establishment (Morrissey 2011a).

5. At this point, CENTCOM also operated 'Security Assistance Offices' in twenty-two countries in its AOR (U.S. Central Command 2007b).

6. Krepinevich and Work (2007, 134) note the three generic types of SOFAs the U.S. JAG Corps developed as standard: "those that offered U.S. personnel administrative and technical staff status under the Vienna Convention on Diplomatic Privileges, commonly

referred to as an A&T SOFA; a 'mini' status-of-forces agreement, often used for short-term visits of U.S. forces, like those in-country to participate in a combined exercise; and a full-blown, permanent status-of-forces agreement for countries where there was a permanent U.S. military presence."

7. Strategizing for enhanced rapid deployability also required planning for the use of private military contractors; on this, see the excellent work of Snukal and Gilbert (2015).

8. Feith signaled too the financial trade-off for participating countries: "we are putting in place so-called cross-servicing agreements so that we can rapidly reimburse countries for support they provide to our military operations" (U.S. Department of Defense 2003b).

9. CENTCOM was interested in RMA theory from an early stage, and especially so in the aftermath of its much-heralded technological success in the Gulf War. The dream of the technological fix is palpably present in its 1992 commissioned report, *Oil and the New World System: CENTCOM Rethinks Its Mission*, for instance: "the solution to a lot of our problems may lie with such technologies as advanced target acquisition, seeker head, and other fire-and-forget weapons" (Pelletiere and Johnson 1992, 22).

10. Since before World War II, 'CINC' was used as the shortened version of 'Commander in Chief' when referring to commanders of unified commands. However, in 2002, Secretary of Defense Donald Rumsfeld cited Article II, Section 2 of the U.S. Constitution, which states that the "President shall be Commander in Chief of the Army and Navy of the United States," to officially replace the 'CINC' title for commanders of unified commands with 'Commander'. 'CINC' is used throughout the book when referring to commanders serving prior to this formal adjustment.

11. CDHQ culminated efforts that were prominent at CENTCOM from the very beginning to facilitate rapid deployment to its Area of Responsibility. In the command's very first deployment to the Middle East, in February 1983, in an operation titled Early Call, CENTCOM intelligence officers tested a "deployed headquarters" in an "isolated field environment" (in Egypt) in terms of the "integration of real-time, all-source intelligence into an extremely dynamic situation"—the test ultimately being about showing capacity to "provide the required support to the deployed commander" and demonstrating "speed and flexibility to react effectively in support of national foreign policy objectives" (U.S. Central Command 1985, 58–59; see also U.S. Central Command 1986a, 204, 221, and U.S. Central Command 1987, 43, 65). These concerns reflected the extent to which the "distance between HQ CENTCOM and its Area of Responsibility presented serious command and control difficulties," particularly during "travel to and from the AOR" by CENTCOM CINCs (U.S. Central Command 1985, 75). This was addressed through the course of the command's first year when the Joint Chiefs of Staff "validated the requirement for a C3 aircraft" with a modified "airframe ready" platform, complete with tailored "electronic and communications systems," to be "permanently assigned to USCENTCOM" (U.S. Central Command 1985, 75).

12. Lawfare overlaps into the political realm of modern war too, of course. It is especially evident in carefully worded pronouncements that take "political responsibility" for military actions but seek to evade "legal culpability" for the consequences. Former UK prime minister Tony Blair, for example, responded to the core finding of the Chilcot Inquiry into the Iraq War—that "the judgements about the severity of the threat posed by Iraq's weapons of mass destruction were presented with a certainty that was not justified"

and that "policy on Iraq was made on the basis of flawed intelligence and assessments" (The Iraq Inquiry 2016, 2, 6)—by accepting "full responsibility" for the fact that the intelligence "turned out to be wrong," yet demarcating a clear position that in the lead-up to the war "there were no lies, Parliament and Cabinet were not misled, there was no secret commitment to war, intelligence was not falsified and the decision was made in good faith" (BBC News 2016).

13. See, for example, the extensive legal support for the command documented in the 'Legal Advisor' and 'Judge Advocate' sections of the command's declassified official histories (U.S. Central Command 1985, 209–211; U.S. Central Command 1986a, 343–345; U.S. Central Command 1987, 135). As sketched in the first command history for 1983, CENTCOM's Legal Advisor division was responsible for developing "exercise and real-world plans in support of all operations, negotiating fly-over rights, staging rights, basing rights, status of forces agreements, and procurement of local goods and labor, while taking into account host country laws and procedures" (U.S. Central Command 1985, 23). CENTCOM JAGS were ultimately "prepared to deploy in support of every contingency wherein legal support was required" (U.S. Central Command 1987, 135).

14. I have made a similar point in relation to the use of the law in the emergent forms of colonial governmentality that coalesced in early modern Ireland (Morrissey 2003).

15. Airman Hatfield was returned to CONUS (Continental United States), a strategy adapted by CENTCOM JAGS from the beginning to protect command personnel from local prosecution in its Area of Responsibility. As detailed in the first command history, for instance, in the case of a pending criminal prosecution in Jordan "arising out of the injury and subsequent death of a local male youth who was struck by an automobile driven by an American soldier," CENTCOM sent a delegation to investigate the "foreign criminal jurisdiction aspects" of the case, with the result that "the soldier was returned to CONUS without being subjected to the criminal justice system of Jordan" (U.S. Central Command 1985, 209–210).

16. A year earlier, the 2007 conference, New Battlefields, Old Laws, held in Washington and jointly organized by the Institute for National Security and Counterterrorism at Syracuse University and the Institute for Counter Terrorism in Herzliya, Israel, addressed the same question. The central conference concern was that "[r]ecent conflicts underscore the continuing shortcomings of international law and policy in responding to asymmetric warfare mounted by non-state terrorist groups" (http://insct.syr.edu/Battlefields/overview.htm, last accessed 10 July 2008). See also the special feature on lawfare in *Joint Force Quarterly* in 2009, in which former U.S. deputy judge advocate general Charles Dunlap (2009, 35) offers a "refined definition" of lawfare that acknowledges it more broadly as a strategy that uses the law "to achieve an operational objective." Efforts to strategically mobilize the use of the law continues. In 2015, for example, the Israel Law Center in Tel Aviv established an annual conference titled Towards a New Law of War. The conference, which features mostly Israeli and U.S. participants, aims "to bring together lead academics, policy makers, and military leaders to exchange ideas regarding the development of armed conflict legal doctrine favorable to Western democracies" (http://israellawcenter.org/activities/law-of-war-conference-towards-a-new-law-of-war, last accessed 31 May 2016).

17. The U.S. Army's most recent legal directive on 'stability operations', for example,

underscores how they "may be performed across the spectrum of conflict" (U.S. Department of the Army 2013, 9-1).

CHAPTER 5. Military-Economic Securitization

1. The housing of a Coalition Village adjacent to its command headquarters is important for CENTCOM in terms of communicating universalist ideas of liberal interventionism and global security. Even the name 'Coalition Village' is significant semantically. It glosses over massive differences between coalition partners regarding the conduct of war and instead implies a united 'village community'. That said, however, CENTCOM has long been active in seeking to develop coalition partnerships, both internally within its AOR and externally via Western allied cooperation. From Exercise Bright Star in the 1980s to Exercise Eagle Lion, Exercise Inherent Resolve, and Exercise Regional Cooperation in more recent years, a range of coalition initiatives have been undertaken inside CENTCOM's AOR (U.S. Central Command 1985; U.S. Central Command 1987; U.S. Central Command 2014b; U.S. Central Command 2015b; U.S. Central Command 2015c). Externally too, the command has been keen from the beginning to foster Western coalition support. In its first year of existence, for instance, the command established "country strategies" for obtaining "allied cooperation" and "allied burden sharing" to offset security shortfalls within its AOR — the old allies, Britain and France, were the original targets (U.S. Central Command 1985, 143).

2. The authors presciently predict CENTCOM's focused deterrence strategy throughout the 1990s, and their warning that "no large scale military action should be considered, unless there is a clear and compelling threat to the system" is something that CENTCOM planners and advisors are no doubt reflecting on anew in the aftermath of the large-scale interventions in Iraq and Afghanistan (Pelletiere and Johnson 1992, 26).

3. Anticipating a wide spectrum of instability and strategizing for military deterrence preoccupied CENTCOM strategists from the beginning, as documented in the first command history: "[n]ormal operations for USCENTCOM include planning for and executing operations in contingencies, limited war, and general war" (U.S. Central Command 1985, 15).

4. Jamey Essex (2013, 110) urges us "not to see geopolitics and geoeconomics as either cleanly separated from one another in a neat strategic and discursive bifurcation or the same." In deconstructing the institution of USAID, Essex (2013, 110) observes how both overlap with "varying degrees of connections" to "specific interests" and how these interests in turn are "intertwined with but distinct from those state apparatuses charged with policing, deploying and articulating" visions and practices of intervention.

5. Such an abstracted mapping denies the impact of prior interventions and negates how ongoing interventions frequently create the conditions for extending and prolonging conflict.

6. Recent theorizations of geoeconomics overlap to some degree with previous work on world-systems analysis, whose documenting of the global economy's unequal asymmetries, maintained and extended by exploitative flows between 'core' and 'periphery', has been helpful in critically reading political economy (Wallerstein 1979; Flint 2010). In CENTCOM's project of geoeconomic deterrence, however, notions of core and periphery do not capture the imprecise endgame of CENTCOM's security mission in a globalized world of corporate capitalism and transnational capitalist accumulation.

7. Matt Sparke (2014) has noted the difficulty of showing how "the ideational and the material are consequentially interarticulated with one another" in the realm of geoeconomics. This has long been a challenge in teasing out how geopolitical calculations are realized in operational grand strategy too.

8. The US-GCC Corporate Cooperation Committee was founded in 1986 with a goal to "promote US-GCC trade, investment, and commercial partnerships, and to raise American awareness of the innumerable benefits to the United States from increased relations with the GCC" (US-GCC Corporate Cooperation Committee 1994). Global companies making up the committee from its inception included AT&T, Exxon, Ford, General Dynamics, Lockheed, Mobil, Oracle, Parsons Corporation, Philip Morris, and Raytheon.

9. See also the follow-up Kauffman Foundation publication "Building Expeditionary Economics: Understanding the Field and Setting Forth an Agenda" (Patterson and Stangler 2010).

10. See the Historical Office of the DoD's Office of the Secretary of Defense for the seven national security strategy documents of the Clinton administration, all of which are remarkably consistent: http://history.defense.gov/HistoricalSources/NationalSecurity Strategy.aspx (last accessed 31 May 2016).

11. As Michael Schwartz (2008, 18) notes, "Bill Clinton's ascension to the White House after twelve years of Republican rule did not alter the trajectory of American policy in the Middle East or relax the Carter Doctrine."

12. Macgregor holds a PhD in international relations from the University of Virginia, and his writings, including four books, have, according to Burke-Macgregor, "profoundly influenced" the "transformation inside America's ground forces, NATO, the Israeli Defense Force and the Chinese People's Liberation Army" (Burke-Macgregor Group 2016c).

CHAPTER 6. No Endgame

1. The mission statement of the Multi-National Security Transition Command in Iraq also extolled the "free market economy" as the critical mechanism in attaining Iraq's "external security and the security of the Gulf Region" (Multi-National Security Transition Command—Iraq 2009).

2. Concerns of access and freedom of navigation led U.S. secretary of defense William Perry to alter the U.S. military's Unified Command Plan in the mid-1990s to assign security responsibility for the Arabian Sea and much of the Indian Ocean to CENTCOM (U.S. Department of Defense 1996).

3. As Kenneth Katzman details, an integral aspect of this economic integration and globalization strategy was a policy of securing free trade agreements, which the United States signed with Bahrain in 2004 and Oman in 2005, for instance. Both served to secure key markets for Exxon Mobil, Royal Dutch Shell, and Totalfina Elf (Katzman 2006, 28–29).

4. The veil of universalism in pronouncements of U.S. grand strategy frequently drops to reveal narrower U.S.-centric concerns. For instance, the new CENTCOM commander, General Joseph Votel, in taking up the leadership of the U.S. military in the Middle East and Central Asia, declared CENTCOM to be "the guarantors of American interests in this vital and deeply challenging part of the world" (U.S. Central Command 2016c).

5. The broader U.S. military and national security establishment have long been active too in strategically anticipating the future: see, for example, the U.S. Army's planning for

"strategic advantage in a complex world" in 2025 (U.S. Department of the Army 2015a) or the U.S. National Intelligence Council's mapping of the "global future" in 2020 or "transformed world" in 2025 (National Intelligence Council 2004, 2008).

6. Gilbert has helpfully outlined the U.S. military's use of money as a "weapons system" in the war on terror, highlighting initiatives such as Operation Adam Smith, a multimillion-dollar operation to regenerate Baghdad's commercial districts in the early stages of the U.S. occupation in Iraq. Her critique is concerned with the U.S. military's aspiration to refashion "economies and populations" in ways that "support liberalization, deregulation, privatization, and entrepreneurialism" (Gilbert 2015, 203)—a grand strategy that echoes earlier iterations of U.S. liberal imperial ambition and mirrors the essence of CENTCOM's military-economic mission solidified in the aftermath of the Gulf War. Gilbert's analysis echoes Roger Mac Ginty's trenchant critique of the type of stability operations the U.S. military is pursuing. As Mac Ginty (2012, 20, 28) argues, the U.S. military's conception of stabilization is centrally based on "ideas of control" and the aspiration to "create compliant, market-friendly any-states that do not threaten the international order."

7. In recent years, the idea of civilian contributions to U.S. military interventions has taken concrete form in DoD initiatives such as the Civilian Expeditionary Workforce (CEW) program (now run by the International/Expeditionary Policy Office at the DoD). As CEW program manager Tom Kelly explains, the U.S. military have "more requirements than military members can fill, and we have some requirements for skill sets that the military doesn't have, so civilian support is critical to mission accomplishment"; for Kelly, it is also an opportunity to "stand shoulder to shoulder with uniformed members in a fight that transcends personal comfort or safety," to "learn more about national defense from the rubber-meets-the-road perspective," and ultimately to "give back to your country" (U.S. Central Command 2015d). Advertisements of a range of civilian support posts throughout CENTCOM's AOR are regularly updated on the command's CEW program website: https://cew.centcom.mil/Landing/Default.aspx (last accessed 4 May 2016). In the DoD's overall CEW program, approximately "400 civilians a year join their military teammates in Afghanistan, Iraq and other locations around the world," of which "roughly 62 percent are serving one-year deployments in support of U.S. Central Command CEW requirements" (U.S. Central Command 2015d).

8. Much of the language here echoes the conflated aid-security discourse of another arm of economic development in war and postwar environments, USAID, which Lisa Bhungalia (2015) has detailed for Palestine and Wes Attewell (2016) for Afghanistan (for a wider critique of USAID, see Essex 2013).

9. Paul Bremer's macroeconomic focus as head of the Coalition Provisional Authority in Iraq in 2004 left little room for locally attuned, politically and socially designed 'stability operations'. Gregory Hooker, the then senior intelligence analyst for Iraq at CENTCOM, has documented the failings of preparations for any postconflict development: "the interagency planning process for the post-hostilities environment for Iraq was weak[; . . .] 'ownership' of the post-hostilities phase fell to civilian agencies, which were not well coordinated [and] had no empowered leadership" (Hooker 2005, xii). This level of postinvasion unpreparedness was matched by the British interventionary effort in Iraq, as detailed in the UK Government's Chilcot Report. It concluded that "despite explicit warnings, the

consequences of the invasion were underestimated" and that "the planning and preparations for Iraq after Saddam Hussein were wholly inadequate" (The Iraq Inquiry 2016, 2).

10. Themes of empire have been variously invoked by a wide range of authors in explaining the U.S.-led war in Iraq and the broader war on terror (Harvey 2003; Foster and McChesney 2004; N. Smith 2005; N. Klein 2007). For John Bellamy Foster (2004, 166), nothing reveals contemporary American imperialism more than U.S. presence in "the critical regions of the Middle East and Caspian Sea basin." For Brian Loveman (2004, xxiv), a U.S. foreign policy of "'forward presence', 'full spectrum threat dominance', 'preemptive deterrence' and covert operations around the globe" equates to that of "a rogue superpower" managing a "global empire through regional military proconsuls." Others have considered the aspects of a 'frustrated', 'incoherent', and 'indifferent' American empire, which, as Michael Mann (2003, 13) remarks, "means well" and "intends to spread order and benevolence" but instead "creates more disorder and violence" (cf. Johnson 2000; Martin 2007; Ryan 2007; Dodge 2009). And vital contributions have emphasized too the enduring abstracted and affective cultural logics of imperialism rehabilitated in subtle ways in contemporary discourses of Western interventionism (Little 2002; Said 2003; Gregory 2004).

11. Copulos used several examples to illustrate: in the Gulf War the approximately 582,000 U.S. troops deployed "used more than twice as much oil on a daily basis as the entire 2-million man Allied Expeditionary Force that liberated Europe in World War II"; in Operation Iraqi Freedom the oil requirement was "20 percent higher"; while for future interventions "the military's oil requirements will be even higher" (Copulos 2006).

12. The U.S. Army's recent publication of its new "Energy Security and Sustainability (ES²) Strategy" sets out how it intends to accomplish future missions "in a world defined by uncertain, adverse, and dynamic conditions" by the "wise use" of "energy, water, and land resources" and "through superior knowledge, technologies, and execution" (U.S. Department of the Army 2015b, i, 13). Despite efforts to signal how green concepts such as 'sustainability', 'adaptability', and 'resilience' will be embraced in mission operations, there is a decidedly old-fashioned take on the human mastering of nature by technology (U.S. Department of the Army 2015b, 3). Environmental discourses are distilled and deployed in a strategy that ultimately centers on managing and controlling resource scarcity. As Nafeez Ahmed (2015) notes, the so-called energy security and sustainability strategy is actually about "maintaining U.S. military dominance despite resource scarcity, while safeguarding the wider fossil fuel system—not changing it" (cf. T. C. Jones 2015; Moore 2015).

13. The former head of the Pentagon's Defense Intelligence Agency, retired U.S. Army lieutenant general Michael Flynn, has acknowledged that "going into Iraq" was "a strategic mistake" (Al Jazeera 2015)—a conclusion echoing a long-held concern of CENTCOM advisors to avoid large-scale military operations with unclear strategic value (Pelletier and Johnson 1992).

REFERENCES

Acharya, Amitav. 1986. "U.S. Strategy in the Persian Gulf: The Rapid Deployment Force as an Instrument of Policy." PhD thesis, Murdoch University, Perth, Australia.

Ackerman, Spencer. 2012. "How the Pentagon's Top Killers Became (Unaccountable) Spies." *Wired*, 13 February, https://www.wired.com/2012/02/jsoc-ambinder (last accessed 29 April 2016).

Africa Center for Strategic Studies. 2008. "About the Africa Center for Strategic Studies." http://www.africacenter.org/iDuneDownload.dll?GetFile?AppId=100&FileID= 433519&Anchor=&ext=.pdf (last accessed 8 February 2008).

Agamben, Giorgio. 1998. *Homo Sacer: Sovereign Power and Bare Life*, translated by Daniel Heller-Roazen. Stanford: Stanford University Press.

Agamben, Giorgio. 2005. *State of Exception*, translated by Kevin Attell. Chicago: University of Chicago Press.

Agnew, John, and Stuart Corbridge. 1995. *Mastering Space: Hegemony, Territory, and International Political Economy*. New York: Routledge.

Ahmed, Nafeez. 2015. "Pentagon Prepares for Century of Climate Emergencies and Oil Wars." *Middle East Eye*, 6 August, http://www.middleeasteye.net/columns/pentagon -prepares-century-climate-emergencies-and-oil-wars-2021134422 (last accessed 12 August 2015).

Al Jazeera. 2015. "Retired U.S. General: Drones Cause More Damage Than Good." *Al Jazeera*, 16 July, http://www.aljazeera.com/news/2015/07/retired-general-drones -damage-good-150716105352708.html (last accessed 28 April 2016).

Amoore, Louise. 2009. "Algorithmic War: Everyday Geographies of the War on Terror." *Antipode* 41 (1): 49–69.

Anderson, Ben. 2010. "Security and the Future: Anticipating the Event of Terror." *Geoforum* 41 (2): 227–235.

Anderson, Ben. 2012. "Rapid Response." *Berfrois*, 17 August, http://www.berfrois.com /2012/08/ben-anderson-emergency-quick (last accessed 1 December 2014).

Aradau, Claudia, and Rens van Munster. 2007. "Governing Terrorism through Risk: Taking Precautions, (Un)knowing the Future." *European Journal of International Relations* 13 (1): 89–115.

Attewell, Wesley Llewellyn. 2016. "'We're Not Counterinsurgents': Development and Security in Afghanistan, 1946–2014." PhD thesis, University of British Columbia, Vancouver, Canada.

Bacevich, Andrew J. 2005. *The New American Militarism: How Americans Are Seduced by War*. New York: Oxford University Press.

Bacevich, Andrew J., ed. 2007. *The Long War: A New History of U.S. National Security Policy Since World War II*. New York: Columbia University Press.

Bacevich, Andrew J. 2008. *The Limits of Power: The End of American Exceptionalism*. New York: Metropolitan Books.

Bacevich, Andrew J. 2016. *America's War for the Greater Middle East: A Military History*. New York. Random House.

Bachman, Jan. 2010. "'Kick Down the Door, Clean Up the Mess, and Rebuild the House': The Africa Command and Transformation of the U.S. Military." *Geopolitics* 15 (3): 564–585.

Bâli, Asli, and Aziz Rana. 2010. "American Overreach: Strategic Interests and Millennial Ambitions in the Middle East." *Geopolitics* 15 (2): 210–238.

Barnes, Trevor J. 2008. "Geography's Underworld: The Military-Industrial Complex, Mathematical Modelling, and the Quantitative Revolution." *Geoforum* 39 (1): 3–16.

Barnett, Thomas P. M. 2004. *The Pentagon's New Map: War and Peace in the Twenty-First Century*. New York: Putnam's.

BBC News. 2016. "Chilcot Report: Tony Blair's Iraq War Case Not Justified." *BBC News*, 6 July, http://www.bbc.com/news/uk-politics-36712735 (last accessed 6 July 2016).

Beck, Ulrich. 1992. *Risk Society: Towards a New Modernity*. London: Sage.

Beck, Ulrich. 1999. *World Risk Society*. Cambridge: Polity Press.

Beckett, Samuel. 1958. *Endgame*. London: Faber and Faber.

Begley, Josh. 2015. "How Do You Measure a Military Footprint?" *Mapping United States Military Installations*, http://empire.is (last accessed 18 February 2015).

Benard, Alexander. 2012. "How to Succeed in Business: And Why Washington Should Really Try." *Foreign Affairs* 91 (4): July/August, http://www.foreignaffairs.com/articles/137684/alexander-benard/how-to-succeed-in-business (last accessed 07 March 2015).

Bender, Brian. 2014. "Raytheon's $50m Will Help Start UMass Lowell Campus in Kuwait." *Boston Globe*, 8 December, http://www.bostonglobe.com/news/nation/2014/12/08/raytheon-fund-umass-lowell-campus-kuwait/kDhReEvNtCEOfufV6yYTPO/story.html (last accessed 15 January 2015).

Benjamin, Walter. 1978 [1921]. "Critique of Violence." In *Reflections: Essays, Aphorisms, Autobiographical Writings*, edited and introduced by Peter Demetz, 277–300. New York: Harcourt Brace Jovanovich.

Benton, Laura. 2010. *A Search for Sovereignty: Law and Geography in European Empires, 1400–1900*. Cambridge: Cambridge University Press.

Bernstein, Peter L. 1996. *Against the Gods: The Remarkable Story of Risk*. New York: John Wiley and Sons.

Bhungalia, Lisa. 2015. "Managing Violence: Aid, Counterinsurgency, and the Humanitarian Present in Palestine." *Environment and Planning A* 47 (11): 2308–2323.

Blank, Stephen. 1995. *Energy, Economics, and Security in Central Asia: Russia and Its Rivals*. Carlisle, Pa.: Strategic Studies Institute, U.S. Army War College.

Blanke, Robert B. 2001. *An Aerospace Power Engagement Strategy for Iraq and the Persian Gulf States after Sanctions*. Maxwell Air Force Base, Ala.: Air Command and Staff College, Air University.

Blomley, Nicholas K. 1989. "Text and Context: Rethinking the Law-Space Nexus." *Progress in Human Geography* 13 (4): 512–534.

Blunt, Alison, and Cheryl McEwan, eds. 2002. *Postcolonial Geographies*. London: Continuum.

Boal, Iain, T. J. Clark, Joseph Matthews, and Michael Watts. 2005. *Afflicted Powers: Capital and Spectacle in a New Age of War*. London: Verso.

Bougen, Philip D. 2003. "Catastrophe Risk." *Economy and Society* 32 (2): 253–274.

Bradford, Jeffrey A. 2001. *Proconsuls and CINCs from the Roman Republic to the Republic of the United States of America: Lessons for the Pax Americana*. Fort Leavenworth, Kans.: School of Advanced Military Studies.

Braverman, Irus, Nicholas Blomley, David Delaney, and Alexandre Kedar, eds. 2014. *The Expanding Spaces of Law: A Timely Legal Geography*. Stanford: Stanford University Press.

Bridge, Gavin, and Philippe Le Billon. 2013. *Oil*. Cambridge: Polity.

Brown, Harold. 1980. *Statement before the House Foreign Affairs Committee*. Washington, D.C.: House Foreign Affairs Committee, 20 February.

Brzezinski, Zbigniew. 1983. *Power and Principle: Memoirs of the National Security Adviser, 1977–1981*. New York: Farrar, Straus, Giroux.

Burke-Macgregor Group. 2016a. "About Us." http://www.burke-macgregor.com/aboutus.html (last accessed 28 April 2016).

Burke-Macgregor Group. 2016b. "Home." http://www.burke-macgregor.com/home.html (last accessed 28 April 2016).

Burke-Macgregor Group. 2016c. "Leadership." http://www.burke-macgregor.com/leadership/executivevicepresident.html (last accessed 28 April 2016).

Bush, George W. 2006. *State of the Union Address 2006*. The American Presidency Project, http://www.presidency.ucsb.edu/ws/index.php?pid=65090 (last accessed 18 June 2014).

Butler, Judith. 1997. *The Psychic Life of Power: Theories in Subjection*. Stanford: Stanford University Press.

Buzan, Barry, and Ole Wæver. 2003. *Regions and Powers: The Structure of International Security*. Cambridge: Cambridge University Press.

Buzan, Barry, Ole Wæver, and Jaap de Wilde. 1997. *Security: A New Framework for Analysis*. Boulder, Colo.: Lynne Rienner.

Byman, Daniel L., and John R. Wise. 2002. *The Persian Gulf in the Coming Decade: Trends, Threats, and Opportunities*. Santa Monica, Calif.: RAND.

Carafano, James Jay. 2003. "The Long War against Terrorism." *The Heritage Foundation*, 8 September, http://www.heritage.org/research/commentary/2003/09/the-long-war-against-terrorism?ac=1 (last accessed 19 June 2014).

Carpenter, Ted G. 2000. "Postwar Strategy: An Alternative View." *Joint Force Quarterly* 27: 40–44.

Carpenter, Ted G. 2007. "Escaping the Trap: Why the United States Must Leave Iraq." *Cato Policy Analysis* 588, 14 February.

Carter, James M. 2008. *Inventing Vietnam: The United States and State Building, 1954–1968*. Cambridge: Cambridge University Press.

Carter, Jimmy. 1980. *State of the Union Address 1980*. The American Presidency Project, http://www.presidency.ucsb.edu/ws/index.php?pid=33079 (last accessed 18 June 2014).

Caspian News Agency. 2003. "During Next 15 Years Investments in Kazakhstan Would Exceed U.S. $80 billion." Caspian News Agency, 21 March (reproduced by Progressive Management. 2004. *Defend America: Defense Department Reports on the War on Terrorism*, DVD-ROM CENTCOM Disc 1, Content 3. Washington, D.C.: Progressive Management).

Center for American Progress. 2004. *Memorandum on the Geneva Conventions*. Center for American Progress, http://www.americanprogress.org/issues/kfiles/b79532.html (last accessed 1 July 2008).

Center for Strategic and Budgetary Assessments. 2016. "Seven Areas to Watch in the FY17 Defense Budget." *Center for Strategic and Budgetary Assessments*, 1 February, http://csbaonline.org/publications/2016/02/sba-fy17-defense-budget-preview (last accessed 11 April 2016).

Central Asia–Caucasus Institute. 2008. "Home." Central Asia–Caucasus Institute, http://www.cacianalyst.org (last accessed 4 February 2008).

Chatterjee, Pratap. 2004. *Iraq, Inc.: A Profitable Occupation*. New York: Seven Stories Press.

Chomsky, Noam. 2003. *Hegemony or Survival: America's Quest for Global Dominance*. New York: Metropolitan Books.

Cieply, Kevin M. 2008. "Rendition: The Beast and the Man." *Joint Force Quarterly* 48: 19–21.

Clayton, Dan. 2004. "Imperial Geographies." In *A Companion to Cultural Geography*, edited by James S. Duncan, Nuala C. Johnson, and Richard H. Schein, 449–468. Oxford: Blackwell.

Cockburn, Patrick. 2014. "Iraq Crisis: How Saudi Arabia Helped ISIS Take Over the North of the Country." *Independent*, 13 July, http://www.independent.co.uk/voices /comment/iraq-crisis-how-saudi-arabia-helped-isis-take-over-the-north-of-the -country-9602312.html (last accessed 26 August 2014).

Coleman, Mat. 2003. "The Naming of Terrorism and Evil Outlaws: Geopolitical Place-Making After 11 September." *Geopolitics* 8 (3): 87–104.

Comaroff, John L., and Jean Comaroff. 2006. "Law and Disorder in the Postcolony: An Introduction." In *Law and Disorder in the Postcolony*, edited by Jean Comaroff and John L. Comaroff, 1–56. Chicago: University of Chicago Press.

Cooper, Melinda. 2007. "Homeland Insecurities." *Postmodern Culture* 18 (1), http://muse .jhu.edu/article/237531 (last accessed 28 April 2016).

Copulos, Milton R. 2006. *Statement before the Senate Foreign Relations Committee*, 30 March. Washington, D.C.: Senate Foreign Relations Committee.

Cowen, Deborah, and Neil Smith. 2009. "After Geopolitics? From the Geopolitical Social to Geoeconomics." *Antipode* 41 (1): 22–48.

Cox, Samuel H., Joseph R. Fairchild, and Hal W. Pedersen. 2000. "Economic Aspects of Securitization of Risk." *ASTIN Bulletin* 30 (1): 157–193.

CREW. 2012. *Strategic Maneuvers: The Revolving Door from the Pentagon to the Private Sector.* Washington, D.C.: Citizens for Responsibility and Ethics in Washington.

Crow, Dennis. 2015. "Review of Stuart Elden's 'The Birth of Territory.'" *Theory, Culture & Society*, Website Reviews, 26 January, http://theoryculturesociety.org/review-of -stuart-eldens-the-birth-of-territory (last accessed 5 March 2015).

Cullen, Peter M. 2008. "The Role of Targeted Killing in the Campaign against Terror." *Joint Force Quarterly* 48: 22–29.

Dalby, Simon. 1991. "Critical Geopolitics: Difference, Discourse, and Dissent." *Environment and Planning D: Society and Space* 9 (3): 261–283.

Dalby, Simon. 2007. "Regions, Strategies, and Empire in the Global War on Terror." *Geopolitics* 12 (4): 586–606.

Dalby, Simon. 2009. *Security and Environmental Change.* Cambridge: Polity.

Dalby, Simon. 2010. "Recontextualising Violence, Power, and Nature: The Next Twenty Years of Critical Geopolitics?" *Political Geography* 29 (5): 280–288.

Dawson, David A. 2010. *The Evolution of U.S. Central Command from Operational to Strategic Headquarters.* Carlisle, Pa.: U.S. Army War College.

Dawson, David A. 2014. "Interview Conducted at CENTCOM Headquarters, 11 April 2014." Tampa, Fla.: MacDill Air Force Base.

Dean, Mitchell. 1999. *Governmentality: Power and Rule in Modern Society.* London: Sage.

Dean, Mitchell, and Kasper Villadsen. 2016. *State Phobia and Civil Society: The Political Legacy of Michel Foucault.* Stanford: Stanford University Press.

Defense Acquisition University. 2016. "Acquisition Community Connection Practice Center." https://acc.dau.mil/CommunityBrowser.aspx (last accessed 27 May 2016).

De Goede, Marieke. 2008. "Beyond Risk: Premediation and the Post-9/11 Security Imagination." *Security Dialogue* 39 (2–3): 155–176.

De la Garza, Paul. 2006. "In Search of Ground Truth." *Tampa Bay Times*, 3 September, http://www.sptimes.com/2006/09/03/Floridian/In_search_of_ground_t.shtml (last accessed 19 March 2015).

De Larringa, Miguel, and Marc G. Doucet. 2008. "Sovereign Power and the Biopolitics of Human Security." *Security Dialogue* 39 (5): 517–537.

DeLong, Mike. 2004. *Inside CentCom: The Unvarnished Truth about the Wars in Afghanistan and Iraq.* Washington, D.C.: Regnery Publishing.

Deni, John R., ed. 2015. *New Realities: Energy Security in the 2010s and the Implications for the U.S. Military.* Carlisle, Pa.: United States Army War College Press.

Dill, Janine. 2014. "Israel's Use of Law and Warnings in Gaza." *Opinio Juris*, 30 July, http://opiniojuris.org/2014/07/30/guest-post-israels-use-law-warnings-gaza (last accessed 19 August 2014).

Dillon, Michael. 2007a. "Governing through Contingency: The Security of Biopolitical Governance." *Political Geography* 26 (1): 41–47.

Dillon, Michael. 2007b. "Governing Terror: The State of Emergency of Biopolitical Emergence." *International Political Sociology* 1 (1): 7–28.

Dillon, Michael, and Julian Reid. 2009. *The Liberal Way of War: Killing to Make Live.* New York: Routledge.

Dodds, Klaus. 2010. "Classical Geopolitics." In *The International Studies Encyclopedia*, volume 1, edited by Robert A. Denemark, 302–322. Oxford: Blackwell.

Dodge, Toby. 2003. *Inventing Iraq: The Failure of Nation-Building and a History Denied.* New York: Columbia University Press.

Dodge, Toby. 2009. "Grand Ambitions and Far-Reaching Failures: The United States in Iraq." In *America and Iraq: Policy-Making, Intervention and Regional Politics*, edited by David Ryan and Patrick Kiely, 92–102. New York: Routledge.

Domosh, Mona. 2013. "Geoeconomic Imaginations and Economic Geography in the Early Twentieth Century." *Annals of the American Association of Geographers* 103 (4): 944–966.

Donzelot, Jacques. 2008. "Michel Foucault and Liberal Intelligence." *Economy and Society* 37 (1): 115–134.

Douzinas, Costas. 2007. *Human Rights and Empire: The Political Philosophy of Cosmopolitanism.* New York: Routledge-Cavendish.

Dowler, Lorraine, and Joanne Sharp. 2001. "A Feminist Geopolitics?" *Space and Polity* 5 (3): 165–176.

Duffield, Mark. 2001. *Global Governance and the New Wars: The Merger of Development and Security.* London: Zed.

Duffield, Mark. 2007. *Development, Security, and Unending War: Governing the World of Peoples.* Cambridge: Polity.

Duncan, James S. 2007. *In the Shadows of the Tropics: Climate, Race, and Biopower in Nineteenth Century Ceylon.* Aldershot: Ashgate.

Dunlap, Charles J. 2007. "Lawfare amid Warfare." *Washington Times*, 3 August, http://www.washingtontimes.com/news/2007/aug/3/lawfare-amid-warfare (last accessed 28 January 2015).

Dunlap, Charles J. 2009. "Lawfare: A Decisive Element of 21st-Century Conflicts?" *Joint Force Quarterly* 54: 34–39.

Elden, Stuart. 2013. *The Birth of Territory.* Chicago: University of Chicago Press.

Epstein, Edward. 2002. "Success in Afghan War Hard to Gauge: U.S. Reluctance to Produce Body Counts Makes Proving Enemy's Destruction Difficult." *San Francisco Chronicle*, 23 March, http://www.sfgate.com/news/article/Success-in-Afghan-war-hard-to-gauge-U-S-2861604.php (last accessed 11 March 2015).

Epstein, Joshua M. 1981. "Soviet Vulnerabilities in Iran and the RDF Deterrent." *International Security* 6 (2): 126–158.

Epstein, Joshua M. 1987. *Strategy and Force Planning: The Case of the Persian Gulf.* Washington, D.C.: Brookings Institution.

Esposito, John L., ed. 2000a. *The Oxford History of Islam.* New York: Oxford University Press.

Esposito, John L. 2000b. "Political Islam and the West." *Joint Force Quarterly* 24: 49–55.

Essex, Jamey. 2013. *Development, Security, and Aid: Geopolitics and Geoeconomics at the U.S. Agency for International Development.* Athens: University of Georgia Press.

EurasiaNet. 2003. "Kazakhstan Daily Digest." EurasiaNet.org, 11 March, www.eurasianet.org/resource/kazakhstan/hypermail/200303/0008.shtml (last accessed 12 February 2008).

Farish, Matthew. 2006. "Frontier Engineering: From the Globe to the Body in the Cold War Arctic." *Canadian Geographer* 50 (2): 177–196.

Farish, Matthew. 2016. "Baseworld." *Los Angeles Review of Books*, 16 March, https://lareviewofbooks.org/review/baseworld (last accessed 18 March 2016).

Ferguson, Charles. 2007. *No End in Sight* (DVD). Los Angeles: Magnolia Pictures.

Filkins, Dexter. 2009. *The Forever War*. New York: Vintage Books.

Flint, Colin. 2010. "Geographic Perspectives on World-Systems Theory." In *The International Studies Encyclopedia*, vol. 5, edited by Robert A. Denemark, 2828–2845. Oxford: Blackwell.

Flint, Colin, and Peter Taylor. 2011. *Political Geography: World-Economy, Nation-State, and Locality*. 6th ed. Harlow: Pearson.

Foster, John Bellamy. 2004. "The New Age of Imperialism." In *Pox Americana: Exposing the American Empire*, edited by John Bellamy Foster and Robert W. McChesney, 161–174. New York: Monthly Review Press.

Foster, John Bellamy, and Robert W. McChesney, eds. 2004. *Pox Americana: Exposing the American Empire*. New York: Monthly Review Press.

Foucault, Michel. 1977. *Discipline and Punish: The Birth of the Prison*, translated by Alan Sheridan. New York: Pantheon Books.

Foucault, Michel. 2003. *Society Must Be Defended: Lectures at the Collège de France, 1975–76*, translated by David Macey. London: Penguin.

Foucault, Michel. 2007. *Security, Territory, Population: Lectures at the Collège de France, 1977–1978*, translated by Graham Burchell. London: Palgrave Macmillan.

Foucault, Michel. 2008. *The Birth of Biopolitics: Lectures at the Collège de France, 1978–1979*, translated by Graham Burchell. London: Palgrave Macmillan.

Friedman, Thomas L. 2005. *The World Is Flat: A Brief History of the Twenty-First Century*. New York: Farrar, Straus and Giroux.

Galleano, Eduardo. 1998. *Upside Down: A Primer for the Looking-Glass World*. New York: Picador.

Gamlen, Elizabeth J. 1993. "United States Strategic Policy toward the Middle East: Central Command and the Reflagging of Kuwait's Tankers." In *The United States and the Middle East: A Search for New Perspectives*, edited by Hooshang Amirahmadi, 213–249. Albany: State University of New York Press.

Gardner, Lloyd C., and Marilyn B. Young, eds. 2007. *Iraq and the Lessons of Vietnam: Or, How Not to Learn from the Past*. New York: The New Press.

Gibson-Graham, J. K. 2004. "Area Studies after Poststructuralism." *Environment and Planning A* 36 (3): 405–419.

Gilbert, Emily. 2015. "Money as a 'Weapons System' and the Entrepreneurial Way of War." *Critical Military Studies* 1 (3): 202–219.

Gillem, Mark. 2007. *America Town: Building the Outposts of Empire*. Minneapolis: University of Minnesota Press.

Glassman, Jim, and Young-Jin Choi. 2014. "The *Chaebol* and the U.S. Military-Industrial Complex: Cold War Geopolitical Economy and South Korean Industrialization." *Environment and Planning A* 46 (5): 1160–1180.

Global Security. 2010. "U.S. Central Command Facilities." Military Facilities, http://www.globalsecurity.org/military/facility/centcom.htm (last accessed 08 August 2010).

Global Security. 2016a. "U.S. Central Command (USCENTCOM)." Military Agencies, http://www.globalsecurity.org/military/agency/dod/centcom.htm (last accessed 4 May 2016).

Global Security. 2016b. "U.S. Central Command Facilities." Military Facilities, http://www.globalsecurity.org/military/facility/centcom.htm (last accessed 3 May 2016).

Glück, Zoltán. 2015. "Piracy and the Production of Security Space." *Environment and Planning D: Society and Space* 33 (4): 642–659.

Gold, Dore. 1988. *America, the Gulf, and Israel: CENTCOM (Central Command) and Emerging U.S. Regional Security Policies in the Middle East.* Jerusalem: Jaffee Center for Strategic Studies.

Goodman, Amy, and Cherif Bassiouni. 2005. "UN Human Rights Investigator in Afghanistan Ousted under U.S. Pressure." *Democracy Now!,* 28 April, http://www.democracynow.org/2005/4/28/un_human_rights_investigator_in_afghanistan (last accessed 30 January 2015).

Goodman, Amy, and Murtaza Hussain. 2014. "How the U.S. Concocted a Terror Threat to Justify Syria Strikes, and the Corporate Media Went Along." *Democracy Now!,* 29 September, http://www.democracynow.org/2014/9/29/how_the_us_concocted_a_terror (last accessed 20 October 2014).

Gopal, Anand. 2014. *No Good Men among the Living: America, the Taliban, and the War through Afghan Eyes.* New York: Metropolitan Books.

Gordon, Colin. 1991. "Governmental Rationality: An Introduction." In *The Foucault Effect: Studies in Governmentality,* edited by Graham Burchell, Colin Gordon, and Peter Miller, 1–51. Chicago: University of Chicago Press.

Graham, Bradley, and Josh White. 2006. "Abizaid Credited with Popularizing the Term 'Long War.'" *Washington Post,* 3 February, http://www.washingtonpost.com/wp-dyn/content/article/2006/02/02/AR2006020202242.html (last accessed 19 June 2014).

Graham, Stephen. 2005. "Remember Fallujah: Demonising Place, Constructing Atrocity." *Environment and Planning D: Society and Space* 23 (1): 1–10.

Greenwald, Glenn. 2015. "Hailed as a Model for Successful Intervention, Libya Proves to Be the Exact Opposite." *Intercept,* 16 February, https://firstlook.org/theintercept/2015/02/16/hailed-model-successful-intervention-libya-proves-exact-opposite (last accessed 18 February 2015).

Greenwald, Glenn, and Murtaza Hussain. 2014. "The Fake Terror Threat Used to Justify Bombing Syria." *Intercept,* 28 September, https://firstlook.org/theintercept/2014/09/28/u-s-officials-invented-terror-group-justify-bombing-syria (last accessed 20 October 2014).

Gregory, Derek. 2004. *The Colonial Present: Afghanistan, Palestine, Iraq.* Oxford: Blackwell.

Gregory, Derek. 2005. "Geographies, Publics and Politics." *Progress in Human Geography* 29 (2): 182–193.

Gregory, Derek. 2008. "The Biopolitics of Baghdad: Counterinsurgency and the Counter-City." *Human Geography* 1 (1): 6–27.

Gregory, Derek. 2010. "War and Peace." *Transactions of the Institute of British Geographers* 35 (2): 154–186.

Gregory, Derek. 2011. "The Everywhere War." *Geographical Journal* 177 (3): 238–250.

Gregory, Derek. 2012. "Rapid Response." *Geographical Imaginations: War, Space, and Security*, 21 August, http://geographicalimaginations.com/2012/08/21/rapid-response (last accessed 1 December 2014).

Gregory, Derek. 2013. "Eyes in the Sky, Boots on the Ground." *Geographical Imaginations: War, Space, and Security*, 15 December, http://geographicalimaginations.com /2013/12/15/eyes-in-the-sky-boots-on-the-ground (last accessed 21 October 2014).

Gregory, Derek. 2014. "Situation Rooms." *Geographical Imaginations: War, Space, and Security*, 17 December, http://geographicalimaginations.com/2014/12/17/situation -rooms (last accessed 18 December 2014).

Gregory, Derek. 2015a. "'That Others May Die.'" *Geographical Imaginations: War, Space, and Security*, 10 January, http://geographicalimaginations.com/2015/01/10/that -others-may-die (last accessed 12 January 2015).

Gregory, Derek. 2015b. "Je Ne Suis Pas Charlie." *Geographical Imaginations: War, Space, and Security*, 17 January, http://geographicalimaginations.com/2015/01/17/je-ne-suis -pas-charlie (last accessed 17 January 2015).

Gregory, Derek. 2015c. "Three Strikes . . ." *Geographical Imaginations: War, Space, and Security*, 29 November, http://geographicalimaginations.com/2015/11/29/three -strikes (last accessed 1 December 2015).

Gregory, Derek, and Allan Pred, eds. 2007. *Violent Geographies: Fear, Terror, and Political Violence*. New York: Routledge.

Grusin, Richard. 2004. "Premediation." *Criticism* 46 (1): 17–39.

Guardian Editorial. 2014. "America's Shame and Disgrace." *Guardian*, 9 December, http://www.theguardian.com/commentisfree/2014/dec/09/guardian-view-on-us -torture-report-america-shame-disgrace (last accessed 10 December 2014).

Hajjar, Sami G. 2002. *U.S. Military Presence in the Gulf: Challenges and Prospects*. Carlisle, Pa.: Strategic Studies Institute, U.S. Army War College.

Halper, Jeff. 2014. "How Israel Undermines International Law through 'Lawfare': Globalizing Gaza." *CounterPunch*, 18 August, http://www.counterpunch.org/2014/08/18 /globalizing-gaza (last accessed 19 August 2014).

Harcourt, Bernard E. 2012. *The Illusion of Free Markets: Punishment and the Myth of Natural Order*. Cambridge, Mass.: Harvard University Press.

Hardt, Michael, and Antonio Negri. 2000. *Empire*. Cambridge, Mass.: Harvard University Press.

Harvey, David. 1985. "The Geopolitics of Capitalism." In *Social Relations and Spatial Structures*, edited by Derek Gregory and John Urry, 128–163. London: Macmillan.

Harvey, David. 2003. *The New Imperialism*. Oxford: Oxford University Press.

Harvey, David. 2005. *A Brief History of Neoliberalism*. New York: Oxford University Press.

Heffernan, Mike. 1996. "Geography, Cartography, and Military Intelligence: The Royal Geographical Society and the First World War." *Transactions of the Institute of British Geographers* New Series 21 (3): 504–533.

Heng, Yee-Kuang. 2006. *War as Risk Management: Strategy and Conflict in an Age of Globalised Risks*. New York: Routledge.

Hines, Jay E. 2000. "From Desert One to Southern Watch: The Evolution of U.S. Central Command." *Joint Force Quarterly* 24: 42–48.

Hooker, Jeffrey. 2005. *Shaping the Plan for Operation Iraqi Freedom*. Washington, D.C.: The Washington Institute for Near East Policy.

Howell, Philip. 2009. *Geographies of Regulation: Policing Prostitution in Nineteenth-Century Britain and the Empire*. Cambridge: Cambridge University Press.

Hoyt, Brian A. 2008. "Rethinking the U.S. Policy on the International Criminal Court." *Joint Force Quarterly* 48: 30–35.

Hyndman, Jennifer. 2000. *Managing Displacement: Refugees and the Politics of Humanitarianism*. Minneapolis: University of Minnesota Press.

Hyndman, Jennifer. 2007. "Feminist Geopolitics Revisited: Body Counts in Iraq." *Professional Geographer* 59 (1): 35–46.

Institute for National Security Studies. 1999. *Strategic Assessment 1999*. Washington, D.C.: Institute for National Strategic Studies, National Defense University.

The Iraq Inquiry. 2016. "Statement by Sir John Chilcot: 6 July 2016." *The Report of the Iraq Inquiry*, http://www.iraqinquiry.org.uk/media/247010/2016-09-06-sir-john -chilcots-public-statement.pdf (last accessed 6 July 2016).

Jager, Sheila M. 2007. *On the Uses of Cultural Knowledge*. Carlisle, Pa.: Strategic Studies Institute, U.S. Army War College.

Jeffrey, Alex, and Michaelina Jakala. 2015. "Using Courts to Build States: The Competing Spaces of Citizenship in Transitional Justice Programmes." *Political Geography* 47: 43–52.

Johnson, Chalmers. 2000. *Blowback: The Costs and Consequences of American Empire*. New York: Metropolitan.

Johnson, Chalmers. 2004. *The Sorrows of Empire: Militarism, Secrecy, and the End of the Republic*. New York: Metropolitan.

Joint Force Quarterly Forum. 2000a. "An Interview with Anthony C. Zinni: Challenges in the Central Region." *Joint Force Quarterly* 24: 26–31.

Joint Force Quarterly Forum. 2000b. "U.S. Central Command." *Joint Force Quarterly* 24: 32–33.

Jones, Craig. 2016. "Lawfare and the Juridification of Late Modern War." *Progress in Human Geography* 40 (2): 221–239.

Jones, Craig, and Michael Smith. 2015. "War/Law/Space: Notes towards a Legal Geography of War." *Environment and Planning D: Society and Space* 33 (4): 581–591.

Jones, Terry. 2001. "Why Grammar Is the First Casualty of War." *Telegraph*, 1 December, http://www.telegraph.co.uk/news/uknews/1364012/Why-grammar-is-the-first -casualty-of-war.html (last accessed 22 April 2016).

Jones, Toby Craig. 2010. *Desert Kingdom: How Oil and Water Forged Modern Saudi Arabia*. Cambridge, Mass.: Harvard University Press.

Jones, Toby Craig. 2012. "America, Oil, and War in the Middle East." *Journal of American History* 99 (1): 208–218.

Jones, Toby Craig. 2015. *Running Dry: Essays on Energy, Water, and Environmental Crisis*. New Brunswick, N.J.: Rutgers University Press.

Joyce, Patrick. 2003. *The Rule of Freedom: Liberalism and the Modern City*. London: Verso.

Kagan, Robert. 2008. *The Return of History and the End of Dreams*. New York: Alfred A. Knopf.

Kaldor, Mary. 1999. *New and Old Wars: Organized Violence in a Global Era*. Cambridge: Polity.

Kaldor, Mary, and Joseph E. Stiglitz. 2013. Introduction. In *The Quest for Security: Protection without Protectionism and the Challenge of Global Governance*, edited by Joseph E. Stiglitz and Mary Kaldor, 1–16. New York: Columbia University Press.

Kalpagam, U. 2000. "Colonial Governmentality and the 'Economy.'" *Economy and Society* 29 (3): 418–438.

Kalpagam, U. 2014. *Rule by Numbers: Governmentality in Colonial India*. London: Lexington Books.

Kaplan, Robert. 2012. *The Revenge of Geography: What the Map Tells Us about Coming Conflicts and the Battle against Fate*. New York: Random House.

Katzman, Kenneth. 2006. *The Persian Gulf States: Issues for U.S. Policy, 2006*. Washington, D.C.: Congressional Research Service Report for Congress.

Kaufman, Edward E., and Howard Berman. 2010. "Send in the Civilians." *Foreign Affairs* 89 (5): 175–176.

Kearns, Gerry. 2009. *Geopolitics and Empire: The Legacy of Halford Mackinder*. Oxford: Oxford University Press.

Kem, Jack. 2008. "The U.S. Army's Doctrinal Renaissance." *World Politics Review*, 14 October, http://www.worldpoliticsreview.com/articles/2773/the-u-s-armys-doctrinal-renaissance (last accessed 27 April 2015).

Kemp, Jack. 2004. "Call in the Private Sector in Iraq." *Foundation for Defense of Democracies*, 21 June, http://www.defenddemocracy.org/media-hit/call-in-the-private-sector-in-iraq (last accessed 2 April 2014).

Kennedy, David. 2006. *Of War and Law*. Princeton: Princeton University Press.

Klare, Michael T. 2002. *Resource Wars: The New Landscape of Global Conflict*. New York: Owl Books.

Klare, Michael T. 2004. *Blood and Oil: The Dangers and Consequences of America's Growing Dependency on Imported Petroleum*. New York: Owl Books.

Klare, Michael T. 2007. "Beyond the Age of Petroleum." *The Nation*, 12 November, http://www.thenation.com/article/beyond-age-petroleum (last accessed 10 October 2014).

Klein, Bradley S. 1988. "Hegemony and Strategic Culture: American Power Projection and Alliance Defense Politics." *Review of International Studies* 14 (2): 133–148.

Klein, Bradley S. 1994. *Strategic Studies and World Order: The Global Politics of Deterrence*. Cambridge: Cambridge University Press.

Klein, Naomi. 2007. *The Shock Doctrine: The Rise of Disaster Capitalism*. New York: Metropolitan Books.

Knights, Michael. 2006. *Troubled Waters: Future U.S. Security Assistance in the Persian Gulf*. Washington, D.C.: Washington Institute for Near East Policy.

Koopman, Sara. 2016. "Beware: Your Research May Be Weaponized." *Annals of the American Association of Geographers* (latest articles), DOI:10.1080/24694452.2016.1145511.

Krepinevich, Andrew, and Robert O. Work. 2007. *A New Global Defense Posture for the Second Transoceanic Era*. Washington, D.C.: Center for Strategic and Budgetary Assessments.

Kuus, Merje. 2010. "Critical Geopolitics." In *The International Studies Encyclopedia*, volume 2, edited by Robert A. Denemark, 683–701. Oxford: Blackwell.

Kuwait News Agency. 2014. "Eagle Resolve 2015 Military Exercise Biggest Regionally, Internationally." *Kuwait News*, 23 September, http://www.kuna.net.kw/ArticlePrintPage .aspx?id=2398923&language=en (last accessed 4 December 2014).

Lawrence, John D. 2008. "Near East South Asia Center for Strategic Studies: Building Relationships, Enhancing Security." *Joint Force Quarterly* 50: 105–108.

Leander, Anna. 2005. "The Power to Construct International Security: On the Significance of Private Military Companies." *Journal of International Studies* 33 (3): 803–825.

Le Billon, Philippe. 2004. "The Geopolitical Economy of 'Resource Wars.'" *Geopolitics* 9 (1): 1–28.

Lefebvre, Henri. 1991. *The Production of Space*, translated by Donald Nicholson-Smith. Oxford: Blackwell.

Legg, Stephen. 2007. *Spaces of Colonialism: Delhi's Urban Governmentalities*. Oxford: Blackwell.

Lesser, Ian O. 1991. *Oil, the Persian Gulf, and Grand Strategy: Contemporary Issues in Historical Perspective*. Santa Monica, Calif.: RAND.

Lester, Alan. 2000. "Historical Geographies of Imperialism." In *Modern Historical Geographies*, edited by Brian Graham and Catherine Nash, 100–120. Harlow, Essex: Prentice Hall.

Lester, Alan. 2001. *Imperial Networks: Creating Identities in Nineteenth-Century South Africa and Britain*. London: Routledge.

Lewis, Bernard. 2004. *The Crisis of Islam: Holy War and Unholy Terror*. New York: Random House.

Li, Tania M. 2007. *The Will to Improve: Governmentality, Development, and the Practice of Politics*. Durham, N.C.: Duke University Press.

Lin, Yiyia, and Samuel H. Cox. 2008. "Securitization of Catastrophe Mortality Risks." *Insurance: Mathematics and Economics* 42 (2): 628–637.

Little, Douglas. 2002. *American Orientalism: The United States and the Middle East since 1945*. Chapel Hill: University of North Carolina Press.

The Long War Journal. 2014. "About *The Long War Journal*." *The Long War Journal*, http://www.longwarjournal.org/about.php (last accessed 19 June 2014).

Loveman, Brian. 2004. "Introduction: U.S. Regional Security Policies in the Post–Cold War Era." In *Strategy for Empire: U.S. Regional Security Policy in the Post–Cold War Era*, edited by Brian Loveman, xiii–xxviii. Lanham, Md.: SR Books.

Lubeck, Paul M., Michael J. Watts, and Ronnie Lipschutz. 2007. *Convergent Interests: U.S. Energy Security and the "Securing" of Nigerian Democracy*. Washington, D.C.: Center for International Policy.

Lupton, Deborah. 1999. *Risk*. New York: Routledge.

Luttwak, Edward N. 1990. "From Geopolitics to Geo-Economics: Logic of Conflict, Grammar of Commerce." *National Interest* 20: 17–23.

Lutz, Catherine, ed. 2009. *The Bases of Empire: The Global Struggle against U.S. Military Posts*. New York: New York University Press.

Mac Ginty, Roger. 2012. "Against Stabilization." *Stability: International Journal of Security and Development* 1 (1): 20–30.

Macgregor, Douglas. 2011. "Thoughts on Force Design in an Era of Shrinking Defense Budgets." *Joint Force Quarterly* 63 (4): 21–29.

Madison, James. 1865 [1795]. "Political Observations." In *Letters and Other Writings of James Madison, Fourth President of the United States*, vol. 4, 483–505. Philadelphia: J. B. Lippincott & Company.

Majorca Partners. 2014. "Home." http://www.majorca.net.au (last accessed 5 May 2014).

Mann, Michael. 2003. *Incoherent Empire*. London: Verso.

Martin, Randy. 2007. *An Empire of Indifference: American War and the Financial Logic of Risk Management*. Durham, N.C.: Duke University Press.

Mason, Michael, and Mark Zeitoun. 2013. "Questioning Environmental Security." *Geographical Journal* 179 (4): 294–297.

McMahan, Jeff. 2009. *Killing in War*. Oxford: Oxford University Press.

McMichael, Philip. 2013. "Land Grabbing as Security Mercantilism in International Relations." *Globalizations* 10 (1): 47–64.

McNaugher, Thomas L. 1985. *Arms and Oil: U.S. Strategy and the Persian Gulf*. Washington, D.C.: Brookings Institution.

Minca, Claudio. 2007. "Agamben's Geographies of Modernity." *Political Geography* 26 (1): 78–97.

Mitchell, Timothy. 2011. *Carbon Democracy: Political Power in the Age of Oil*. London: Verso.

Moore, Jason W. 2015. *Capitalism in the Web of Life*. London: Verso.

Morrissey, John. 2003. *Negotiating Colonialism*. London: Royal Geographical Society Historical Geography Research Series.

Morrissey, John. 2009. "The Geoeconomic Pivot of the Global War on Terror: U.S. Central Command and the War in Iraq." In *America and Iraq: Policy-Making, Intervention, and Regional Politics*, edited by David Ryan and Patrick Kiely, 103–122. New York: Routledge.

Morrissey, John. 2011a. "Architects of Empire: The Military-Strategic Studies Complex and the Scripting of U.S. National Security." *Antipode* 43 (2): 435–470.

Morrissey, John. 2011b. "Liberal Lawfare and Biopolitics: U.S. Juridical Warfare in the War on Terror." *Geopolitics* 16 (2): 280–305.

Morrissey, John. 2011c. "Closing the Neoliberal Gap: Risk and Regulation in the Long War of Securitization." *Antipode* 43 (3): 874–900.

Morrissey, John. 2012. "Foucault and the Colonial Subject: Emergent Forms of Colonial Governmentality in Early Modern Ireland." In *At the Anvil: Essays in Honour of William J. Smyth*, edited by Patrick Duffy and William Nolan, 135–150. Dublin: Geography Publications.

Morrissey, John. 2015. "Securitizing Instability: The U.S. Military and Full Spectrum Operations." *Environment and Planning D: Society and Space* 33 (4): 609–625.

Morrissey, John. 2016. "U.S. Central Command and Liberal Imperial Reach: 'Shaping the Central Region for the 21st Century.'" *Geographical Journal* 182 (1): 15–26.

Morrissey, John. 2017. "Geoeconomics in the Long War." *Antipode* 49 (s1): 94–113.

Morrissey, John, Simon Dalby, Gerry Kearns, and Gerard Toal. 2009. "Geography Writes Back: Responses to Kaplan's 'The Revenge of Geography.'" *Human Geography* 2 (2): 33–51.

Morrissey, John, David Nally, Ulf Strohmayer, and Yvonne Whelan. 2014. *Key Concepts in Historical Geography*. London: Sage.

Mountz, Alison. 2011. "The Enforcement Archipelago: Detention, Haunting, and Asylum on Islands." *Political Geography* 30 (3): 118–128.

Mountz, Alison. 2012. "Mapping Remote Detention: Dis/Location through Isolation." In *Beyond Walls and Cages: Prisons, Borders, and Global Crisis*, edited by Jenna M. Loyd, Matt Mitchelson, and Andrew Burridge, 91–104. Athens: University of Georgia Press.

Multi-National Security Transition Command—Iraq. 2009. "Mission Statement." http://www.mnstci.iraq.centcom.mil (last accessed 11 February 2009).

Mythen, Gabe, and Sandra Walklate, eds. 2006. *Beyond the Risk Society: Critical Reflections on Risk and Human Security*. Maidenhead, Berkshire: Open University Press.

Nally, David. 2011. *Human Encumbrances: Political Violence and the Great Irish Famine*. Notre Dame, Ind.: University of Notre Dame Press.

National Intelligence Council. 2004. "Mapping the Global Future." National Intelligence Council, https://www.dni.gov/files/documents/Global%20Trends_Mapping%20the%20Global%20Future%202020%20Project.pdf (last accessed 3 June 2016).

National Intelligence Council. 2008. "Global Trends 2025: A Transformed World." National Intelligence Council, https://www.dni.gov/files/documents/Global%20Trends_2025%20Report.pdf (last accessed 3 June 2016).

Neal, Andrew W. 2010. *Exceptionalism and the Politics of Counter-Terrorism: Liberty, Security, and the War on Terror*. New York: Routledge.

Neocleous, Mark. 2008. *Critique of Security*. Edinburgh: Edinburgh University Press.

Nichol, Jim. 2003. *Central Asia's New States: Political Developments and Implications for U.S. Interests*. Washington, D.C.: Congressional Research Service Issue Brief for Congress.

O'Hanlon, Michael. 2008. *Unfinished Business: U.S. Overseas Military Presence in the 21st Century*. Washington, D.C.: Center for a New American Security.

Ohlin, Jens D. 2015. *The Assault on International Law*. Oxford: Oxford University Press.

O'Malley, Pat. 2004. *Risk, Uncertainty, and Government*. London: Glasshouse Press.

Ó Tuathail, Gearóid. 1996. *Critical Geopolitics: The Politics of Writing Global Space*. Minneapolis: University of Minnesota Press.

Paglen, Trevor. 2008. "Mapping Ghosts." *An Atlas of Radical Cartography*, http://www.an-atlas.com/contents/pag_em_vis.html (last accessed 28 November 2013).

Paglen, Trevor. 2009. *Blank Spots on the Map: The Dark Geography of the Pentagon's Secret World*. New York: Dutton.

Painter, David S. 1986. *Oil and the American Century: The Political Economy of U.S. Foreign Oil Policy, 1941–1954*. Baltimore: Johns Hopkins University Press.

Palmer, Michael A. 1992. *Guardians of the Gulf: A History of America's Expanding Role in the Persian Gulf, 1833–1992*. New York: Free Press.

Patrick, Stewart, and Kaysie Brown. 2007. *The Pentagon and Global Development: Making Sense of the DoD's Expanding Role*. Working Paper No. 131. Washington, D.C.: Center for Global Development.

Patterson, Rebecca, and Dane Stangler. 2010. "Building Expeditionary Economics: Understanding the Field and Setting Forth an Agenda." *Kauffman Foundation Research Series*, November: 5–17.

Paye, Jean-Claude. 2007. *Global War on Liberty*, translated by James H. Membrez. New York: Telos Press.

Pease, Donald E. 2000. "U.S. Imperialism: Global Dominance without Colonies." In *A Companion to Postcolonial Studies*, edited by Henry Schwarz and Sangeeta Ray, 203–220. Oxford: Blackwell.

Peay, James H. Binford, III. 1995a. *Five Pillars of Peace: A Blueprint for Achieving Peace and Stability in the Central Region*. Washington, D.C.: US-GCC Corporate Cooperation Committee.

Peay, James H. Binford, III. 1995b. "The Five Pillars of Peace in the Central Region." *Joint Force Quarterly* 9: 32–39.

Peck, Jamie. 2013. "Explaining (with) Neoliberalism." *Territory, Politics, Governance* 1 (2): 132–157.

Pelletiere, Stephen C. 2004. *America's Oil Wars*. Westport, Conn.: Praeger.

Pelletiere, Stephen C. 2007. *Losing Iraq: Insurgency and Politics*. Westport, Conn.: Praeger.

Pelletiere, Stephen C., and Douglas V. Johnson II. 1992. *Oil and the New World System: CENTCOM Rethinks Its Mission*. Carlisle, Pa.: Strategic Studies Institute, U.S. Army War College.

Peña, Charles. 2003. "Bush's National Security Strategy Is a Misnomer." *Cato Policy Analysis* 496, 30 October.

Piketty, Thomas. 2014. *Capital in the Twenty-First Century*, translated by A. Goldhammer. Cambridge, Mass.: Harvard University Press.

Powell, Colin L. 1993. "A Word from the Chairman." *Joint Force Quarterly* 1: 4–5.

Prados, Alfred B. 2001. *Middle East: Attitudes toward the United States*. Washington, D.C.: Congressional Research Service Report for Congress.

Prashad, Vijay. 2002. *War against the Planet: The Fifth Afghan War, Imperialism, and Other Assorted Fundamentalisms*. New Delhi: LeftWord Books.

Prashad, Vijay. 2014. "Blowback Time." *Frontline*, 25 July, http://www.frontline.in/cover-story/blowback-time/article6185216.ece (last accessed 26 August 2014).

Rapid Deployment Joint Task Force. 1981. *Command History 1980*. MacDill Air Force Base, Fla.: RDJTF Headquarters.

Rapid Deployment Joint Task Force. 1982. *Command History 1981*. MacDill Air Force Base, Fla.: RDJTF Headquarters.

Rapid Deployment Joint Task Force. 1984. *1982 Command History*. MacDill Air Force Base, Fla.: United States Central Command Office of the Commander in Chief.

Raytheon. 2003. "Raytheon-Developed Deployable Headquarters Now Operating in Qatar." News Release, 3 February, http://investor.raytheon.com/phoenix.zhtml?c=84193&p=irol-newsArticle&ID=377804 (last accessed 4 December 2014).

Record, Jeffrey. 1981a. "The Rapid Deployment Force: Problems, Constraints, and Needs." *Annals of the American Academy of Political and Social Science* 457: 109–120.

Record, Jeffrey. 1981b. *The Rapid Deployment Force and U.S. Military Intervention in the Persian Gulf*. Washington, D.C.: Institute for Foreign Policy Analysis.

Reveron, Derek S., ed. 2004. *America's Viceroys: The Military and U.S. Foreign Policy*. New York: Palgrave Macmillan.

Reveron, Derek S., and Michelle D. Gavin. 2004. "America's Viceroys." In *America's Viceroys: The Military and U.S. Foreign Policy*, edited by Derek S. Reveron, 1–16. New York: Palgrave Macmillan.

Riggle, Al. 2007. "The Global War on Terrorism: The Long War." Miami, Fla.: Defense Industrial Base Critical Infrastructure Protection Conference, April 10–12. National Defense Industrial Association.

Rishikof, Harvey. 2008. "Juridical Warfare: The Neglected Legal Instrument." *Joint Force Quarterly* 48: 11–13.

Robbins, James S. 2004. "U.S. Central Command: Where History Is Made." In *America's Viceroys: The Military and U.S. Foreign Policy*, edited by Derek S. Reveron, 163–184. New York: Palgrave Macmillan.

Roggio, Bill. 2014. Personal E-mail Communication, 1 April. University of Cambridge: Emmanuel College.

Romero, Pia. 2012. "Quick Wins Show the Benefits of DoD's Rapid Acquisition Program." Federal News Radio, http://www.federalnewsradio.com/394/2897741/Quick-wins-show-the-benefits-of-DoDs-Rapid-Acquisition-Program (last accessed 7 March 2015).

Rubin, Philip. 2003. "Introduction." In *The Geographical Dimensions of Terrorism*, edited by Susan L. Cutter, Douglas G. Richardson, and Thomas J. Wilbanks, ix–xi. New York: Routledge.

Ryan, David. 2007. *Frustrated Empire: U.S. Foreign Policy, 9/11 to Iraq*. London: Pluto Press.

Ryan, David, and Patrick Kiely, eds. 2009. *America and Iraq: Policy-Making, Intervention, and Regional Politics*. New York: Routledge.

Said, Edward W. 1978. *Orientalism: Western Conceptions of the Orient*. London: Routledge & Kegan Paul.

Said, Edward W. 1993. *Culture and Imperialism*. New York: Alfred A. Knopf.

Said, Edward W. 2003. *Orientalism*. Penguin classic edition. London: Penguin.

Sandars, Christopher T. 2000. *America's Overseas Garrisons: The Leasehold Empire*. New York: Oxford University Press.

Sassen, Saskia. 2010. "A Savage Sorting of Winners and Losers: Contemporary Versions of Primitive Accumulation." *Globalizations* 7 (1–2): 23–50.

Savage, Charlie. 2015. *Power Wars: Inside Obama's Post-9/11 Presidency*. New York: Little, Brown and Company.

Scahill, Jeremy. 2007. *Blackwater: The Rise of the World's Most Powerful Mercenary Army*. New York: Nation Books.

Scahill, Jeremy. 2013. *Dirty Wars: The World Is a Battlefield*. London: Serpent's Tail.

Schlosser, Kolson. 2008. "Bio-Political Geographies." *Geography Compass* 2 (5): 1621–1634.

Schramm, Carl J. 2010. "Expeditionary Economics: Spurring Growth after Conflicts and Disasters." *Foreign Affairs* 89 (3): 89–99.

Schwartz, Michael. 2008. *War without End: The Iraq War in Context*. Chicago: Haymarket Books.

Schwarzkopf, Norman II. 1992. *It Doesn't Take a Hero*. New York: Bantam Books.

Scott, David. 1995. "Colonial Governmentality." *Social Text* 43: 191–220.

Shaw, Ian G. R. 2013. "Predator Empire: The Geopolitics of U.S. Drone Warfare." *Geopolitics* 18 (3): 536–559.

Sidaway, James. 1998. "What Is in a Gulf? From the 'Arc of Crisis' to the Gulf War." In *Rethinking Geopolitics*, edited by Gearóid Ó Tuathail and Simon Dalby, 224–239. London: Routledge.

Simmons, Jeremy, Chris Manuel, and John Arquilla. 2003. *Closing the Gaps: A Strategy for Gaining the Initiative in the War on Terror*. Monterey, Calif.: Center for Terrorism and Irregular Warfare, Naval Postgraduate School.

Singer, P. W. 2003. *Corporate Warriors: The Rise of the Privatized Military Industry*. Ithaca, N.Y.: Cornell University Press.

Smith, Neil. 2003a. *American Empire: Roosevelt's Geographer and the Prelude to Globalization*. Berkeley: University of California Press.

Smith, Neil. 2003b. "After the American *Lebensraum*: 'Empire,' Empire, and Globalization." *Interventions: International Journal of Postcolonial Studies* 5 (2): 249–270.

Smith, Neil. 2005. *The Endgame of Globalization*. New York: Routledge.

Smith, Neil. 2008. *Uneven Development: Nature, Capital, and the Production of Space*. 3rd ed. Athens: University of Georgia Press.

Smith, William C. 2003. "Lawyers at War." *ABA Journal* February: 14–15, 70.

Snukal, Katia, and Emily Gilbert. 2015. "War, Law, Jurisdiction, and Juridical Othering: Private Military Security Contractors and the Nisour Square Massacre." *Environment and Planning D: Society and Space* 33 (4): 660–675.

Sparke, Matthew. 2007. "Geopolitical Fears, Geoeconomic Hopes, and the Responsibilities of Geography." *Annals of the American Association of Geographers* 97 (2): 338–349.

Sparke, Matthew. 2013. *Introducing Globalization: Ties, Tensions, and Uneven Integration*. Chichester, West Sussex: Wiley-Blackwell.

Sparke, Matthew. 2014. "Book Review of Jamey Essex, Development, Security, and Aid: Geopolitics and Geoeconomics at the U.S. Agency for International Development." Academia.edu, http://washington.academia.edu/MattSparke/Papers (last accessed 25 March 2015).

Stafford, W. A. 2000. "How to Keep Military Personnel from Going to Jail for Doing the Right Thing: Jurisdiction, ROE, and the Rules of Deadly Force." *Army Lawyer*, November: 1–25.

Stahl, Roger. 2014. "Life Is War: The Rhetoric of Biomimesis and the Future Military." *Democratic Communiqué* 26 (2): 122–137.

Szanton, David L., ed. 2004. *The Politics of Knowledge: Area Studies and the Disciplines*. Berkeley: University of California Press.

Taw, Jennifer Morrison. 2012. *Mission Revolution: The U.S. Military and Stability Operations*. New York: Columbia University Press.

Telhami, Shibley. 2002. *The Stakes: America and the Middle East*. Boulder, Colo.: Westview Press.

Terry, James P. 2008a. "Habeas Corpus and the Detention of Enemy Combatants in the War on Terror." *Joint Force Quarterly* 48: 14–18.

Terry, James P. 2008b. "The International Criminal Court: A Concept Whose Time Has Not Come." *Joint Force Quarterly* 48: 36–40.

Thayer, Bradley A. 2003. *The Pax Americana and the Middle East: U.S. Grand Strategic Interests in the Region after September 11*. Ramat Gan, Israel: The Begin-Sadat Center for Strategic Studies, Bar-Ilan University.

Thomas, Jason. 2012. "Multi-National Corporations and Stability Operations: A New Role?" *Small Wars Journal* 8 (10), October, http://smallwarsjournal.com/jrnl/iss /201210 (last accessed 7 March 2015).

Timm, Trevor. 2014. "Stop Believing the Lies: America Tortured More than 'Some Folks'—and Covered It Up." *Guardian*, 10 December, http://www.theguardian.com /commentisfree/2014/dec/09/america-torture-cia-report-defenders (last accessed 10 December 2014).

Ullman, Harlan K., James P. Wade, Leon A. Edney, Frederick M. Franks, Charles A. Horner, Jonathan T. Howe, and Keith Brendley. 1996. *Shock and Awe: Achieving Rapid Dominance*. Washington, D.C.: Institute for National Strategic Studies, National Defense University.

U.S. Africa Command. 2009. *Statement before the Senate Armed Services Committee and the House Armed Services Committee on the Posture of United States Africa Command by AFRICOM Commander General William E. Ward*. 17–18 March. Washington, D.C.: Senate Armed Services Committee and House Armed Services Committee.

U.S. Army Judge Advocate General's Legal Center. 2016. *Operational Law Handbook*. Charlottesville, Va.: International and Operational Law Department, The Judge Advocate General's Legal Center and School.

U.S. Central Command. 1985. *1983 Command History*. MacDill Air Force Base, Fla.: Office of the Commander in Chief.

U.S. Central Command. 1986a. *1984 Command History*. MacDill Air Force Base, Fla.: Office of the Commander in Chief.

U.S. Central Command. 1986b. *Statement before the Senate Armed Services Committee on the Posture of United States Central Command by CENTCOM Commander in Chief General George Crist*. 11 March. Washington, D.C.: Senate Armed Services Committee.

U.S. Central Command. 1987. *1985 Command History*. MacDill Air Force Base, Fla.: Office of the Commander in Chief.

U.S. Central Command. 1990. *Statement before the Senate Armed Services Committee on the Posture of United States Central Command by CENTCOM Commander in Chief General Norman Schwarzkopf*. 8 February. Washington, D.C.: Senate Armed Services Committee.

U.S. Central Command. 1995. *Posture Statement*. MacDill Air Force Base, Fla.: Office of the Commander in Chief.

U.S. Central Command. 1997a. *Strategic Plan II, 1997–1999: Shaping U.S. Central Command for the 21st Century*. MacDill Air Force Base, Fla.: Office of the Commander in Chief.

U.S. Central Command. 1997b. *Report to the House Appropriations Committee Subcommittee on National Security by CENTCOM Commander in Chief General James*

Binford Peay III. 17 March. Washington, D.C.. House Appropriations Committee Subcommittee on National Security.

U.S. Central Command. 1997c. *Posture Statement.* MacDill Air Force Base, Fla.: Office of the Commander in Chief.

U.S. Central Command. 1998. *Statement before the Senate Armed Services Committee on the Posture of United States Central Command by CENTCOM Commander in Chief General Anthony C. Zinni.* 3 March. Washington, D.C.: Senate Armed Services Committee.

U.S. Central Command. 1999a. *Shaping the Central Region for the 21st Century.* MacDill Air Force Base, Fla.: Office of the Commander in Chief.

U.S. Central Command. 1999b. *Statement before the Senate Armed Services Committee on the Posture of United States Central Command by CENTCOM Commander in Chief General Anthony C. Zinni.* 13 April. Washington, D.C.: Senate Armed Services Committee.

U.S. Central Command. 2000. *Statement before the Senate Armed Services Committee on the Posture of United States Central Command by CENTCOM Commander in Chief General Anthony C. Zinni.* 29 February. Washington, D.C.: Senate Armed Services Committee.

U.S. Central Command. 2005. *Statement before the House Armed Services Committee on the Posture of United States Central Command by CENTCOM Commander General John Abizaid.* 2 March. Washington, D.C.: House Armed Services Committee.

U.S. Central Command. 2006a. *Statement before the Senate Armed Services Committee on the Posture of United States Central Command by CENTCOM Commander General John Abizaid.* 16 March. Washington, D.C.: Senate Armed Services Committee.

U.S. Central Command. 2006b. "Current Operations in the Long War." Presentation of CENTCOM Director of Logistics Major General Brian Geehan, National Defense Transportation Association Forum and Expo, Memphis, Tenn., 23–27 September.

U.S. Central Command. 2007a. "U.S. CENTCOM History." CENTCOM Office of History, http://www.centcom.mil/sites/uscentcom2/CENTCOM%20History/History.aspx (last accessed 5 February 2007).

U.S. Central Command. 2007b. "CENTCOM FAQ." U.S. Central Command, http://www .centcom.mil/sites/uscentcom2/FAQ/CENTCOM%20FAQ.htm (last accessed 5 February 2007).

U.S. Central Command. 2007c. *Statement before the House Armed Services Committee on the Posture of United States Central Command by CENTCOM Commander Admiral William J. Fallon.* 18 April. Washington, D.C.: House Armed Services Committee.

U.S. Central Command. 2008. "Change of Command." Ceremony Booklet, 31 October. MacDill Air Force Base, Fla.: United States Central Command.

U.S. Central Command. 2009a. "Our Mission." United States Central Command, http:// www.centcom.mil/en/about-centcom/our-mission (last accessed 22 March 2009).

U.S. Central Command. 2009b. *Statement before the Senate Armed Services Committee on the Afghanistan-Pakistan Strategic Review and Posture of United States Central Command by CENTCOM Commander General David H. Petraeus.* 1 April. Washington, D.C.: Senate Armed Services Committee.

U.S. Central Command. 2010. *Statement before the Senate Armed Services Committee on the Posture of United States Central Command by CENTCOM Commander General David H. Petraeus.* 16 March. Washington, D.C.: Senate Armed Services Committee.

U.S. Central Command. 2011. "Eagle Resolve Exercise Concludes Today in United Arab Emirates." Press Releases, http://www.centcom.mil/en/news/press-releases/eagle -resolve-exercise-concludes-today-in-united-arab-emirates (last accessed 5 December 2014).

U.S. Central Command. 2012. *Statement before the Senate Armed Services Committee on the Posture of United States Central Command by CENTCOM Commander General James N. Mattis.* 6 March. Washington, D.C.: Senate Armed Services Committee.

U.S. Central Command. 2013a. "Officials Agree to Hold Eagle Resolve 2015 in Kuwait." News Articles, http://www.centcom.mil/en/news/articles/officials-agree-to-hold -eagle-resolve-2015-in-kuwait (last accessed 4 December 2014).

U.S. Central Command. 2013b. *Statement before the Senate Armed Services Committee on the Posture of United States Central Command by CENTCOM Commander General James N. Mattis.* 5 March. Washington, D.C.: Senate Armed Services Committee.

U.S. Central Command. 2014a. *Statement before the Senate Armed Services Committee on the Posture of United States Central Command by CENTCOM Commander General Lloyd J. Austin III.* 6 March. Washington, D.C.: Senate Armed Services Committee.

U.S. Central Command. 2014b. "Exercise Regional Cooperation 2014 Kicks Off." News Articles, 17 September, http://www.centcom.mil/news/news-article/exercise-regional -cooperation-2014-kicks-off (last accessed 3 May 2016).

U.S. Central Command. 2015a. *Statement before the House Appropriations Committee– Defense Committee on the Posture of United States Central Command by CENTCOM Commander General Lloyd J. Austin III.* 5 March. Washington, D.C.: House Appro-priations Committee–Defense Committee.

U.S. Central Command. 2015b. "Participants Say Coalition Teamwork Makes for Successful Exercise, Key to Future Operations." News Articles, 20 May, http://www .centcom.mil/news/news-article/participants-say-coalition-teamwork-makes-for -successful-exercise-key-to-fu (last accessed 3 May 2016).

U.S. Central Command. 2015c. "Coalition United to Defeat Daesh." News Articles, 26 May, http://www.centcom.mil/news/news-article/coalition-united-to-defeat -daesh (last accessed 3 May 2016).

U.S. Central Command. 2015d. "Civilians Serve Their Country, Deploy with Military Teammates." News Articles, 6 May, http://www.centcom.mil/news/news-article /civilians-serve-their-country-deploy-with-military-teammates (last accessed 4 May 2016).

U.S. Central Command. 2016a. *Statement before the Senate Armed Services Committee on the Posture of United States Central Command by CENTCOM Commander General Lloyd J. Austin III.* 8 March. Washington, D.C.: Senate Armed Services Committee.

U.S. Central Command. 2016b. "Mission and Vision." About Us, http://www.centcom .mil/about-us/mission-vision (last accessed 3 May 2016).

U.S. Central Command. 2016c. "Leaders Praise Central Command for Meeting Every Challenge." News Articles, 30 March, http://www.centcom.mil/news/news-article

/leaders praise central-command-for-meeting-every-challenge (last accessed 3 May 2016).

U.S. Central Command. 2016d. "CENTCOM Releases Iraq and Syria Civilian Casualty Assessments." Press Releases, 22 April, http://www.centcom.mil/news/press-release /april-22-u.s.-central-command-releases-iraq-and-syria-civilian-casualty (last accessed 4 May 2016).

U.S. Central Command. 2016e. "CENTCOM Releases Investigation into Airstrike on Doctors Without Borders Trauma Center." Press Releases, 29 April, http://www .centcom.mil/news/press-release/april-29-centcom-releases-kunduz-investigation (last accessed 4 May 2016).

U.S. Congressional Budget Office. 1983. *Rapid Deployment Forces: Policy and Budgetary Implications.* Washington, D.C.: U.S. Congressional Budget Office.

U.S. Department of Defense. 1980. *Authorization for Appropriations for Fiscal Year 1981: Hearings of the Senate Armed Services Committee.* Washington, D.C.: Senate Armed Services Committee.

U.S. Department of Defense. 1995a. *United States Security Strategy for the Middle East.* Washington, D.C.: Department of Defense, Office of International Security Affairs.

U.S. Department of Defense. 1995b. "Working with Gulf Allies to Contain Iraq and Iran." Speeches, 18 May, http://www.defenselink.mil/speeches/speech.aspx?speechid =909 (last accessed 30 January 2015).

U.S. Department of Defense. 1996. "Unified Command Plan Changes Announced." News Articles, 7 February, http://www.defenselink.mil/news/Feb1996 (last accessed 9 February 2008).

U.S. Department of Defense. 2001a. *Annual Report to the President and to Congress by Secretary of Defense William S. Cohen.* Washington, D.C.: Department of Defense.

U.S. Department of Defense. 2001b. "Exercise Bright Star to Begin Oct. 8." News Releases, 3 October, http://www.defense.gov/Releases/Release.aspx?ReleaseID=3085 (last accessed 25 March 2015).

U.S. Department of Defense. 2002. "Rumsfeld Thanks Kyrgyzstan for Support." News Articles, 27 April, http://www.defense.gov/news/newsarticle.aspx?id=44124 (last accessed 10 April 2015).

U.S. Department of Defense. 2003a. "Briefing on Coalition Post-War Reconstruction and Stabilization Efforts." News Transcripts, 12 June, http://www.defense.gov /Transcripts/Transcript.aspx?TranscriptID=2737 (last accessed 19 November 2014).

U.S. Department of Defense. 2003b. "Transforming the U.S. Global Defense Posture." Speeches, 3 December, http://www.defense.gov/speeches/speech.aspx?speechid=590 (last accessed 30 January 2015).

U.S. Department of Defense. 2004a. "Bush Announces Global Posture Changes over Next Decade." News Articles, 16 August, http://www.defenselink.mil/news /newsarticle.aspx?id=25515 (last accessed 9 July 2008).

U.S. Department of Defense. 2004b. *Strengthening U.S. Global Defense Posture.* Washington, D.C.: Department of Defense.

U.S. Department of Defense. 2005a. *The National Defense Strategy of the United States of America.* Washington, D.C.: Department of Defense.

U.S. Department of Defense. 2005b. *Directive 3000.05: Military Support for Stability,*

Security, Transition, and Reconstruction (SSTR) Operations. Washington, D.C.: Department of Defense.

U.S. Department of Defense. 2006. *National Military Strategic Plan for the War on Terrorism.* Washington, D.C.: Office of the Chairman of the Joint Chiefs of Staff.

U.S. Department of Defense. 2007a. *Dictionary of Military and Associated Terms, Joint Publication 1-02.* Washington, D.C.: Department of Defense.

U.S. Department of Defense. 2007b. "U.S. Africa Command." Briefing Slides, 7 February, http://www.defense.gov/dodcmsshare/briefingslide/295/070207-D-6570C-001.pdf (last accessed 7 March 2015).

U.S. Department of Defense. 2008. *National Defense Strategy.* Washington, D.C.: Department of Defense.

U.S. Department of Defense. 2010. *Active Duty Military Personnel Strengths by Regional Area and by Country.* 31 December, http://siadapp.dmdc.osd.mil/personnel/MILITARY/history/hst0912.pdf (last accessed 10 June 2010).

U.S. Department of Defense. 2012. *Sustaining U.S. Global Leadership: Priorities for 21st Century Defense.* Washington, D.C.: Department of Defense.

U.S. Department of Defense. 2014. *United States Department of Defense Fiscal Year 2015 Budget Request Overview.* Washington, D.C.: Office of the Under Secretary of Defense.

U.S. Department of Defense. 2015a. *Active Duty Military Personnel Strengths by Regional Area and by Country.* 31 March, https://www.dmdc.osd.mil/appj/dwp/dwp_reports.jsp (last accessed 10 April 2015).

U.S. Department of Defense. 2015b. *Law of War Manual.* Washington, D.C.: Department of Defense.

U.S. Department of Defense. 2016a. "Unified Command Plan." United States Department of Defense, http://www.defense.gov/Sites/Unified-Combatant-Commands (last accessed 6 April 2016).

U.S. Department of Defense. 2016b. *DoD 101: An Introductory Overview of the Department of Defense.* http://www.dod.gov/pubs/dod101 (last accessed 6 April 2016).

U.S. Department of State. 2004. "Office of the Coordinator for Reconstruction and Stabilization." *U.S. Department of State Archive.* http://2001-2009.state.gov/s/crs (last accessed 2 December 2013).

U.S. Department of State. 2014. *Congressional Budget Justification: Department of State, Foreign Operations, and Related Programs, Fiscal Year 2015.* Washington, D.C.: Department of State.

U.S. Department of State and U.S. Joint Warfighting Center. 2005. *United States Joint Forces Command J7 Pamphlet Version 1.0: U.S. Government Draft Planning Framework for Reconstruction, Stabilization, and Conflict Transformation.* Washington, D.C.: Department of State.

U.S. Department of the Army. 2008a. *Field Manual 3-0: Operations.* Washington, D.C.: Department of the Army Headquarters.

U.S. Department of the Army. 2008b. *Field Manual 3-07: Stability Operations.* Washington, D.C.: Department of the Army Headquarters.

U.S. Department of the Army. 2009. "Full Spectrum Operations." Army Posture Statement 2009, http://www.army.mil/aps/09/information_papers/full_spectrum_operations.html (last accessed 2 December 2013).

U.S. Department of the Army. 2013. *Field Manual 1-04: Legal Support to the Operational Army*. Washington, D.C.: Department of the Army Headquarters.

U.S. Department of the Army. 2015a. "The Army Vision: Strategic Advantage in a Complex World." United States Army, https://www.army.mil/e2/rv5_downloads/info/references/the_army_vision.pdf (last accessed 3 June 2016).

U.S. Department of the Army. 2015b. *Energy Security and Sustainability (ES²) Strategy*. Washington, D.C.: Department of the Army.

US-GCC Corporate Cooperation Committee. 1994. *Building Bridges: Business to Business and People to People*. http://ncusar.org/publications/Publications/1994-01-15-Building-Bridges.pdf (last accessed 07 March 2015).

U.S. House Committee on the Budget. 1981. *Statement before the House Committee on the Budget by Secretary of Defense Caspar Weinberger*. 23 September. Washington, D.C.: House Committee on the Budget.

U.S. House International Relations Committee. 2002. *Statement before the House International Relations Committee by Secretary of Energy Spencer Graham*. 20 June. Washington, D.C.: House International Relations Committee.

U.S. House of Representatives. 1963. *Hearings on Military Posture and HR 9751, Fiscal Year (FY) 1963*. Washington, D.C.: House Armed Services Committee.

U.S. Joint Chiefs of Staff. 1982. *Military Posture FY 1982*. Washington, D.C.: Department of Defense.

U.S. Joint Chiefs of Staff. 2006. *Joint Publication 3-0, Joint Operations*. http://www.dtic.mil/doctrine/docnet/courses/operations/jfcon/jp3_0.pdf (last accessed 2 December 2013).

U.S. National Security Council. 2006. *The National Security Strategy of the United States of America*. Washington, D.C.: The White House.

U.S. National Security Council. 2010. *The National Security Strategy of the United States of America*. Washington, D.C.: The White House.

U.S. National Security Council. 2015. *The National Security Strategy of the United States of America*. Washington, D.C.: The White House.

U.S. Office of the Assistant Secretary of Defense for Logistics and Materiel Readiness. 2015. Materiel Readiness Product Support Manager Annual Conference, 13–15 January. http://www.acq.osd.mil/log/mr/PSM_conference.html (last accessed 07 March 2015).

U.S. Overseas Basing Commission. 2005. *Commission on Review of the Overseas Military Facility Structure of the United States: Report to the President and Congress*. Arlington, Va.: Commission on Review of Overseas Military Facility Structure of the United States.

U.S. Senate. 1997. "American Interests in the Caspian Sea Region." Congressional Record—Senate, 8 May, https://www.congress.gov/crec/1997/05/08/CREC-1997-05-08-pt1-PgS4207.pdf (last accessed 10 April 2015).

Valenta, Markha. 2015. "Charlie Hebdo—One Week Later." *openDemocracy*, 16 January, https://www.opendemocracy.net/can-europe-make-it/markha-valenta/charlie-hebdo-—-one-week-later (last accessed 19 January 2015).

Vinch, Peter M. 2012. *A New Paradigm for Defense Rapid Acquisition*. Carlisle, Pa.: U.S. Army War College.

Vine, David. 2009. *Island of Shame: The Secret History of the U.S. Military Base on Diego Garcia*. Princeton: Princeton University Press.

Vine, David. 2015. *Base Nation: How U.S. Military Bases Abroad Harm America and the World*. New York: Metropolitan Books.

Vitalis, Robert. 2006. *America's Kingdom: Mythmaking on the Saudi Oil Frontier*. Stanford: Stanford University Press.

Von Clausewitz, Carl. 1989 [1832]. *On War*, translated by Michael Howard and Peter Paret. Princeton: Princeton University Press.

Wacquant, Loïc. 2009. *Punishing the Poor: The Neoliberal Government of Social Insecurity*. Durham, N.C.: Duke University Press.

Wallerstein, Immanuel. 1979. *The Capitalist World-Economy*. Cambridge: Cambridge University Press.

Waltz, Kenneth N. 1981. "A Strategy for the Rapid Deployment Force." *International Security* 5 (4): 49–73.

Watts, Michael. 2008. "Imperial Oil: The Anatomy of a Nigerian Oil Insurgency." *Erdkunde* 62 (1): 27–39.

Weizman, Eyal. 2009. "Lawfare in Gaza: Legislative Attack." *openDemocracy*, 1 March, http://www.opendemocracy.net/article/legislative-attack (last accessed 10 July 2009).

Weizman, Eyal. 2011. *The Least of All Possible Evils: Humanitarian Violence from Arendt to Gaza*. London: Verso.

The White House. 2005. *National Security Presidential Directive/NSPD-44: Management of Interagency Efforts Concerning Reconstruction and Stabilization*. Washington, D.C.: The White House.

The White House. 2012. *National Strategy for Global Supply Chain Security*. Washington, D.C.: The White House.

Wickramasinghe, Nira. 2015. "Colonial Governmentality and the Political Thinking through '1931' in the Crown Colony of Ceylon/Sri Lanka." *Socio* 05: 99–114.

Williams, Michael. 2007. *Culture and Security: Symbolic Power and the Politics of International Security*. London: Routledge.

Wolfowitz, Paul D. 1994. "Book Review. Crusade: The Untold Story of the Persian Gulf War by Rick Atkinson." *Joint Force Quarterly* 3: 123–124.

Woodward, Rachel. 2005. "From Military Geography to Militarism's Geographies: Disciplinary Engagements with the Geographies of Militarism and Military Activities." *Progress in Human Geography* 29 (6): 718–740.

Wrage, Stephen D. 2004. "U.S. Combatant Commander: The Man in the Middle." In *America's Viceroys: The Military and U.S. Foreign Policy*, edited by Derek S. Reveron, 185–202. New York: Palgrave Macmillan.

Young, Robert J. C. 2001. *Postcolonialism: An Historical Introduction*. Oxford: Blackwell.

INDEX

Abizaid, John, 7, 53, 57–59, 70, 76–77, 84, 100, 103
Afghanistan: Soviet Union invasion of, 6, 42, 107nn5–6; U.S. war in, 7, 39, 53, 56, 93, 103, 114n2
AFRICOM (U.S. Africa Command), 82–83, 108–109n11
Agamben, Giorgio, 53, 107n4
Anthony, John Duke, 78
AOR (Area of Responsibility), 3–5, 26, 57, 88–89, 108n11, 110n18
Aradau, Claudia, 53
Army Lawyer, The (U.S. Department of the Army), 60
Austin, Lloyd J., III, 52, 71, 89

Bacevich, Andrew, 41
Bahrain, 25, 41, 58, 64, 115n3
Bâli, Asli, 85
Barnett, Thomas, 45–46, 77
Bassiouni, Cherif, 64
Beck, Ulrich, 92
Begley, Josh, 56
Benard, Alexander, 82
Benjamin, Walter, 14, 49, 68
Benton, Lauren, 12, 15, 49, 54
Berman, Howard, 97
biopolitics, 12, 15–16, 49–53, 68–69, 104
Blomley, Nicholas, 15
Bremer, Paul, 32–33, 116n9
Britain, 30, 71–72, 114n1
Brown, Harold, 18
Brzezinski, Zbigniew, 18, 21–22, 41–42
Bush, George W., 7, 28, 32–33, 62–64, 90–92, 96

capitalism, 11–13, 32–33, 80–81, 111n3
Carpenter, Ted, 46–47

Carter, Jimmy, 1–2, 18, 20–22, 33, 72, 81, 94
CENTCOM (United States Central Command): as Guardians of the Gulf, 3–7, 16, 28–29, 70, 72, 102; origin of, 1, 15, 19–25; studies and sources on, 2–3, 105n4
Central Region, 5, 31, 39, 71, 76–77, 80–81, 89, 98–102
Cieply, Kevin, 66
Clinton, Bill, 30, 80–81, 92
Cold War, 15, 23–24, 33, 59–60
Comaroff, Jean and John, 63
Combat Equipment Group—Europe, 19
communication: management of media, 6, 27; military field systems of, 26–27, 112n11; public relations, 5–6, 65, 76–77, 79, 98–100, 104, 105n4, 114n1; use of law for, 62–66, 69
Cooper, Melinda, 93
Copulos, Milton, 101
counterinsurgency, 46–47, 65, 95
Country Books, 4, 110n4
Cowen, Deborah, 12–13, 93
Crist, George, 27
Crow, Dennis, 103
Cullen, Peter, 66

Dawson, David, 3, 7, 9–10, 38, 57, 76–77, 90–91
defense contractors, 81–84
Desert Spring, Operation, 9, 31, 75
deterrence: geoeconomic, 9, 77–79, 85–86, 90, 101; post–Gulf War strategy (1990s), 29–32, 55–56, 61, 73–77; preemptive intervention, 93–95, 117n10; RDJTF and, 24–25; as shaping activities, 16; against Soviet Union, 19–20, 60; territorial access and, 12–13

CPSIA information can be obtained
at www.ICGtesting.com
Printed in the USA
LVOW03s0112050517

533274LV00002B/149/P

9 780820 351056